WESTERMARCK

First published in 2014 by
Sean Kingston Publishing
www.seankingston.co.uk
Canon Pyon

In association with
the Anglo-Finnish Society

British Library Cataloguing in Publication Data
A catalogue record for this book is available from the British Library.

The moral rights of the authors have been asserted.

Printed by Lightning Source

ISBN 978-1-907774-31-7

Westermarck

Edited by David Shankland

Occasional Paper No. 44 of the Royal Anthropological Institute

Published in association with the Anglo-Finnish Society

Sean Kingston Publishing
www.seankingston.co.uk
Canon Pyon

Westermarck on a mule in Morocco.

FOREWORD

Professor Edward Westermarck (1865–1939) is possibly the most internationally famous of Finnish social scientists. His *The History of Human Marriage*, published in 1891, was soon translated into more than half a dozen other languages, including Japanese. Indeed, from the 1890s onwards Westermarck enjoyed worldwide fame as a social anthropologist, moral philosopher and sociologist, whose students at the London School of Economics included such distinguished future scholars as Malinowski, Ginsberg, Evans-Pritchard, Ashley Montagu and Talcott Parsons. For us Finns he was an important international supporter of Finnish independence and, above all, a man who did not forget his home country, but who continued throughout his illustrious career to teach part of each year at the University of Helsinki and the Swedish-speaking university Åbo Akademi in Turku.

This publication originates from an international seminar on Westermarck's life and legacy organized at the University of London in December 2011 by the Anglo-Finnish Society, who wished to honour one of their founding fathers in their centenary year. This event would not have been possible without the generosity of Professor Geoffrey Crossick, Vice-Chancellor of the University of London, and of Mr Terry Walsh, who with his team helped in many practical arrangements. Mrs Marjatta Bell of the Anglo-Finnish Society, who had devised the project, acted as coordinator. The Society is also grateful for grants from the Svenska Kulturfonden, the Stiftelsen för Åbo Akademi and the Alfred Kordelin Foundation.

As there are signs of a reawakening international interest in Westermarck's work, it is a great pleasure for me to see the seminar papers, together with some new articles by other Westermarck scholars, becoming available to a wider international audience. We are grateful to the Royal Anthropological Institute for including them in their series of publications, and in particular we thank Dr David Shankland, Director of the RAI, for editing all the materials into a pleasing and informative volume.

Pekka Huhtaniemi
Finnish Ambassador in London
Honorary President of the Anglo-Finnish Society

ACKNOWLEDGEMENTS

The genesis of this volume lies in a one-day symposium on Edward Westermarck's life and legacy held at the University of London in order to commemorate the dedication of a 'Blue Plaque' to Westermarck. These famous plaques dot the London urban scenery, and mark the house where a named distinguished person lived. In the case of Westermarck, it turns out that the house he was living in is now no longer in existence, having been pulled down to build the imposing University of London Senate House buildings that dominate the Bloomsbury landscape. However, the plaque is safely placed there onto an outside wall. We in turn had the pleasure of celebrating his life in the Chancellor's Hall within, in the presence of the Ambassador of Finland, His Excellency Mr Pekka Huhtaniemi, the Vice-Chancellor, Professor Geoffrey Crossick, and academic colleagues and members of the Westermarck family. The organization of the day itself was put into place by the Anglo-Finnish Society, ably led by Mrs Marjatta Bell, to whom the credit should go for an extremely successful event.

As editor of the volume I should like to thank His Excellency for his constant and generous support for this project, and for the foreword which he has so kindly contributed. I should also like to thank Professor Olli Lagerspetz from the Åbo Akademi University, who has assisted at every turn in the most productive and friendly way as the book has gradually come together. Mr Tommy Lahtinen from the Åbo Akademi University Archives helped in finding the illustrations and Mrs Bell assisted in the technical production of this volume. I am also grateful to Mr Pekka Isosomppi for his most pertinent comments on Westermarck's work. At the RAI, I should thank all the staff and Fellows for their constant inspiration and support, and especially with regard to this project, Clive Gamble, Tim Ingold, Wendy James, Jeremy MacClancy, James Staples and Anthony Leigh.

Westermarck is a fascinating figure, one whose neglect is quite unwarranted. This is a great pity, because it could easily be argued from the point of view of the history of anthropology that he is a 'missing link', that is a towering intellectual figure who helps us to understand the extraordinary complex transition from nineteenth-century anthropology to modern social anthropology in the twentieth century, and one who was linked to both. As well as providing more information concerning Westermarck's life, we hope that this volume illustrates some of the ways in which this claim may be justified. Although it covers certain important aspects of Westermarck's life and works, an equally useful work could be prepared that assesses his contribution from the point of view of today's biological and evolutionary anthropology. We hope that this may act as a stimulus for such a project to be undertaken. There is still very little exegesis on Westermarck, but it is suggested that the interested reader who wishes to look further may find the edited volume by Stroup (*Edward Westermarck: Essays on His Life and Works*, Philosophical Society of Finland, 1982) a useful starting point.

David Shankland
Director, Royal Anthropological Institute

Westermarck's parents.

CONTENTS

KEY DATES IN WESTERMARCK'S PUBLIC LIFE

1862	Edward (Edvard) Westermarck is born 20 November, Helsinki, Finland
1881	Matriculates with high marks, and enrolls as a student in Helsinki University
1886	Receives Bachelor's and Master's degree
1887–8	First trip to the British Library, for his Ph.D. research.
1890	Obtains Ph.D. with *The Origin of Human Marriage*.
1890–1906	Lecturer in Sociology, University of Helsinki
1890–5	Appointed Master: Nylands Nation (student fraternity), University of Helsinki
1891	*The History of Human Marriage* is published, Macmillan
1894–7	Acting Professor of Philosophy, University of Helsinki
1898	Travels to Morocco commence
1899	Active in soliciting signatures for the *Pro Finlandia* petition to the Tsar
1904–7	Delivers lectures in Sociology, University of London (LSE)
1905	Elected fellow of the Royal Anthropological Institute
1906–18	Professor of Philosophy, University of Helsinki
1906–8	*The Origin and Development of the Moral Ideas*, 2 volumes, Macmillan
1907	First becomes RAI Council member
1907–31	Martin White Professor of Sociology, University of London (LSE)
1910	Strikes up friendship with Malinowski, with whom he later goes on to teach
1911	Co-founder of the Anglo-Finnish Society established in London to promote Finland's case during the second period of Russian oppression
1914	*Marriage Ceremonies in Morocco* published, Macmillan
1918–21	First Rector of Åbo Akademi University
1918–32	Professor of Philosophy, Åbo Akademi University
1918	*Sex år i Marocko* published, Schildts Förlag
1920–1	Member of delegation presenting Finland's case to the League of Nations over the Åland question
1921	*The History of Human Marriage*, extended to 3 volumes, Macmillan

1926   *Ritual and Belief in Morocco,* 2 volumes, Macmillan
        Receives the Rivers Medal of the Royal Anthropological
        Institute for his fieldwork in Morocco.
1927   *Minnen ur mitt liv* published, Schildts
1929   *Memories of My Life* published, Allen & Unwin Ltd.
1930   *Wit and Wisdom in Morocco: A Study of Native Proverbs*
        published, Routledge
1930   Retires from the LSE
1932   *Ethical Relativity* published, Paul Kegan
1934   *Three Essays on Sex and Marriage.* Macmillan
1936   *The Future of Marriage in Western Civilisation* published,
        Macmillan
        Receives the Huxley Medal of the Royal Anthropological
        Institute
        Delivers Huxley lecture: `Methods in Social Anthropology'
1939   *Christianity and Morals* published, Paul Kegan
1939   Westermarck dies 3 September, Tenhola, Finland

CONTRIBUTORS

Jan Antfolk (Department of Philosophy, and Department of Psychology and Logopedics, Åbo Akademi University) is a philosopher and psychologist. His academic interests include evolutionary biology and the human family system. Both his empirical and theoretical research has been guided by Westermarck's work – especially his theory about the evolutionary origin and the development of human inbreeding aversion.

Maurice Bloch is Emeritus professor of Anthropology at the London School of Economics. His two latest books are *Anthropology and the Cognitive Challenge* (2012) and *In and Out of Each Other's Bodies: Theory of Mind, Evolution, Truth and the Nature of the Social* (2013).

Juhani Ihanus is Adjunct Professor of Cultural Psychology (University of Helsinki) and of the History of Science and Ideas (University of Oulu), Senior Lecturer (Open University, University of Helsinki). He has published books and articles on cultural and clinical psychology and the history of psychology and the human sciences.

Camilla Kronqvist is a post-doc researcher at Åbo Akademi University. Her main research and teaching interests are the philosophy of emotion, in particular love, moral philosophy, feminist philosophy and the philosophy of science. She is the co-editor of *Emotions and Understanding: Wittgensteinian Perspectives* (2009) and *Ethics and the Philosophy of Culture: Wittgensteinian Approaches* (2013).

Olli Lagerspetz is senior lecturer in philosophy at Åbo Akademi University. He studied sociology and philosophy at Åbo and at Illinois, Urbana-Champaign. Lagerspetz has previously worked at the University of Wales, Swansea. His research interests include Wittgenstein, the philosophy of mind, moral philosophy. Together with Kirsti Suolinna, he is the author of *Edward Westermarck and his Intellectual Networks*.

Pekka Rantanen is currently secretary of the Westermarck Society. He is on the editorial board of the Finnish sociological journal *Sosiologia*, and has been journal's editorial secretary. His research interests include migration, historical sociology, cultural studies, discourse theory and ethnography.

David Shankland is Director of the Royal Anthropological Institute, and Reader in Anthropology at the University of Bristol. Amongst his specialist areas of study are the history of anthropology, particularly disciplinary diversity and the emergence of Social Anthropology in the twentieth century.

Timothy Stroup is Professor of Philosophy at John Jay College (CUNY). He is the author of *Westermarck's Ethics* and editor of *Edward Westermarck: Essays on His Life and Works*. He has written the entries on Westermarck in *Oxford Dictionary of National Biography*, *Encyclopaedia of Ethics*, and *Dictionary of Anthropology*, as well as articles on him in *Man*, *The Journal of the History of Philosophy*, *Ajatus* etc.

Kirsti Suolinna has a Ph.D. from Helsinki University and is currently a free researcher at Åbo Akademi University. Her research interests cover the sociology of religion and the history of sociology in Finland. She has studied Edward Westermarck's fieldwork, as well as that of his students, and the decline and fall of the Westermarck School. Together with Olli Lagerspetz, she is the author of *Edward Westermarck and his Intellectual Networks*.

Arthur P. Wolf is Professor of Anthropological Sciences and David and Lucile Packard Foundation Professor of Human Biology at Stanford University. He is editor of *Religion and Ritual in Chinese Society* and *Family and Population in East Asia;* coauthor with Chieh-shan Huang of *Marriage and Adoption in Chinese Society, 1845–1945;* and author of *Sexual Attraction and Childhood Association: A Chinese Brief for Edward Westermarck.* A second book concerning incest avoidance and the incest taboos is in press.

Introduction

Westermarck

A missing link

DAVID SHANKLAND

Edward Westermarck (1862–1939) was one of the greatest anthropologists there has ever been. He made fundamental contributions to at least three areas of the discipline: to the study of kinship and marriage; to the ethnography of North Africa; and to the philosophy of anthropology, notably to questions of ethics and moral relativism. He wrote with enviable clarity. His success was immediate and long lasting. His *History of Human Marriage*, his first and perhaps his most popular work, burst alive from the press into the international academic world in 1891, and went through five editions in his lifetime.[1] From the outset, it was supported by his academic peers on the highest level. Wallace, for example, wrote the foreword to the first edition, saying:

> Having read the proofs of Mr Westermarck's book, I am asked by the
> publishers to say a few words by way of introducing the work to English
> readers. This I have great pleasure in doing, because I have seldom read
> a more thorough or a more philosophic discussion of some of the most
> difficult, and at the same time interesting, problems of anthropology...With
> such an array of authority on the one side and a hitherto unknown student
> on the other, it will certainly be thought that all the probabilities are against
> the latter. Yet I venture to anticipate that the verdict of independent thinkers
> will ... be in favour of the new comer who has so boldly challenged the
> conclusions of some of our most esteemed writers.
>
> (Westermarck 1921:ix–x)

Faced with this formidable early renown in the English-speaking world, renown upon which he built throughout his career by regularly publishing major volumes, it is easy to forget that he wrote equally in Swedish, Finnish, French and Italian. Likewise, he was a continual and thoughtful contributor to learned journals, producing on average a dozen papers a year, often of great length.[2] His remarks on feasting, for example, take up thirty-one pages of *Folklore* in 1907, as do those on the Feast of Sacrifice in Morocco in the same journal in 1911. Whether article or book, his work was equally frequently translated, meaning that he was read widely by a huge range of persons across Europe, from Scandinavia to the Mediterranean.

Born of a Swedish-speaking family in Finland, Westermarck graduated from Helsinki University. After graduation, he continued with his studies – a period, as he described himself in his memoirs Westermarck (1929), that was active and full of debate. In illustration of this, Antfolk kindly provides for this volume the first English translation of a lecture that the young Westermarck gave to the Helsinki Student Union in 1889. It shows a profound understanding of the issues to which evolutionary theory may give rise. Indeed, two years before the publication of his *Human Marriage*, it shows how remarkably thought through his ideas already were at the age of twenty-seven. As Antfolk points out, he airs in that early lecture the central theses that are so crucial in his work: that there is no such thing as a promiscuous society, and nor has there ever been; and that proximity in childhood reduces the probability of mating, which Westermarck famously regarded as being an explanation of prescriptions avoiding incest.

Westermarck's promise was recognized, and he was appointed to a Chair at the University of Helsinki from 1906. After the First World War, upon Finland's independence, Westermarck changed universities, accepting a Chair in Philosophy and the Rectorship of a new, private university that would concentrate on Swedish-language education at Turku (Åbo), an old university town in south-west Finland (Lagerspetz and Suolinna, in this volume).

Just as Malinowski, though, Westermarck was drawn to Britain, and to the London School of Economics. Having lectured in sociology to the School, he was appointed the Martin White Professor of Sociology in 1907. To these two occupations, he added a third, that of fieldworker, going regularly to Morocco. He made extensive fieldwork trips from 1898 onwards, until 1923, acquiring in order to do so a house that he bought from the Swedish Consul in Tangier.

This creative triangle lies at the heart of Westermarck's life and scholarly endeavours. Yet, it did lead to tensions, which Lagerspetz and Suolinna describe, concerning his tenure at Åbo Akademi University as Rector. Equally, Westermarck was caught between conflicting loyalties. The following unpublished letter, written to his parents, and kindly been provided by the Westermarck family, gives an insight into this.[3] By 1899, the date the letter was written, Westermarck's fieldwork in Morocco is established. Prefiguring the later social anthropologists and their arrangements in the field, he has struck up a close relationship with a Berber who has acted to guide him in the complexities of local life. However, the political situation in Morocco at that time was unstable. The European nations were seeking to expand their colonial influence, though Morocco officially only became a French protectorate in 1906, and it was not clear in 1899 which of these external powers was to prevail. Further, as Gellner (1969) as well as many others have described, there is an internal tension between the central power of the Sultan and the independence of the Berber notables. In such a fluid situation, Westermarck feared that his friend could be compromised, as he writes: 'I cannot be certain to find him still here when I come back.' The solution he adopts is to bring him back to Europe with him.

The reason that he wishes to go to Europe at this point is to aid Finland, then an autonomous Grand Duchy within the Russian Empire, in her struggles to be free of Russian dominance. Indeed, though his academic reputation was international, he appears to have reserved political and social ambitions largely for his home country. As Rantanen outlines (Chapter 3), motivated strongly by patriotism, Westermarck was active as one of the leading co-ordinators for an international petition that was taken, unavailingly, to present to the Tsar. This petition was published by the Germans in a handsome facsimile (*Pro Finlandia* 1899), presumably happy to embarrass their continental rival. The signatures reprinted within are a tribute to Westermarck's success in collecting support from the luminaries of the day. Our letter appears to describe the point when he is tearing himself away from his fieldwork, to see what he can do to help the resistance movement, ultimately leading to the petition. The footnotes to the letter are kindly provided by Professor Lagerspetz.

Tangier 31st March 1899

My dear parents,

I wrote a card this morning but could not then express what I wanted to say. Lately I have prepared myself for a journey to the Atlas Mountains. The Russian ambassador is on his way to meet the Sultan in Marrakesh. A Russian warship came here to fetch him and with him all his entourage. He promised me that he will get me the Sultan's permit to travel to the Glaui Passage, which cannot be visited without such permission as his governor must make sure that no strangers go there. My horses have been receiving extra fodder to prepare them for the journey, and I have selected the two men who will be accompanying me together with the Shereef.[4] My plan was to take the high road along the coast, but at slow speed so that I could collect notes during the journey. Kaid Maclean[5] has invited me to be his guest when in Marrakesh. But now all this has to wait. I am not going to travel to the Atlas Mountains *now*; it is not possible. On Monday I will go to Gibraltar and on Tuesday by steamer to London. Even I must try to add my little straw to the stack. Yesterday I heard from Sully[6] that in London there is a protest committee[7] being formed. This is the right time as the Peace Conference is due to start soon.[8] I have seen how uninformed the English press is about the facts of the matter. However, I believe I can clarify a thing or two and perhaps get an article in the *Nineteenth Century*, the most important periodical there. I will try to do this and in addition visit some influential people. I am not optimistic but know that I must do what little I can. Indeed, I have better contacts in England than most of us. How long will I stay in London? I don't know yet, but I will leave my things behind me here. There is no question of leaving my work here half done. Lately I have got so much new material and good ideas that I am sure that, provided I have got the time, I can produce something valuable to put alongside my work on ethics. So I must go back. I am certainly not going round like this for fun. Now is the best time to travel when the whole country is decorated with early summer blooms and the rains have stopped. But I *cannot* with a good conscience leave undone what I had decided to do. And I must travel now to London.

Yesterday I informed the Shereef of my decision. He received it with resignation and offered to send 1,000 men from his own tribe to help me! His political understanding is somewhat hazy. Furthermore Russia is his great ideal and he would like to make his village the starting point of a Russian occupation of the whole of Morocco. However, he started to ponder how much money I was owing him and then announced that he wanted to use that to come to London with me. On considering the matter further I found this suggestion quite satisfactory also from my point of view. I cannot be certain to find him still here when I come back. The fact that he had travelled with me without a single soldier, which was contrary to the pasha's orders, had made him most unpopular in the eyes of the latter. I have not mentioned earlier that when I was in London I once received a telegram telling me that he was in danger of being put in jail. I telegraphed to the Russian ambassador who simply had the soldiers carted away who had been keeping an eye on his hiding place. The cause was that he had been travelling without a military escort; to this was added some private dispute. Certainly Russian protection has been granted him for life after I leave him, but the whole of the Russian legation has now embarked on a long journey and God only knows what would happen if he were left on his own. I have therefore decided to allow him to follow me to London. He has to pay his own travel costs, and he does not expect any salary, but moneys he has are not enough for his upkeep. I do not believe, however, that it would be much more expensive if I were to pay him the fee he was due here when I was away. And above all, I cannot let him be left here without protection. He is now snorting with delight at being able to see railways, cars and lions.

You may perhaps think that all this is somewhat fanciful, but I have thought over this matter carefully and find that there is nothing else I can do. Of my own money I have just over 1,200 marks in English pounds and in addition some Moorish money. This should be enough until 1 June, i.e. for two months. From London I will send a new authorization for further credit, but will do it in good time so that there will not be any complications. It is likely that the bank will renew the loan already in May but should they wish to get some securities until 1 June then I must ask Pappa to kindly help me with some shares or such. It could happen that my English money will not last as long as is needed; I do not know at all how long I will stay in London.

As to the newspapers, I would like Mamma to be kind enough to send them to London, to the old address, 18 Keppel Street, Russell Square, London WC. – It is so wonderful and like summer here that one feels really bad about leaving the country. Southern Morocco must now be radiantly beautiful. And all those genial Moors and interesting matters which become more and more interesting every day the more one begins to feel at home. It is no fun to return to the cold and 'civilization'. But I am not doing it for fun. When I said in an earlier letter that I would probably leave Morocco in April, it was partly because of my depressed state of mind and partly because I had not seen clearly how huge an amount there is still to be studied, and that by more thorough research I could write a whole book about this subject, the first of its kind not only on Morocco but also on Arabic folk religion as it exists today. But that is enough now. I will send a card from Gibraltar and then from London, where I should arrive around 10 April.

Finally a few words to Helena. I intended to write her a separate letter but this letter is indeed to all of you. I thanked her already for the bother with the music sheets. But I have not said anything about a request for a contribution to the album. I do not know whether I have time to get anything done by June. I had thought to provide a description of travel to the Atlas Mountains together with illustrations, but now that is delayed, I do not know for how long. It is better not to promise too much and to do what one has not precisely promised. I have now so many irons in the fire. But the album should not be left uncompleted. With many greetings to you all, Valter's family, the Ehrströms[9] and the Aunts,

Yours affectionately

Edvard

Politically committed, an active fieldworker, careful of his conduct in the field, explicitly grateful to his closest local helper, acutely conscious of the philosophical basis of anthropology, widely read and soon to be recipient of the first Chair of Sociology at the LSE where he was to teach for more than twenty years, one could suppose that Westermarck, rather than a later figure such as Evans-Pritchard or Malinowski, would be regarded as the founder of modern anthropology. Indeed, given his extraordinary renown outside anthropology as well as within, he would seem to be the most logical person to choose for such an accolade. Yet, in Britain there is no Westermarck lecture, no history devoted to his contribution, and – until the celebration that marked the conference from which this book derives – it appears that recognition from the University where he made his reputation, and where he helped to found anthropology, steadily declined from his retirement onwards. As Stroup writes: 'While everyone has heard of Westermarck his actual contributions to the social sciences and philosophy have largely been ignored in the more than forty years since his death, and when his writings have not been neglected they have more often than not been misinterpreted.' Stroup (1982:ix).[10]

Why then, has he been so widely eclipsed? This is a matter which I treat in a little more detail in my chapter on Westermarck's links with the RAI, but in essence it is possible to identify a number of possibilities that may help us to understand this. Though he did realize that fieldwork was quite essential for the development of anthropology, and equally supported the idea of detailed case studies – which he referred to as 'monographs' – he never quite convinced himself that functionalist or single-village studies were sufficient in themselves to tackle major intellectual questions, questions which were suggested to him by his reading of the previous generation of anthropologists, particularly Tylor and Frazer. Though he frequently disagreed with them, he emulated their method in as much as he drew in dozens of ethnographic comparisons. His early work, then, bears a strong resemblance to the scissors and paste method of Frazer. A perhaps rather grudging obituary of Westermarck in the *American Journal of Sociology* illustrates this uncertainty:

> *History of Human Marriage* ... brilliantly exposed the errors and inadequacies of the evidence upon which the theory of primordial promiscuity had been based ...
>
> These early works of Westermarck were distinguished by their literary style, ability in organization, capacity for generalization and emphasis on the biological and psychological explanations of behavior. The chief limitation in his use of the comparative method was his disposition to draw far-reaching conclusions from comparisons of customs and ideologies detached from their organic setting in the social life of the people.

> ... Westermarck's later writings were characterized by much the same qualities as his earlier work...
>
> (Anon.:451)

Lowie, in his *History of Ethnological Theory*, is even more damning:

> This approach is doubly suspect: first of all, the classification does not grow naturally out of the material, but is imposed on it; secondly, the collector is likely to concentrate only on what seems to fall under his rubrics, omitting correlated phenomena of the utmost significance...Westermarck is not primarily interested in culture; he is a philosopher who uses its phenomena to illustrate his points... With Westermarck the reader has the uncomfortable feeling that nothing interests him less than to comprehend primitive tribes... Sweeping generalizations of his, chosen here and there, will illustrate his ethnographic inadequacy...
>
> (Lowie 1937:97)

As well as being uncertain as to the value of the 'organic' studies lauded by the anonymous obituarist, and devoted to the comparative method so disliked by Lowie, he was unable to accept the idea of an ethnographic present as it later came to be understood. Even when he is writing ethnography at its densest, for example in his *Ritual and Belief in Morocco*, the sort of questions that he wished to ask were imbued often with a sense of sequence and history, an unfolding over time that Radcliffe-Brown quite explicitly wanted to remove from his definition of Social Anthropology, and consign to archaeology or to ethnology.[11] Thus, Westermarck never really fitted in with the 'modern' definition of social anthropology.

Nevertheless, unlike Evans-Pritchard's explicit statement of anthropology as history, Westermarck did not conceive anthropology as part of the humanities only. His early hypothesis, discussed by Wolf in this volume, concerning incest avoidance is as neat an example as one could wish to find of a scientific approach. Furthermore, Westermarck just as the nameless obituarist above pointed out, was as interested in psychology as he was in locating behaviour in the biological basis of mankind, breaking the Durkheimian insistence on excluding psychology from anthropological investigations. Even more than this, he explicitly regarded evolution as the basis of his explanatory framework. It is precisely because he found regular social patterns in the sexual interaction in the higher primates that he believed that there could be no indiscriminate promiscuity in human groups, at whatever time in history or prehistory. This appears very close to the idea that human beings must have developed in a consistent way toward the present, something that Lubbock certainly would have considered as the first President of the Anthropological Institute in 1871,[12] but not the modern social anthropologists fifty years later, who became very suspicious of anything that even smacked of evolutionary models of human civilization. Handler, remarked in 1985, surely representing many, 'Today, Westermarck is forgotten as yet another of the 19th century evolutionists.' (1985:684).

How then, may Westermarck be regarded as a 'missing' link? I would argue that in fact he is so in multiple ways. He is a direct line of transmission between the older, English school which he himself lauded, and the emergence of Malinowski and his school at the LSE. In order to appreciate this, we need to realize that at that time institutional support for anthropology, let alone social anthropology, was still comparatively weak within British universities. Martin White's support of Westermarck was therefore a vital act, one fully seven years before Seligman was awarded his first part-time senior position in ethnology. Of course, White was primarily interested in Sociology, and this was the name initially of Westermarck's endowed lectures, and then his Chair, but it should be recalled that in this period 'sociology' often referred to the anthropological search for comparative social institutions, and Westermarck himself seems to have continued to do exactly what he had always done.[13]

Later, as students of anthropology came to the LSE, and Malinowski's presence became significant, Westermarck first befriended him, and later taught together with him as a colleague. His intellectual influence at the LSE is therefore palpable. It was Westermarck, of all the English school, who actually conducted fieldwork of a kind that was recognizably similar to that which Malinowski would 'pioneer'. Westermarck himself had not invented the idea of fieldwork, of course, any more than Malinowski was to do, but above all he did it, and did so through precisely that one-to-one intense interaction that later was to become de rigueur. Malinowski acknowledged Westermarck's skills in this respect, particularly with regard to his learning the fieldwork language (Young 2004:173).[14]

Westermarck was also an excellent teacher and colleague; warm, supportive and popular. Montague writes:

> As I remember it, Westermarck gave a seminar for one term each year ...
> at the London School of Economics. The seminars were anthropologically
> based and a trifle sociologically oriented, and since Malinowski regularly
> attended them they were very lively. Applications of anthropological
> findings to the illumination of problems of contemporary society, as well
> as those of non-literate societies, made the seminars very attractive, so that
> from an initial ten or so members they grew to about thirty. Sometimes
> in the vicinity of 1925, I recall a regular visitor to the seminar, a young

American sociologist named Talcott Parsons. Among other members of
both Malinowski's and Westermarck's seminars were Evans-Pritchard ... and
Raymond Firth... Malinowski was an active contributor to the enjoyment of
the seminars, and Westermarck a most stimulating guide...[15]

Young, in describing Westermarck's teaching writes:

The syllabus was extra-ordinarily comprehensive and indicative of the scope
of Westermarck's interests. A brief sample:

> The characteristics of social phenomena as distinguished from
> biological and psychological phenomena. The systems of paternal
> and maternal descent. The family, joint family, clan, tribe, nation. The
> biological and psychological facts on which the formation , scope and
> coherence of society depend. Customs and laws as rules of conduct.
> Moral approval and disapproval. The origin and functions of marriage.

Several of Malinowski's abiding anthropological interests are here
– marriage, the family, and primitive law. The syllabus of Westermarck's
second lecture course, on social rights and duties, refers to additional topics
such as warfare, magic, and religion that Malinowski subsequently made his
own.

(Young 2004:172)[16]

The summary of Westermarck's course is remarkably close to the theory
of institutions that Malinowski later came to develop. Further than this
even – and this is also discussed by Young – crucially, Malinowski's theory
of the family, which he published in his early volume *The Family among
the Australian Aborigines,* is directly related to Westermarck's *History of
Human Marriage,* particularly in its understanding of the causal relationship
between family and marriage (Young 2004:179–82). Indeed, Malinowski can
be regarded as having based his work on Westermarck's example, writing as
he does:

They [Westermarck's researches] must be regarded as a starting point. It is
the most exhaustive treatise on the individual family; all the essential parts
of the problem are sketched in a masterly manner in this fundamental work,
and the outlines of a more specialist investigation indicated.
(Malinowski 1913:34)

Westermarck's influence upon and interaction with other anthropologists
at that time could be traced further. What is already amply clear, however, is
that Westermarck should be regarded as a direct ancestor, not a peripheral or
indirect one. In other words, even though Gellner is quite right when he says:
'Westermarck like Malinowski was attracted by British empiricism [but] the
fusion of empiricist philosophical background and fieldwork practice did not,
in this case, engender the new functionalist style' (1995:235–6), the breadth
and brilliance of Westermarck's teaching was an immediate and discernable
influence on shaping anthropology at, in Goody's (1995) suggestive phrase,
the 'Expansive Moment', the epoch when it coalesced into its modern form.

There are further reasons. Survivals, or the rejection of survivals, is
associated with the creation of the new social anthropology under Malinowski
and, above all Radcliffe-Brown. It is, indeed, a central pillar of that anthropology
that what used to be thought of as survivals, whatever social manifestation
may be considered under that rubric, must have some contemporary function,
especially in as much as culture may be said to support or maintain the social
structure of a society. This is a more powerful idea than later sceptics often
realize, but important for the argument here is not the inherent worth of that
approach, but rather that Westermarck was in the forefront of the attack on
survivals.

This is reiterated in a paper by Westermarck published here for the first
time. Written late in his career, it consists of his presentation to the first major
anthropological congress in the UK, organized by the Royal Anthropological
Institute in 1934. The 'International Congress of Anthropological and
Ethnological Sciences' founded by Professor John Myres, eventually became
the International Union of Anthropological and Ethnological Sciences,
which is still flourishing today. Here, Westermarck is presenting in Section
F: 'Sociology', along with a number of others who gathered to address the
question of ritual at that session, amongst them Evans-Pritchard, Hocart,
Lévy-Bruhl, Mauss, Bateson, Marett, Piddington, Aubrey Richards, Firth
and Fortune. Westermarck opens simply, 'The object of this paper is to warn
against interpreting without sufficient reason existing rites as survivals of
something else in the past', and goes on to renew his criticism of Freud and
Briffault, a contemporary with whom he had held heated discussions.[17] It is
true that Westermarck did not go as far as Radcliffe-Brown in rejecting the
importance of the past for the present. He was rather looking for a way of
accommodating conceptual difficulties with survivals that would permit him
to incorporate the importance of history within his anthropological writings.
This attempt would perhaps merit revisiting, but again, the point for our
argument is that he had a leading role in debates surrounding these issues,

a role that is not now acknowledged. Stocking, for instance, overlooks him completely in his important work *Functionalism Historicized* (1984).[18]

So we return to our original question, if in fact he had such a great influence and was not merely a nineteenth-century evolutionist, why the eclipse? It is impossible to be sure how history or historiography becomes shaped: the inner debates, quarrels, multiple borrowings and inspirations are so intertwined that rarely can we disentangle things precisely, let alone strip away the subsequent misleading writings and impressions that are so often penned after the event. What I suspect is the case, however, is that his most substantial intellectual contribution, that which we may regard as being so important as to have changed the course of anthropology, is his work on the family and marriage. The study of kinship was at the heart of social anthropology as it came to be formed in the twentieth century, the only topic, as the late Gellner used to remark, that it could claim that no other discipline was able to tackle. Essential to it was the presumption that all societies have some form of kinship organisation, and that there has never been a primordial time when the family did not exist. It was Westermarck who demonstrably created that new paradigm in his first and most famous work.

Yet, if recognized for the great contribution that it surely was, this immediately leads us to a paradox. Westermarck realized this insight through methods which were anathema to the social anthropologists who nevertheless incorporated it into their system; it was armchair based, universalist, comparative in method, and rooted in biology, psychology and evolutionary theory. As the new movement reversed almost all these presumptions, they were hardly in a position to laud him as a founding figure. So, it became more convenient to ignore him, other than in the most perfunctory fashion, even whilst they were using his insight as a founding principle of their movement.

This whole argument could be put another way. It is a well-known and indeed fascinating exercise in academic and intellectual history to seek ways in which later theories were already anticipated by an earlier person, but forgotten because they were ignored by their peers, only to be discovered by a subsequent generation. This might be called the cul-de-sac vision of intellectual progress. The extreme version of it would be Leonardo de Vinci's anatomical drawings only being rediscovered long after scientists had reached his conclusions centuries later. Closer to home, I myself have attempted a modest exercise along those lines with regard to F.W. Hasluck, and his innovative work at the British School at Athens, research which led him to anticipate much that lies within Radcliffe-Brown's and Malinowski's positions. Seemingly, he had no influence whatsoever at that time, but he is constantly referred to today by specialists in the Balkans (Shankland 2013:intro.).

Yet, the cul-de-sac vision does not apply to Westermarck, or more precisely only in part. We need to differentiate. His fieldwork, which *was* modern in execution, is brilliant but difficult to digest for the modern social anthropologist used to highly contextualized cross-cutting material that illustrates the complexities of life in a small-scale community. Given its inherent quality, it is possible that a Westermarckian school of field research could emerge, but as yet none has done so. Thus his fieldwork has not been influential, other than indirectly by example of his actually being a fieldworker.

An even more negative argument could be made for his extensive philosophical writings. In terms of amount published, Westermarck clearly devoted as much of his attention to ethics as any other subject, if not more. His two major works, *The Origin and Development of the Moral Ideas* (1906–8) and *Ethical Relativity* (1932), offer a description of approaches to ethics, and a new system of his own, that are written with persuasive clarity. Yet, they appear to have had no progeny.[19] This is in spite of the fact that anthropologists later in the twentieth century and in this have become fascinated by ethics and by the question of cultural relativity. In this volume, Bloch and Kronqvist revisit Westermarck's writings afresh, and find great interest in doing so. Nevertheless, Westermarck's insistence that moral ideas are rooted in emotions was not at the time sufficiently attractive to be regarded as being worthy of incorporation into the anthropological canon. Today, if we as anthropologists return to his writings on this subject, it is not with a sense of revisiting classics, but rather with a sense of surprise that they exist at all.

Yet all this contrasts with his work on kinship and marriage. Here, the trail both in terms of his published work, *A History of Human Marriage*, and his personal influence as a teacher and a scholar is discernable. That inspiration fed into the very school of anthropology that later became dominant. That they came later to ignore his contribution was at great cost to the historical accuracy of our accounts of the way that anthropology developed, yet illustrates modern anthropology's failure to recognise its debt to a school of thought that was essential to its founding.

Notes

1   A second edition appeared in 1894, a third in 1901 and a reprint in 1903. Stroup (1982:274) suggests that a distinct fourth edition may have been published in 1911, though I too have been unable to locate one. Either way, the initial one-volume edition was expanded and rewritten to three volumes in 1921, and published as the fifth edition.

2   A detailed bibliography of Westermarck's writings is provided by Stroup (1982:274–92).

3   I am most grateful to Mrs Bell for the translation, and to Dr Bell, and Professor Lagerspetz for their comments on it.

4   Shereef sîdi Abdessalam El-Baqqâli (1876–1942) was Westermarck's crucial contact and friend in Morocco. The Shereef was employed as Westermarck's guide and the head of his household, but he also gave him language instruction and collected fieldwork data. El-Baqqâli is explicitly acknowledged as the co-author in *Wit and Wisdom in Morocco*, a collection of proverbs.

5   General Sir Harry Maclean (1848–1920), who was in the Sultan's employ as an army commander (*qaid*).

6   James Sully (1842–1923), professor of psychology at University College, London. Westermarck first met Sully on a hiking tour in the Norwegian mountains in 1885, after which they remained close friends.

7   Relating to alleged violations of the Finnish Constitution by the Russian central government.

8   The Hague Peace Conference, convening in July 1899 on the initiative of Nicholas II of Russia.

9   In Edward's childhood, the Westermarcks spent several summers at Träskända (Järvenpää) manor north of Helsinki, then owned by the Ehrströms. Walter, Edward's brother, married the daughter, Alfhild Ehrström, and took over the estate in 1899.

10   See also Stroup 1984.

11   A meeting of teachers from Oxford, Cambridge and London was held to discuss the terminology of our subject. We agreed to use "ethnography" as the term for descriptive accounts of non-literate peoples. The hypothetical reconstruction of "history" of such people was accepted as the task of ethnology and prehistoric archaeology. The comparative study of the institutions of primitive society was accepted as the task of social anthropology, and this name was preferred to "sociology". (Radcliffe-Brown 1952:276).

12   See for instance, Lubbock 1871:esp. 29.

13   The changing use of the word sociology is an interesting issue. That Westermarck himself regarded sociology as similar to social anthropology is clear, for example from his inaugural lecture to the LSE, which is reprinted in this volume. Sociology was clearly used also to mean social anthropology at the 1934 international conference of anthropology organized in London (Anon. 1934:iii, 268–88), where it became Section F, and at which Westermarck spoke. His address there is also reprinted in this volume. See also the comment by Radcliffe-Brown: 'Frazer, in 1906, had already defined social anthropology as the branch of sociology that deals with primitive people. Westermarck held the position of Professor of Sociology, even though his work was in the field of social anthropology.' (Radcliffe-Brown 1952:276).

14   See also Westermarck's translations of Moroccan proverbs (1930).

15   Montague in Stroup (1982:65–6).

16   The internal quotation is from the *LSE Calendar* 1910–11:190–1.

17   The quotation is taken from the published abstract (Anon. 1934:269). The paper
     itself was deposited in the RAI archives, with Westermarck's corrections, but not
     to our knowledge subsequently published.

18   Stocking, of course, is fully aware of Westermarck (e.g. Stocking 1987). The point
     is that he doesn't feel the need to integrate that awareness into his account of the
     emergence of the later anthropologists who came to dominate.

19   The detailed discussion by Stroup in his dissertation (1982b) is a noticeable
     exception to this neglect, though it may be noted that it was published in Finland,
     by the Westermarck society, rather than in Britain.

References

Anon. [J. L. Myres]. 1934. *Congres International des Science Anthropologiques
     et Ethnologiques. Compte-rendu de la premiere Session, Londres, 1934.*
     Londres: Institut Royal D'Anthropologie.

Anon. 1939. Obituary: Edward Alexander Westermarck: 1862–1939. *American
     Journal of Sociology* 45(3):452.

Evans-Pritchard, E. 1950. Social Anthropology past and present. *Man*:118–24

Gellner, E. 1969 *Saints of the Atlas.* London: Weidenfeld and Nicholson.

Gellner, E. 1995 *Anthropology and Politics.* Oxford: Blackwell.

Goody, J. 1995 *The Expansive Moment: the Rise of Social Anthropology in Britain and
     Africa, 1918–1970.* Cambridge: Cambridge University Press.

Handler, R. 1985. Edward Westermarck: essays on his life and works by Timothy
     Stroup [review]. *American Anthropologist* (NS) 87(3):684–5.

Lowie, R. 1937. *The History of Ethnological Theory.* New York: Farrar and Rinehart.

Lubbock, J. 1871. On the development of relationships. *The Journal of the
     Anthropological Institute* 1:1–29.

Malinowski, B. 1913. *The Family among the Australian Aborigines.* London:
     University of London Press.

Montague, A. 1982. Edward Westermarck; recollections of an old student in young
     age. In T. Stroup 1982a:63–70.

Pro Finlandia. 1899 *Pro Finlandia, Les adresses internationals á S.M. l'émpereur-
     grand-duc Nicolas II. International Peace Conference.* Berlin: Mertz.

Radcliffe-Brown, A. 1952. Historical note on British Social Anthropology. *American
     Anthropologist* (NS) 54(2):275–7.

Shankland, D. (ed.) 2013. *Archaeology, Anthropology and Heritage in the Balkans and
     Anatolia: The Life and Works of FW Hasluck, 1878–1920.* Istanbul: Isis
     Books.

Shankland, D. Forthcoming. *The Roots of International Co-operation in Anthropology
     and the founding of the IUAES.* Warsaw: Polish Institute of Anthropology.

Stocking, G. (ed.) 1984. *Functionalism Historicized: Essays on British Social
     Anthropology.* Wisconsin: University of Wisconsin Press.

Stocking, G. 1987. *Victorian Anthropology.* New York: Free Press.

Stroup T. (ed.) 1982a. *Edward Westermarck: Essays on his Life and Works.* Helsinki:
     Societas Philosophica Fennica 34.

Stroup, T. 1982b. *Westermarck's Ethics.* Åbo: Publications of the Research Institute of
     the Akademi Foundation.

Stroup, T. 1984. Edward Westermarck: a reappraisal. *Man* (NS) 19(4):575–92.

Westermarck, E. 1891. *A History of Human Marriage,* London: Macmillan.

Westermarck. E. 1906–8. *The Origin and Development of the Moral Ideas* (2 vols). London: Macmillan.

Westermarck, E. 1907. The principles of fasting. *Folklore* 18(4):391–422.

Westermarck, E. 1913. The popular ritual of the great feast in Morocco. *Folklore* 22(2):131–82.

Westermarck, E. 1926. *Ritual and belief in Morocco*. London: Macmillan and Co.

Westermarck, E. 1929. *Memories of my Life* (trans. A. Barwell). London: George Allen and Unwin.

Westermarck, E. 1930. *Wit and Wisdom in Morocco: A Study of Native Proverbs by Edward Westermarck with the assistance of Shereef 'Abd-es- SalamEl-Baqqali*. London: George Routledge & Sons.

Westermarck, E. 1932. *Ethical Relativity*. London: Kegan Paul, Trench, Trubner.

Young, M. 2004. *Malinowski: Odyssey of an Anthropologist, 1884–1920*. New Haven: Yale University Press.

Part 1 – On Westermarck

1

Westermarck, anthropology and the Royal Anthropological Institute

David Shankland

My acquaintance with Westermarck as a writer and ethnographer goes back some twenty-five years, to a period in which I was writing up my fieldwork in Morocco. Almost routinely, I ordered up his researches on North Africa at the library of the Royal Anthropological Institute, at that time based in the Museum of Mankind, at the British Museum. The books arrived at my table, and I was astonished at the quality, richness and thoroughness of the work that they contained. Who, I wondered, is this Westermarck? And why was he so puzzlingly absent in modern anthropology curricula? From that point on, I have retained a fondness for his memory, and I willingly join in now our public celebration of his name.

It may help to revisit, very briefly, the main works with which he made his reputation as a fieldworker. They are *Marriage Ceremonies in Morocco* (1914), *Ritual and Belief in Morocco* (1926), and an accompanying work on proverbs, with simultaneous Arabic and English versions, *Wit and Wisdom in Morocco* (1930). These of course accompany his much wider theoretical speculations on marriage, on the origins of the family, and on philosophy and ethics, as well as his other volumes not strictly professionally devoted to his subject, such as his autobiography and his final monograph, on theology. His approach is unusual in its breadth. Immediately, to a modern anthropologist, this presents something of a puzzle. His writings appear to be a reflection of the previous era from one point of view, and an anticipation of the future in another.

I should explain. Modern anthropology, though it may sometimes regret this, is divided between two periods: AM and PM, or *ante Malinowski*, and *post Malinowski*. However much the sharpness of the distinction is to be deplored, however much anthropologists have despairingly – as did Herbert so long ago – 'Struck the board, and cry'd, "No more!"', Malinowski really did revolutionize the way the discipline went about its business.[1] Before Malinowski, there were a number of leading figures who treated anthropology as the rightful speculation of mankind's origins, whether from the physical point of view, or cultural. These were most notably represented by Robertson Smith, Tylor, Marett and, above all, Frazer, in volumes as extensive in scope as they were learned. After Malinowski and his brilliantly dense researches in the Trobriand Islands, the emphasis changed sharply. History becomes much less emphasized, and the quality of fieldwork instead became judged on just that, the minute contextualization of detail accompanied by the assumption that everything within a particular location may become equally relevant: here economy, politics and kinship become as important as the magic and religion that pre-occupied Frazer and so many of his contemporaries.

This transformation produced a huge leap in the overall quality of the work that was produced. In some ways, it is analogous to the transition in archaeology between the early period before stratigraphic excavation and that after.[2] One can do so much more with data, if one knows where the information is coming from. Yet, and this is something that the PM anthropologists did not always appreciate, the questions that their forebears asked remain just as valid and just as potentially interesting as before. In their steadfast desire to avoid examining the issues which distinguished their ancestors, PM anthropologists have tended to leave the great questions concerning diffusion, for example, to archaeologists, leading without a doubt to an impoverishment and splintering of the field. The emergence of an unnecessarily acute disciplinary boundary between archaeologists and anthropologists, and between biological and social anthropology, has still not entirely been overcome.[3]

Westermarck, though, relished these earlier questions, even as they were becoming less frequently the preoccupation of the younger generation of anthropologists. Not just this, his treatment of these questions in his work remains pertinent. His early proposition that proximity results in incest avoidance is simple but brilliant and, as is often noted, a precise antidote to the fantasies of Freud. His work on the origins of marriage, denying the possibility of primitive promiscuity, is a cornerstone of modern kinship, even if unacknowledged as such.

Emotionally, as well as intellectually, Westermarck appears to have been entirely at home with this group of anthropological elders. Far from the ambitious unease which permeates Malinowski from the outset, Westermarck in moving to London found in Frazer, Seligman, Marett, Haddon, Rivers and others a congenial field of enquiry with which he was entirely content.[4] It is as if, having left Finland to broaden his acquaintance of broader scholarly worlds, he was thoroughly pleased with what he has found, devotes his life to it, and takes an active role within it, without for a moment wishing to replace this network of collegiality with a new team, and a new paradigm.

An instance of this can be seen in his successful interaction with the Royal Anthropological Institute. The RAI was by that time, in the early part of the twentieth century, settled down in Bedford Square. Its council, library, lecture series, fellows and intellectual pre-occupations are recognizably similar to today, and notably amongst anthropological bodies it has never recognized the divisions into which university anthropology fell in the twentieth century, assuming that a multi-field approach must remain the most fruitful way of tackling the subject. Westermarck fitted comfortably into this already established framework. He was elected a Fellow of the Institute, nominated by Seligman, his colleague at the LSE in 1905. He contributed to the institute's journal, still the periodical of record in the UK today (Westermarck 1904). He was elected a member of Council in 1907–9, and again in 1911–12. He was awarded the Rivers medal for his researches in Morocco in 1926, then – the most significant accolade that the RAI can offer – was invited to give the Huxley lecture in 1936.

The Huxley lecture is a very revealing event, in that it puts a lecturer firmly in the public eye in front of his or her peers. It remains a significant date in the social calendar to this day, regularly filling the lecture theatre at the Clore Centre in the British Museum. Some speakers use it to survey the field, or to offer a tour de force of the sort of analysis they find interesting, an illustration, as it were, of their scholarly technique. Others take a more reflective approach, and meditate on what they have found over the course of their careers, almost as a form of intellectual autobiography. Westermarck takes this latter approach, but goes further than this even, and warming to his audience, takes the opportunity to offer thanks and acknowledge the intellectual home that he has found. He also defends the AM group of anthropologists, who had offered him intellectual friendship, rigorously. Here, he appears to be specifically responding to Radcliffe-Brown and the more ahistoricist approach that was beginning to become popular.

> Although it has been said that the 'new anthropology' avoids all discussion of hypotheses as to historical origins, I think on the contrary that, in many cases, it belongs to the task of the field-anthropologist to be concerned with the question of such origins, after he has studied the cultural phenomena and their relations as they exist at present. I fail to see how my researches in Morocco could have avoided this question, and how anybody but a field-worker could have tackled it with any prospect of success.
>
> Westermarck (1936:247)[5]

And, at the conclusion of his lecture, he states his allegiance quite clearly:

> Ladies and Gentlemen! I am afraid that I ought to make an apology for the
> rather egotistic character of my lecture. The greater part of it consists of an
> account of the methods, illustrated by examples, which I have applied in my
> own researches, both as an armchair anthropologist and as a field-worker.
> They are in essential points similar to those which have been characteristic
> of what may be called the classical school of English social anthropology;
> and I hope that this may serve me as an excuse for repeating much that
> has been said by others before. I have felt an eager wish to express my
> indebtedness to English anthropology for what I have learned from it. And
> at the same time I have desired to raise a protest against what has recently
> been said by the esteemed advocate of the 'new anthropology' about the
> 'unsoundness' of its methods, culminating in the allegation that 'in England
> we have very little of anything that is called sociology.' I am convinced that
> there is no country in the world that can rival it in its achievements in social
> anthropology, whether pursued in the study or in the field, largely owing to
> its sterling qualities of lucidity and good sense.
>
>   Westermarck (1936:248)

North Africa

If Westermarck was nineteenth century in his anthropological approach or, to
put it another way, was clear that the prime purpose of anthropology was to
seek the origins and developments of man and his culture, how did he turn into
such an outstanding fieldworker, and how was his fieldwork influenced by this
theoretical orientation? Here, again, Westermarck should be given immense
credit, for he realized even as a young man that the only way to justify the
elaborate claims of anthropology was to conduct fieldwork. In this, he was
unusual. No other practitioner of generalized theories felt simultaneously
the urge to spend so much time with a strange society. Even Marett, who in
some respects is the most modern of this group in his approach, conducted
no ethnography at all, even if he acknowledged its desirability (Marett 1912).
Westermarck, of course, actually put his claims into actions, and did so
supremely effectively.

With the benefit of hindsight, we can see already some attributes that made
Westermarck into the fine fieldworker that he was. Perhaps alone of this early
group, he was ready to espouse ethical relativism. This was later to become a
hallmark of modern social anthropology, leading to criticisms sometimes from
outsiders that it has become too Panglossian in its thinking. Perhaps there is
something in this. Nevertheless, some level of ethical relativism is absolutely

vital, otherwise the empathy that is essential to understand another way of thinking from the inside simply is not there.

In addition, Westermarck was not just a remarkable scholar in the sense that he could draw together, study and synthesize a vast range of material. He was also an empiricist, with that fieldworker's knack of finding every detail about a strange people of interest in itself; more than this, as he frequently mentions, he used to check and recheck his findings at every opportunity, meaning that his comments are based on an unusual level of ethnographic thoroughness. Then, having obtained the material, he was assiduous in recording it, meaning that the detail is very carefully written down at the time of its obtaining.

He also realized very soon that good fieldwork takes time. The seven years that he spent in total in Morocco is, I would certainly say, about the right time to get to know a society. The disentangling of the immensely complicated social interactions, ritual, beliefs, politics and economics that one encounters in the field simply cannot be undertaken adequately in a brief spell.

Accompanying this already formidable set of qualities, we may add that he was a superb linguist. His English is excellent; simple, clear and accurate, not just in his published texts, but also his letters. His Arabic was, by all accounts, as good. He gives throughout his works abundant transliterations of the original phrases, and is confident enough to publish in *Wit and Wisdom in Morocco* a parallel text of proverbs (something even today many fieldworkers would hesitate to do), explaining precisely that to translate the pithy linguistic nuances of everyday sayings is a key to gaining insights into a strange culture.

As a result, the fieldwork in Morocco through which he sought such answers has scarcely been bettered by anyone, then or now, in Morocco or elsewhere. Though now nearly a hundred years has passed since his work has been published, he is quoted frequently today. For example, his long essay on the evil eye, received well at the time and reprinted in *Ritual and Belief*, was used equally appreciatively by Michael Herzfeld (1981), a leading contemporary anthropologist working on the other side of the Mediterranean. It is indeed an outstanding piece of writing.

Why then, the eclipse? Why should he be so utterly ignored in all anthropology curricula? The answer lies not just in the way that fashions change, though this is part of the problem. Evans-Pritchard noted already in his Marett lecture in 1950 that the search for origins had become unpalatable for anthropologists, writing perhaps a little harshly: 'It had in any case ceased to stimulate research, because once the stages of human development had been marked out further investigation on these lines offered nothing more exciting than attachment of labels written by dead hands.' (Evans-Pritchard 1950:198).[6] The split, the division of intellectual labour that has emerged here between social anthropology and archaeology, is obvious, and clearly Westermarck's varied theoretical contribution was going to find little succour in a discipline that eschewed his approach so forcefully. What of his fieldwork, however? Why is this not used?

Here, we come across a problem that is not only one of fashion. However thoroughly Westermarck conducted his research, he had not developed a strong idea of place or context. Though of course he knew Malinowski well, having been one of his tutors at the LSE, he did not borrow from him that ability to see how it is possible to see all social life in terms of an expanding series of interwoven events which give meaning to and influence each other.[7] Malinowski characterized these guiding frameworks as 'institutions', treating the word very widely. The American anthropologist Murdock, who knew Malinowski well, writing sadly in his obituary after his early death from a heart attack, summed up these 'institutions' as follows,

> *(1) personnel,* a group of individuals cooperating in the performance of
> a common task; *(2) material apparatus,* the artifacts employed in their
> activities; *(3) norms,* the rules or ideal patterns to which behavior is
> expected to conform; *(4) activities,* the behavior, including deviation from
> norms, which actually takes place in the performance of the joint tasks; *(5)*
> *charter,* the express cultural definition of the common aims or purpose of
> the institution; and *(6) function,* the actual effect of the collective enterprise
> in satisfying human needs.
>
> (Murdock 1943:442)

In Malinowski's hands, the ethnographic details and linguistic turn, so ably demonstrated by his teacher Westermarck, become much more clearly clustered in these multiple layers, so that one can see how all becomes interrelated around a single social phenomenon. *Argonauts of the Western Pacific,* the scintillating founding text of this new school, demonstrates this through the multiple approaches to the *kula,* the ceremonial gift exchange practised by the Trobriand Islanders. Evans-Pritchard, more influenced by Malinowski than he would have liked to admit, takes this approach one step further in *Magic, Witchcraft and Oracles amongst the Azande,* in producing what is perhaps the most influential work of all of that modern school of social anthropology, showing that thought can be utterly bound up in itself, so that the external world becomes hardly relevant. Westermarck, with his emphasis on magic, ritual and charms in North Africa, would not have been surprised at Evans-Pritchard's analysis. Indeed, he concludes after his seven years in Morocco that everything is pervaded by these forces of belief and magic. However, the way that he wrote up his researches means that the interlocking sense of mutual reinforcement of the different elements of social life is almost always absent, to the disappointment of the social anthropologists who succeeded him and who have searched for this now familiar method in his fieldwork accounts.

Yet, even here, I would argue that there is a danger of being too hasty on a number of levels. It should be reiterated that Westermarck was committed to an exploration of magic and religion that had in mind not the modernist theories of Malinowski and Radcliffe-Brown, but the example of Frazer, with whom he politely but firmly disagrees. He does, it is true, divide up the material in a way that apparently destroys much of the social context that today we find so interesting, but taken individually, the successive chapters in *Ritual and Belief in Morocco*, for instance, are still first class if taken on their own terms. His explanation of the transfer of design in the evil eye as sequential steps from the human body, to the material, to the architectural is, even if not the way that we might phrase the question today, a piece of analysis of the very first rank. It is, just as his other sociological insights, both surprising and convincing.

Further, even though he does not provide the clear account of the social background of the region that we would now regard as necessary, a careful reading of volume one of *Ritual and Belief* does in fact provide a fascinating overview of Moroccan society at that time, one that is from the point of view of the tribesman. He shows how, just as Gellner (1981) was to claim some decades later, political forces are balanced between the ruling power of the Sultan and the *baraka* of local saints, who provide with their sacred potential a temporal focal point of social action through their physical presence (and of the shrines which are built after them). It is unfair to wish that an author had provided something that they had no intention or desire to, but such is the wealth of scattered detail that a fruitful reanalysis would here be possible. Indeed, I cannot help but think that fifty pages on dispute settling from as accomplished a pen as Westermarck's would have saved ten times as many pages of subsequent dispute amongst anthropologists of the next generation on this aspect of Moroccan society. Perhaps it may also be possible, such is the quality of Westermarck's notes, to go back to them and distil further, supplementary information.

Finally, if one reads carefully, the social context does occasionally come alive in a way that is palatable even to the most committed of modern social anthropologists. Take, for example, his detailed description of the way oaths and curses may be exchanged, which helps to put a social context to the earlier descriptions of saints, their followers and those who would seek magical relief, so that the everyday interaction, and invective, between men becomes clear.

Following this, there is a remarkable chapter, one that has no exact parallel until the work of Bourdieu, and was perhaps an influence upon his concept of *habitus*, which he was to develop amongst the Berbers in the 1970s, and with which he was to make his name (Bourdieu 1977). I refer to Westermarck's dense description in volume one, chapter ten, of a custom known as *Ar*, one that is halfway between a challenge to help, a commitment to protect the weak and a mechanism of shame. It may be invoked by a poor man to a richer, a husband to a wife, a wife to her husband, and even between a supplicant and a saint, alive or dead. Here is social anthropological writing at its very best, it describes the way that social actors are bound together in a hierarchical negotiation which none can escape, but which may be brought into play on either side depending on how the actors see each other in terms of their mutual interplay. Rereading it now suddenly enabled me to understand something that has puzzled me for twenty-six years, ever since I appealed for help to a Berber family of the Ait Buggmez. The family took me in immediately, protected me and helped me without question: they had accepted me according to their rules, rules of which I as a young anthropologist in the field was woefully ignorant, but which Westermarck the master fieldworker had already delineated beautifully so many years before.

Notes

1   There are many histories of this modern movement, amongst the most useful are Jarvie (1967), and Kuper (1996).

2   On theoretical changes within archaeology, see Trigger (2006).

3   On the split between archaeology and anthropology, see Shankland (2012:intro).

4   As well as Westermarck's own comments on his life in this respect (for example, in Westermarck 1929), see Stroup's intellectual biography (1982).

5   The lecture is reprinted in this volume.

6   The previous sentence is equally dismissive: 'The reaction against the attempt to explain social institutions in terms of parallel, seen ideally as unilinear, development came at the end of the century; and though this so-called evolutionary anthropology was recast and re-presented in the writings of Westermarck and Hobhouse it had finally lost its appeal.'

7   Malinowski actually seems to have been influenced by Westermarck's use of the term 'social institutions' in teaching in developing this idea (see Introduction above, pp. 8–9). This is curious, and leads us to the conclusion that for Westermarck this was one of a number of possible analytical approaches, whereas for Malinowski it became the defining principle of his ethnographic approach and writings. Westermarck, though clearly aware of what his erstwhile pupil was developing, didn't warm to it sufficiently to change his own fieldwork style.

References

Bourdieu, P. 1977. *Outline of a Theory of Practice*. Cambridge: Cambridge University Press.

Evans-Pritchard, E., 1950. Social anthropology past and present. *Man* 50:118–24.

Gellner, E. 1981. *Muslim Society.* Cambridge: Cambridge University Press.

Herzfield, M. 1981. Meaning and morality: a semiotic approach to the evil eye accusations in a Greek village. *American Ethnologist* 8(3):560–74.

Jarvie, I. 1967. *The Revolution in Anthropology.* London: Routledge and Kegan Paul Books.

Kuper, A. 1996. *Anthropology and Anthropologists: The Modern British School* (3rd edn.). London: Routledge.

Marett, R.R. 1912. *Anthropology.* London: Williams and Norgate.

Murdock, G. Malinowski [obituary]. *American Anthropologist* 45(3):441–51.

Shankland, D. (ed.) 2013. *Archaeology and Anthropology: Past, Present and Future* (Association of Social Anthropologists Monographs Series Number 48). London: Berg.

Stroup, T. 1982. *Westermarck's Ethics* (Publications of the Research Institute of the Åbo Akademi Foundation). Åbo: Åbo Akademi.

Suolinna, K. 2000. Hilma Granqvist: a scholar of the Westermarck school in its decline. *Acta Sociologica* 43(4):317–23.

Trigger, B. 2006. *A History of Archaeological Thought* (2nd edn.). Cambridge: Cambridge University Press.

Westermarck, E. 1904. The magic origin of Moorish design. *Journal of the Anthropological Institute of Great Britain and Ireland* 34:211–22.

Westermarck, E. 1914. *Marriage Ceremonies in Morocco.* London: Macmillan.

Westermarck, E. 1926. *Ritual and Belief in Morocco.* London: Macmillan.

Westermarck, E. 1929. *Memories of my Life* (trans. A. Barwell). London: George Allen and Unwin.

Westermarck, E. 1936. Methods in social anthropology. *Journal of the Royal Anthropological Institute of Great Britain and Ireland* 66:223–48.

2

Edward Westermarck at the
Academy of Åbo, 1918–32

OLLI LAGERSPETZ AND KIRSTI SUOLINNA

For most of his working life, Edward Westermarck held teaching positions in two countries simultaneously. His position at the London School of Economics (LSE) gave him a platform in international scholarly debate, but he was intent on making his mark on Finnish academic life as well. He was active in founding a completely new university. From 1906, Westermarck held a professorship at Helsingfors (Helsinki). In 1918 he resigned from there and took up the chair of philosophy in the newly founded Academy of Åbo (today, Åbo Akademi University),[1] which he would lead as its first Rector.

At the time of his move to Åbo (Turku), Westermarck was an accomplished scholar with an international research network. His students, who had profited from his academic contacts, were gradually establishing themselves as scholars in their own right. Westermarck's move to Åbo did not imply any major disturbance on this score. As before, he was engaged to teach in London in the summer terms. After the early 1920s this was in close cooperation with his former student, Malinowski. Important members of Westermarck's Finnish academic network also moved to Åbo. The new university obviously profited from these contacts. It could attract a wider group of academics and it was able at once to start a series of high quality research volumes. But there were problems too. As we will see, Westermarck's set descended on Åbo complete with aspirations, fears, and prejudices that sometimes blinded them to the unexplored possibilities and acute needs of the new university; mainly, the need to attract students. As university finances deteriorated, Westermarck became the centre of many interwoven conflicts in a close-knit academic milieu.

Figure 1   Rolf Lagerborg, Westermarck's disciple and colleague, kept up a correspondence with Westermarck for 45 years. By courtesy of Veronica Wirseen, digitized by www.filosofia.fi.

In *Memories of My Life*, written in 1927, Westermarck writes of his time at Åbo,

> It is perhaps rare to find that a person of my age, who leaves his old home and birthplace for another neighbourhood, gets on so excellently in his new environment.
>
> (Westermarck 1929:282)

He mentions old and new friends, generous sponsors and beautiful surroundings. Nothing is said of his relations to colleagues. The most obvious omission is his failure to mention that his rectorate was cut unexpectedly short. The university senate failed to re-elect him for Rector for a new triennium in 1921.

Published memoirs are a notoriously selective source of information. No doubt this is especially true with regard to comments on living persons with whom the author is actively working, as Westermarck still was at the time of writing (he retired only in 1932). Fortunately, Westermarck, who typically spent a large part of the year abroad, kept up a lively correspondence with his closest colleagues at Åbo. His most important correspondent was the philosopher Rolf Lagerborg (1874–1959), a former student and old friend. Some more dramatic developments at the Academy were also reported and debated in newspapers. Some are described in memoirs written by others. By looking at contemporary documents of this kind we hope to present the outlines of Westermarck's years at Åbo.[2]

Background: Swedish cultural autonomy in Finland

Westermarck's involvement with the Academy of Åbo had an explicitly political background, as did the creation of the Academy itself. The Academy of Åbo was founded in late 1918 as a private university, after fundraising among local businessmen and among the Swedish-speaking population in Finland generally.[3] At the time, Swedish-speakers made up about a tenth of the total population. The campaigners hoped that the Academy would constitute a new nucleus of autonomous Swedish culture on Finnish soil. The first students were admitted in January 1919. The new university started its work in a country that had recently gained its independence (1917) and gone through a civil war (1918). However, preparations for the new site of learning had started earlier in the 1900s, when Finland was still part of the Russian Empire.

Finnish university life in the late nineteenth and early twentieth century was strongly committed to nation building, in what was then the Russian Grand Duchy of Finland. The nation's only full university, Imperial Alexander University at Helsingfors (later, the University of Helsinki), served as a training ground for future leaders of public life. University appointments were often politically charged. Bourgeois politics c.1885–1917 was dominated by two central concerns: relations to Russian central government and the rivalry between ethnic Finns and ethnic Swedes.[4] Nationalist politicians in Russia hoped to dismantle the constitutionally guaranteed Finnish autonomy.[5] In domestic Finnish politics, the language of instruction at the Alexander University was a central bone of contention. Academic conflicts tended to have a language dimension. Westermarck's conflicts at Helsingfors were connected with his support of Swedish.[6] Swedish had traditionally held a strong position in all walks of public life. The university, like other public institutions, was committed to bilingualism, but as Finnish was advancing, it was widely believed that Swedish would soon be elbowed out. There were also fears that Russian dominance was waiting in the wings.

Preparations for a new university at Åbo were responses to these two issues.[7] As a private university with Swedish as its medium of instruction, the new institution would be immune to pressures from either the Russian central government or Finnish ethnic nationalists. As a final piece of the jigsaw, the idea of a university at Åbo captured the imagination of the local high bourgeoisie. They fondly recalled that Åbo had been a university town until 1828. At first, the activists organized a programme of public academic lectures and campaigned for money. Westermarck joined the preparatory work. Arthur Rindell, the future Vice-chancellor, who contacted him with the offer of a chair at Åbo, assumed he would enjoy an environment less disturbed by ethnic politics and being 'rid of Finnish and the lot'.[8]

Figure 2   Åbo Academy main building. The new Academy gradually took over most of the property in the area of the original Academy of 1640–1828. By courtesy of Åbo Akademi University (ÅAU) Library.

Moving to a fledgling university may look like an odd career move for a scholar of Westermarck's stature. He had received and turned down feelers from prestigious universities abroad.[9] But he liked, as he put it, 'the fascinating task of organizing a new university for Swedish-speaking Finland, whose foundation I had greeted with enthusiasm and which was now begging for my services' (Westermarck 1929:275–6). Many of those who took the initiative, including Rindell, were his personal friends, and some were relatives. As his students from Helsingfors grew older, he managed to secure some of them teaching positions at Åbo. A Faculty of Politics was created, the first of its kind in Scandinavia.

It almost looks as if Westermarck was hoping to re-create a likeness of LSE on Finnish soil: a seat for modern research and education, unencumbered by obsolete research traditions such as Theology and German Idealism. A letter by Rindell (after Westermarck had already accepted the chair) held out the additional prospect of an international research institute to be headed by Westermarck,[10] an idea that was, however, never realized. The university at Helsingfors was the other obvious model for the new university. It was often assumed that the Academy of Åbo would gradually take over most of the 'Swedish' functions of Helsingfors.

Figure 3   Westermarck (left) with donors at Åbo. He seems to have felt thoroughly at home with the local haute bourgeoisie (ÅAU Library).

Westermarck as Rector

On paper at least, the Rector had a central position at the Academy. He would chair the meetings of the senate (*konsistorium*). The senate included all professors who held regular chairs. Except for the Registrar (*akademisekreterare*), who had no vote but acted as secretary, other staff were not included. The Registrar at the time was Svante Dahlström (1883–1965), a historian by education. Dahlström, who had studied at Helsingfors, had also been taught by Westermarck. They were also fellow former members of Prometheus, a Helsingfors student club devoted to secularism and freedom of religion. Dahlström had campaigned actively for the new university. There was also a Chancellor and a Vice-Chancellor,[11] whose powers, technically, were mainly limited to monitoring the legality of university decisions. However, they wielded considerable informal influence. Vice-Chancellor Rindell negotiated with prospective new staff on the university's behalf. He also kept Westermarck informed of the situation at Åbo during his absences.

Figure 4   The original Senate of the Academy of Åbo (ÅAU Library). From left to right: Helge Backlund (Geology), Per-Olof von Törne (Scandinavian History), Karl F. Lindman (Physics), Severin Johansson (Mathematics), Edward Westermarck (Philosophy), Svante Dahlström (Registrar).

All these officials were known to Westermarck from his time as a student and young scholar at Helsingfors.

The main donors, mostly elderly heads of big commercial houses, constituted a Board of Trustees.[12] They would secure the funding and had a strong say in the affairs of the new university. Any new ideas that involved money needed the green light from the Trustees. Westermarck had excellent relations also with them. In sum, he could count on the support of important sections of the new academic community.

Yet the situation was somewhat unstable from Westermarck's point of view. At this stage, the university was diminutive. It was agreed that it should include faculties of Science, Engineering, Arts and Politics. But not all the chairs had been permanently filled. Temporary teachers were not included in the senate, which initially was only comprised of two professors from the Arts (including Westermarck) and four from the Sciences.[13] When the interests of the Arts and the Sciences clashed, Westermarck was frequently outvoted.

Figure 5   Westermarck in Rector's robes, procured in Britain for the inauguration of 1919 (ÅAU Library). The outfit prompted a comment from the LSE: 'We are looking forward at the School to great developments and let us hope to ample funds though whether we shall ever be able to do our chief in the princely style of Äbo [sic] "I hae ma doots" as we say in Scotland.' (C.S. Mactaggart to Westermarck, 20 January 1919, ÅAB: EW).

Arts vs. sciences, basic vs. applied

In his introductory address at the opening of the university in 15 January 1919, Westermarck outlined his academic vision. He returned to the theme in his inauguration speech of 11 October (Westermarck 1927:369–70, 379; 1929:279–80).[14] The Academy would be a full-fledged research university. The emphasis should lie on basic research rather than applied science. There should be no expectation of immediate economic profit. Nor should one immediately hope to attract great student numbers. In fact he hinted that the shortage of students would be an advantage from a research point of view (Westermarck 1927:369). The scholars should publish for an international audience. A series of publications, Acta Academiæ Aboensis, was initiated, with the first volume carrying Westermarck's paper on 'The belief in spirits in Morocco' as well as four other ethnological pieces by his former students Rafael Karsten, Gunnar Landtman and K. Rob. V. Wikman.[15]

At the initiatory phase of the Academy, very different hopes had been pinned on the future seat of learning. Both a pure research institute and a vocational university had been envisioned. Some members of the Science faculty were opposed to Westermarck's approach. Mainly they suspected him of prejudice against natural and applied science. To quote a description of how they were thinking,

> Art History, Heredity Research, and other fine things which also required a costly apparatus around the Chair, were favoured more than simple and respectable sciences that help their students forward to useful activities and daily bread. The first Rector was rather dismissive of experimental science, whose methods and goals he would often, in discussions, polemically chastise as somewhat impure and muddled. He never set foot in chemical laboratories and he would only absent-mindedly hear Professor Wahl's pleas for adequate apparatus. The relation between the Rector and the Trustees was good, but perhaps not quite of the right kind.... The donors ought to have been kept informed of difficulties, and new donors should have been traced. But that did not lie in Westermarck's nature. He was far too sunny and urbane to take up unpleasant topics and ruin the quiet afternoons of the captains of commerce.
>
> (Huldén 1935:116–17)

Westermarck took exception to this description, which was published in 1935.[16] Nevertheless, it describes the thinking of those sceptical of his rectorate, or at least how they wanted to remember it later.

Post-war economic hardship

Westermarck might still have pulled it off except for two things. He was required for a diplomatic mission to the League of Nations, relating to the dispute between Finland and Sweden over the Åland Islands.[17] As the proceedings dragged on, he ended up being away from Åbo for the entire academic year of 1920–1, during which time the Vice-rector stood in as the acting head of the university. Vice-rector Severin Johansson (1879–1929) was

Figure 6   Severin Johansson at his desk (ÅAU Library). Johansson believed he had to bear the brunt of the administration during Westermarck's leaves of absence.

the Professor of Mathematics, and he believed he was burdened with the brunt of the administrative work without corresponding formal authority (Huldén 1935:121). He was, however, free to influence the senate in the absence of the incumbent.

The second problem was funding. Because of post-war inflation and economic depression, there was suddenly much less money to go around. To be sure, Finland was spared the galloping inflation that, for instance, Germany famously experienced a few years later. Nevertheless, as it was said, 'we all woke up one morning and found we owned just one tenth of what we had the night before. The Academy woke up and it had ten millions instead of a hundred' (Söderhjelm 1938:64).

The donated capital was severely depleted. Even the existing donors were already in dire straits by late 1920.[18] A year later it was noted that the university funds would be twice the size if they had been converted to Swedish crowns two years earlier.[19] In 1924 Westermarck privately described the Academy as 'fit for bankruptcy'.[20] Johansson, in charge during Westermarck's leave of absence, was active and successful in looking for new sponsors. His feverish quest for funding perhaps reflected a motivated sense of panic, as the whole future of the Academy suddenly seemed uncertain.[21] Some colleagues, however, were sceptical:

A gentleman I know claimed to be persecuted by Professor Johansson to the
degree that he could not sneak into the smallest and most secluded room at
[the local hotel] Hotell Börs without Professor Johansson standing up by the
door and declaring it will cost 5.000 Marks.

(Söderhjelm 1938:56)

Severin Johansson believed that more should be done to find students and
to cultivate the interest of the business community. For him, the main thing
was not abstract learning but usefulness to society. It must be admitted that
Johansson had identified a problem that Westermarck's set ignored. Initially,
it was believed that Åbo would attract most of the 'Swedish' students from
Helsingfors, as well as additional sponsors from that city. As that was not
happening, Åbo needed to look beyond the urban middle class, the traditional
student recruiting base. Johansson hoped to reach out to rural and working-
class students, and to new sponsors, by introducing bread-and-butter subjects
like divinity, engineering, economics and modern languages. In a letter to
Westermarck in 1920, Rindell expressed his dread of an endless queue of
modern-language Chairs knocking at the door. Westermarck sympathized
with his fears.[22]

Their contrasting attitudes to theology are revealing. Johansson argued
early on for including divinity at Åbo.[23] This was anathema to Westermarck.
When it was decided in 1923 that the academic year would commence with
a church service, Westermarck reacted with 'a paroxysm of rage', as reported
by Arthur Montgomery, the professor of political economy[24]. Westermarck's
resistance only seemed to egg on the religious sympathies of Johansson,
'otherwise hardly very Christian'. Montgomery wrote he 'could only dislike
both parties'. In a letter to his friend Dahlström, Westermarck predicted a 'war
of religion'.[25] But this was only the beginning. In 1924, Anna von Rettig donated
the funds for a Faculty of Theology. Westermarck thought there were better
ways to use the money.[26] The reaction by Rolf Pipping, his nephew and *docent*
(Adjunct Professor) at Åbo, was an extreme one:

Here we are then! and obviously, no protest. – It is good in a way that you
aren't at home now. Hence you are not responsible and have no reason to
resign as a protest. I think on the contrary it is of utmost importance that
you should stay on as long as possible in order to resist theology in the
senate and in your lectures.[27]

In brief, the university received a substantial amount of money, and now
we read that Westermarck should not resign *in protest* but, on the contrary,
use his influence to sabotage the aim of the donation.[28]

Figure 7 The Senate with Severin Johansson as Chair (ÅAU Library). Three members outside natural science were added once Johansson's election was secured. From left to right: Backlund, Wahl, von Törne, Lindman, Westermarck, Johansson, Nikander, Sundwall, Gadolin, Hägglund and Dahlström (at the corner desk).

A vote of no confidence

Things came to a head in the spring of 1921. Rindell repeatedly asked Westermarck to come home, as academic politics seemed to be getting out of control.[29] Lagerborg wrote to his friend on 29 March: 'I suspect ambitious plans, far too presumptuous and ruinous for the reputation of the Academy, amongst some of the mathematical profession.'[30] On 16 April, the senate proceeded to elect the Rector for the next triennium. The mathematician Severin Johansson was elected to succeed Westermarck. Lagerborg saw the vote as a power grab by Johansson and his retinue in the Science faculty (Lagerborg 1951:110). The new Vice-rector, K.F. Lindman, also came from the Sciences. The coup was possible because the senate had not yet cleared the appointments of new professors in Arts and Politics – as Westermarck and his friends believed, with the express purpose of not upsetting the favourable power balance in the senate.[31]

The election implied a vote of no confidence in Westermarck. But it also reflected general rivalries between Arts and Sciences and between basic research and applied science (Nordström 1968:158–61). Johansson's supporters cited the need for a more determined leadership. They argued that Westermarck had treated the Rectorate as merely an honorary post.[32]

Professor Wahl, who had voted for Johansson, justified the decision with a comparison with the newly founded Polish republic:

> We did what the Poles did. When they wished to make the new republic known, they elected a world famous pianist [Paderewski] for President, but when there was work to do for the consolidation of the Republic, they turned to a general [Piłsudski].[33]

Westermarck, abroad at the time, was informed in writing.[34] In a letter to Lagerborg, he describes his feelings:

> Today I received the letter about the election. Your earlier conjectures did not surprise me the least. Already in the autumn of 1919 I clearly saw what was in the offing, and several events during the academic year have further supported my conviction. I mainly experienced a sense of relief for not having to shoulder the final responsibility for decisions made by a senate where I remain in the minority. And now I am in a better position also to defend the interests of the Humanities in that same body, than I sometimes was when I was chairing it.[35]

The election received wide public attention. There were worries that Westermarck would leave the Academy altogether, and he had to write to reassure one of the Trustees.[36] On the surface, Westermarck shook off his defeat gracefully. Nevertheless, it implied loss of prestige. Westermarck developed antipathies to his rivals. Now back in his teaching job, his feelings can be divined from a letter he sent to Lagerborg:

> You may want to hear news of your former colleagues. Johansson has let blood – 400 grams to ease his high blood pressure. Lindman is all puffed up of fat and Vice-rectorial dignity.... Wahl has taken a handsome wife, and were I twenty years younger I would pay court to her just to irritate him.... Homén [Professor of Swedish Literature] is all worried about the speech he should give at the Student Ball, and Rolf Pipping has suggested the topic of parvenu types in literature.[37]

One feels the hostility, perhaps particularly against Wahl who had voted against Westermarck. Oddly, Westermarck lays stress on his talent for womanizing. The butt of the final joke appears to be Johansson. He came from a rural working-class family and never felt quite at ease in the class-conscious company of the Trustees (Söderhjelm 1938:71).

There were attempts at reconciliation. In late 1922, Westermarck's sixtieth birthday was marked with a Festschrift and a stream of congratulations and newspaper articles. The new university leadership put their best foot forward. In good academic spirit, the former antagonists greeted each other with conciliatory speeches (see Lagerborg 1951:101–11). Yet the grudges were not overcome. The new leadership still felt an evident need to justify themselves in the context of sceptical public opinion, while Westermarck's friends nourished hopes of turning the tables.

The conflict was remembered once again when the Registrar, Svante Dahlström, celebrated his fortieth birthday in select company on 14 October 1923. In his address, Westermarck noted, in what appears to be an implicit comparison between Johansson and Dahlström, that '[t]here are different ways of doing one's work. There are those who do little but make everyone believe they work miracles; others work unseen…. We know how to appreciate a friend who always speaks his mind regardless of the unpleasantness that it may cost him.' (Lagerborg 1951:422).

The salaries dispute, 1923–4

The 'unpleasantness' Westermarck referred to had hit the Registrar a few months earlier, in the summer of 1923, when his salary had been more than halved. The acute economic crisis that had hit the Academy gave rise to a bitter conflict between university leadership and junior staff.[38] The senate had made a decision about hefty pay cuts, but the salaries of the professors – who of course could vote in the senate – were not touched. Furthermore, the Registrar had been cut much more than the others.[39] Dahlström had worked in close tandem with Westermarck and had supported him against Johansson. It seems that the plan was to force Dahlström out of the university (Nordström 1968:178). Dahlström's panicked letter to Westermarck reveals that he was pinning his hopes on his reinstatement: 'If anything still is to be saved, one needs to make Johansson let go of the result he has secured by a thousand low means.'[40]

A bitter public debate ensued. The easily recognisable *nom de plume* R.P. (Rolf Pipping) appeared in 1 August 1924 alongside a polemic piece in the magazine *Nya Argus*, under the title '*Åbo Akademi i en återvändsgränd*' ('Åbo Academy at a dead end').[41] Pipping was the President of the Teachers' and Clerics' Guild (*Åbo Akademis Lärare- och tjänstemannaförening*), which had been created in the autumn of 1923. He warned of a moral and economic vicious circle. The Academy needs money, but it cannot attract sponsors because its policies have undermined public trust (ibid.:162). First and foremost, its moral standing must be restored. It is easy to read all this as a call for new leadership. The targets of Pipping's criticism construed his article

Figure 8 Future professors (ÅAU Library). Westermarck and his nephew Hugo E. Pipping in the summer home of Anna and Hugo Pipping in 1897.

as part of a systematic smear campaign. Disciplinary measures were discussed (Westerlund 1985:20). Johansson was so upset he took leave for treatment at a nursing home for the mentally ill (Huldén 1935:77–9, 141).

Subsequent events certainly improved Johansson's spirits. On 12 September 1924, the local newspaper carried a brief letter signed by fifteen members of the Guild. Only the names of Svante Dahlström, Rolf Pipping and his brother (hence also Westermarck's nephew) Nils Pipping[42] were conspicuously absent. The signatories declared in a few words their 'confidence in the current leadership of the Academy'.[43] It was commonly assumed that the declaration had come about under pressure from the Rector, or even that he was literally the author.[44] Pipping, drawing his conclusions, resigned from the presidency

*Figure 9   Severin Johansson leading the procession of the degree ceremony in 1927,
the symbolic high point of his career (ÅAU Library). Westermarck declined the task.*

of the Guild. In October 1924, Montgomery described the situation as calm
for the time being, except that the antagonism between Johansson and
Westermarck was unresolved, and there was more or less a state of war
between Johansson and Pipping.[45]

This was apparently the last serious attempt to reinstate Westermarck
as the Rector of the Academy of Åbo. Severin Johansson continued his work
as an energetic and controversial head of the university, and a *modus vivendi*
developed between him and Westermarck until his premature death in 1929,
aged fifty.[46]

The conflict replayed

In the spring of 1927, it was suggested that Westermarck act as the leader
(*promotor*) of the degree ceremony (*promotion*), the first to be arranged by
the Academy. The request can be seen as an act of goodwill by the Rector,
otherwise the obvious person for the symbolic task. Westermarck believed the
ceremony was absurd.

> In my young days only the example of my most intimate friends could
> induce me to go through the degree ceremony, even though I laughed at it

Figure 10   From the degree ceremony of 1927 (ÅAU Library). Johansson (middle, in front) with graduates outside the main building.

and then already made fun of degree ceremonies. In Sweden, ceremonies for the Master's degree are no longer held, and I believe it would be wise for Åbo to follow the example.[47]

Westermarck had enthusiastically led the inauguration of the Academy in 1919, although he does note, at that juncture, that he had generally 'never taken much interest in academic ceremonies' (Westermarck 1929:280).[48] But to lead the ceremony now would have given the impression of symbolic reconciliation with Johansson. Perhaps he was not prepared to go to such lengths. Johansson headed the degree ceremony himself on 24 September 1927 (Nordström 1968:229–33).

A final, posthumous, replay of the Johansson-Westermarck conflict was acted out in 1935–6, with Johansson already dead and Westermarck in retirement. A biography of Severin Johansson was published by an admiring colleague (Huldén 1935). It was generally critical of Westermarck's rectorate, with the obvious objective of justifying Johansson's election *ex post facto*. A polemic exchange unfolded, with responses by both Westermarck and Dahlström.[49] Soon afterwards, the Westermarck party scored a symbolic victory when Rolf Pipping, Westermarck's nephew and once Johansson's vocal opponent, was elected Rector by a narrow majority.[50]

Figure 11   The Humanities building, originally the home of a donor (ÅAU Library). The bay windows to the left belonged to a family chapel which was converted to Westermarck's study.

On the whole, Westermarck's position at Åbo was not quite what he had initially envisioned. But in hindsight it was perhaps a blessing in disguise for him to be spared the Rector's responsibilities in a time of acute economic crisis.

Professor of Philosophy at Åbo

Westermarck continued his work as professor and faculty member. Among other things, he secured the donation of a new Humanities building.[51] On Westermarck's initiative, teaching positions in Nordic Ethnology and Sociology were created and filled according to his recommendations.[52] The future Professor of Sociology, K. Rob. V. Wikman, wrote his doctoral thesis for Westermarck. A chair in Political Economy was created and given to the Swedish Arthur Montgomery. He described himself as Westermarck's 'loyal disciple'.[53] Rolf and Nils Pipping were appointed professors in 1927 and 1930, respectively.

Starting in 1919 (with the exception of his leave of absence in the academic year of 1920–1), Westermarck was engaged to teach at Åbo for the entire academic year (running from September to end of May), excepting May and the latter half of April. In April, he would go to London for the Summer term at LSE. The Christmas holidays would often be spent in Morocco. At 65, Westermarck took semi-retirement, and taught at Åbo in the Autumn terms only, spending the springs in Morocco. He retired completely from Åbo in 1932 and from London in 1930.

Westermarck's lecture courses would typically be general overviews of topics such as Early Modern Philosophy, Philosophy of the Enlightenment, Moral Philosophy, Psychology, Comparative Religion or History of the Family.[54] He would present the main authors on the subject in an orderly textbook manner, mostly just inserting minor comments of his own.[55] In addition, he conducted seminars that other staff were encouraged to attend. At Åbo, Westermarck held a chair of philosophy rather than sociology or anthropology. On the other hand, for Westermarck at least, both social science and general philosophy tended to blend rather seamlessly into moral philosophy, largely of the Enlightenment variety. Before the establishment of the social sciences and psychology as independent disciplines, they were generally taught in Nordic universities under the heading of 'Practical Philosophy'.

In Westermarck's absence, his friend Lagerborg would stand in as acting professor. He would also take over Westermarck's flat, housekeeper Mari included. Lagerborg was given a personal chair in 1929, with funding organized by Westermarck and P.O. von Törne, Dean of the Faculty.[56] He later succeeded Westermarck to his chair.

Westermarck's research in the 1920s and 30s

Westermarck published actively during his years at Åbo. Arguably, this was more a time of reaping than of sowing, with earlier research efforts coming to fruition. In a revised and enlarged edition of his book on marriage, he responded to critics of the original work. After his spell as Rector, Westermarck took up his visits to Morocco again and summed up his results in several volumes between 1926 and 1933 (Westermarck 1926, vols. I–II; 1930; 1933). French translations of *The Origin and Development of the Moral Ideas, Ritual and Belief in Morocco,* and *The History of Human Marriage* were published in the 1920s. Westermarck was especially happy to gain visibility in France, as he was generally sceptical of French sociology (Lagerborg 1951:259).[57]

In 1932 Westermarck published what he called his 'dearest book',[58] *Ethical Relativity.* It was a restatement of his theoretical position in *The Origin and Development of Moral Ideas,* now with more focus on philosophical argument. Westermarck argued that ethics cannot be a normative discipline. Normative ethical systems that claim rational grounds, such as Utilitarianism and Kantianism, in fact reach their conclusions on the basis of emotions. Ethics must be reconstituted as the study of the human emotions that give rise to moral judgements.[59]

Westermarck was active still in retirement. *Three Essays on Sex and Marriage* (1934a), includes arguments against Freud and a more explicit

Figure 12   At home in Åbo in 1932 (ÅAU Library). Ethical Relativity was finished about this time. Photo by Alma Söderhjelm.

statement of his theory of incest (known as 'the Westermarck Hypothesis').[60] The book *Christianity and Morals* (1939) is a summary of Westermarck's moral arguments against Christianity. Shortly before he died, in the spring and summer of 1939, Westermarck told his friends he was planning a monograph called *The Essence of Holiness*.[61] He planned to emphasize 'the socially most important characteristic of the holy – its extraordinary sensitivity to external influences'.[62]

Comparative method vs. functionalism

A question that needs addressing is whether Westermarck's work in this period was influenced by the paradigm change that was well under its way in anthropology.[63] As versions of functionalism were increasingly being embraced also by anthropologists in Britain (notably, by A.R. Radcliffe-Brown and Bronisław Malinowski), it could no longer be ignored simply as a parochial French invention. Malinowski's *Argonauts of the Western Pacific* had established his reputation in 1922.

First of all, it must be noted that Westermarck explicitly defended the comparative method and did not wish to disown his earlier work. This was still the case in his last major public lecture, the Huxley Memorial Lecture of 1936 (Westermarck 1936). On the other hand, in his memoirs Westermarck conceded that he did 'see the weak points of the comparative method without the need of reminders from others' (Westermarck 1929:300). Large-scale syntheses required that the author should master a huge amount of material.

Their main weak point, as he saw it, was that they tended to detach cultural phenomena 'from the organic whole' of the local culture.

> [S]ocial phenomena are not isolated facts, but are largely influenced by local conditions, by the physical environment, by the circumstances in which the people are living, by their habits and mental characteristics. And all these factors can of course be taken into account much more easily when the investigation is restricted to a particular group of men than when it comprises things that are common to widely separated peoples or to mankind in general.
>
> (Westermarck 1929:298–9)

This passage shows that Westermarck had taken some of the functionalist criticism to heart, although he still saw comparative synthesis as the desired end result. He justified himself by suggesting that different methods should complement each other. Fieldworkers should produce monographs that could later be brought together as elements of a synthesis (Westermarck 1936:248).[64] Westermarck furthermore points out that his Moroccan studies were 'free from such defects', as he had 'confined [him]self to a much narrower field – namely, the religious and magical ideas and rites of a single people' (Westermarck 1929:298, 300).[65] Even though Westermarck did not give up the idea of a comparative synthesis – as shown by his late plan on *The Essence of Holiness* – he was devoting much of his time to more focused tasks.

A certain *détente* occurred in Westermarck's relations to French sociology in the 1920s. In June 1928, The University of London hosted the visit of Marcel Mauss. In his Presidential Address to Mauss on 4 June, Westermarck stated that English and French sociology had much to learn from each other (Lagerborg 1951:133–4; 1953:19–20). 'I invited him to an *entente cordiale*, which was also accepted, and we became good friends', he wrote to Lagerborg.[66] During Westermarck's absence in the spring of 1931, Lagerborg organized the visit of Lucien Lévy-Bruhl to Åbo. He was expecting to entertain Lévy-Bruhl in Westermarck's flat, with the assistance of other faculty and Mari the housekeeper. Westermarck's letters show his appreciation of Lagerborg's initiative. Tragically, Lagerborg's wife was taken ill and died shortly before the planned reception. Lagerborg was unable to attend, and von Törne hosted the occasion (Lagerborg 1945:198–200).

Westermarck's Finnish students

Student numbers were diminutive at the Department of Philosophy at Åbo – the Faculty of Arts as a whole had 57 students in 1919–20, and enrolment did not grow significantly during the 1920s (Nordström 1968:242). Westermarck's most important Finnish disciples date from his time at Helsingfors at the turn of the century. They included the anthropologists Hilma Granqvist (1890–1972), Rafael Karsten (1879–1956) and Gunnar Landtman (1878–1940), the folklorist Uno Harva (1882–1949), the ethnologist K. Rob. V. Wikman (1886–1975), the art and literature scholar Yrjö Hirn (1870–1952) and the philosopher Rolf Lagerborg. With Westermarck's support, Wikman and Lagerborg secured teaching positions at Åbo. Wikman got his doctorate at Åbo in 1937 with Landtman as the oral examiner. Harva got a chair of Sociology at the neighbouring University of Turku, while Karsten, Landtman and Hirn became professors in Helsingfors. Granqvist was already a student of Landtman, but she submitted her dissertation at Åbo with Westermarck as the oral examiner.

Landtman and Karsten had particularly close connections with the emerging British anthropology in the early 1900s. They worked together at the British Museum Library in 1903–4. Their plan was to go together to South America for field research. However, at the suggestion of A.C. Haddon, Landtman chose instead to study the Kiwai Papuans, staying for two years in 1910–12. He subsequently stayed in Britain in 1912–13, 1925–6 and 1931, working especially with Haddon. Westermarck and Landtman were good friends. Westermarck told Landtman he was distressed that Karsten rather than Landtman succeeded him to the chair he had left at Helsingfors.[67] He also was a godfather of one of Landtman's children.

Westermarck's cooperation with Lagerborg was a central element of his years at Åbo. Lagerborg's philosophical profile was reminiscent of Westermarck's. At a time when philosophy was increasingly separating itself from empirical investigations – partly a result of the development known as the linguistic turn – Lagerborg continued in the tradition of 'practical philosophy', where this distinction did not apply. A prolific writer, Lagerborg tended to address theoretical questions within psychology, sociology and comparative religion in addition to 'pure' philosophy. Like Westermarck, he adhered to the traditions of Enlightenment and positivism. Both were critical of established religion and both were believers in moral relativity. Lagerborg was loyal to Westermarck in academic matters and defended him in public debates.

However, Lagerborg's approach to the social sciences was clearly different from Westermarck's. Lagerborg, who had written his dissertation for Durkheim in Paris, remained in close touch with French and Continental thought, to which his friend was at best indifferent. In his correspondence with Westermarck, he expressed sympathies with Freud, whereas his friend made fun of the 'absurdities' of the Freudian incest theory.[68] Lagerborg agreed with Durkheim that morality and religion were collective phenomena. According to

Figure 13   The Philosophy Seminar Room in the Humanities building (ÅAU Library). The portrait of Westermarck, by his friend Hugo Backmansson, was commissioned in 1922.

Westermarck, writing to Lagerborg in 1901, Durkheim 'writes with no deeper insight and fantasises quite unreasonably. His essay on blood feud, recently published in Année sociologique, seems to me quite Leftist [*venstervridet*]; he suffers from totem craze [*totem-dille*], if you know what that means.'[69] In his letters, Lagerborg was constantly trying to moderate his friend's criticism of French sociology. This exchange continued from 1894 to the very end of Westermarck's life.

Conflicts with former students

The late 1920s saw something of a rupture between Westermarck and one of his most outstanding students at Helsingfors. Rafael Karsten had studied the natives of Ecuador, Peru and Bolivia in the 1910s. He published his main results as *The Civilization of the South American Indians* in 1926. Karsten's British publisher wanted Westermarck to write an Introduction, though Karsten no doubt believed that his own stature should be enough. Despite some foreboding,[70] Westermarck agreed to contribute an introductory note (Karsten 1926:v–xii), even though there was a long-standing disagreement between them concerning tattoos, mutilations and other body embellishments.[71] Karsten argued they were charms against evil influences, while Westermarck, like Darwin, believed they were meant to attract the opposite sex. Their exchange of letters failed to bring about rapprochement, with Karsten stating that 'the two of us are utterly unable to understand each other on this matter.'[72]

Westermarck discussed the painful situation with several friends, including his sister Helena, Landtman (then in Britain), and Malinowski. Karsten, too, wrote to Malinowski, who did not reply at once.[73] Malinowski argued that Westermarck, if he were to write an Introduction, should stand his ground:

> So if the bugger is such a bloody fool as not to accept your suggestions & persists in misrepresenting − I think you are scientifically, morally & in all other respects justified in slashing him & slashing hard. It will do him no harm & will make the production rather unconventional & rare! ... there seem to be no earthly reasons, why you should moderate your lash or restrain your pen.[74]

Westermarck's *Introductory Note* was more conciliatory than that. He praised Karsten's work, but included a defence of his own views against the implicit critique. He ventured the suggestion that their two positions were actually compatible. Karsten, in his turn, inserted a response of his own into a Preface (Karsten 1926:xiii–xiv), insisting that there was, 'in certain particular points, a more or less radical disagreement' between them. Westermarck took offence (Lagerborg 1951:375, 448–9), and their correspondence effectively came to an end. The dispute apparently had much to do with personal chemistry. Their relations were not completely cut off, however, as we know that Karsten visited Westermarck's London seminar in 1929.[75]

Another conflict occurred between Karsten and Landtman, on the one hand, and Granqvist and Westermarck on the other. This was more a matter of opposing paradigms. But now Westermarck sympathized with the 'new' impulses against the conservative leanings of his two former students.

Hilma Granqvist was writing her dissertation for Landtman, professor of Sociology at Helsingfors.[76] On Landtman's suggestion, Granqvist travelled to Palestine in 1925 in order to collect background data on 'The women of the Old Testament'. But once there, she decided to stay in one village (Artas, in the vicinity of Bethlehem) for an in-depth study of the local culture and of the role of women in it. She believed that hunting for comparative material would lead to superficiality: 'I was successful in resisting the temptation which often assailed me to carry on comparative studies in the other parts of the country', she wrote (Granqvist 1931:4).[77] In her work she combined statistical data, participant observation and local commentary on people and events, whereby she could point at differences between ideals and reality (Suolinna 2000:20). Her style of reporting was also modern. By quoting her informants directly, instead of digesting the information extracted from them into general overviews, she allowed them to appear with distinct voices and also the reader to feel part of the fieldwork situation (Suolinna 2000:18). Landtman disliked the turn that her thesis, now entitled Marriage Conditions in a Palestinian Village, was taking. He believed the topic was too narrow for a Ph.D.

At this juncture, Granqvist appealed to Westermarck, whose sister Helena she had known for many years (Widén 1989:30).[78] In early 1929 Granqvist complained to him of the narrow-mindedness of Landtman and 'the gentlemen of the senate'[79] at Helsingfors. She asked Westermarck for help, believing him to be 'more open-minded and not viewing it simply as a crime to take a somewhat different approach.'[80] Granqvist was of course familiar with Westermarck's Moroccan studies. Like hers, they were detailed descriptions of a single culture, not comparative syntheses. Westermarck took her on as a research student at Åbo. As a compromise, he suggested that she might collect complementary data elsewhere in the Middle East in order to placate her critics.[81] He also made the shrewd suggestion that she should approach Karsten, as Landtman and Karsten were at loggerheads.[82] In his referee's statement, he finally recommended the highest possible mark (*laudatur*) for Granqvist's Ph.D. thesis in 1932.

Despite their considerable international contacts and field experiences, Karsten and Landtman failed to see the point of a more modern take on fieldwork, and Granqvist's career suffered in the process.[83] Westermarck, on the other hand, understood that her approach was quite acceptable, considering the general development of anthropology at the time.

The encounter between 'classical' and 'new' anthropology at LSE

At this time, LSE was the main centre of the development of British anthropology.[84] Throughout the 1920s, Westermarck steadily conducted his London seminars in the summer terms. He arranged his teaching in close tandem with Malinowski, a good friend ever since his arrival in England in 1910.[85]

Westermarck's support had been crucial in the early years of Malinowski's career in Britain. He had recommended him for grants and helped him bring out his first English book, *The Family among the Australian Aborigines*. Westermarck's emotional support was no less important. In a letter, Malinowski thanked him for recommending him for a grant from J. Martin White, but most of all for his friendship: 'You know how much I appreciate your kindness for me – and not only for such big & important things like this, but especially for your general kindness to me. I am always very grateful indeed.'[86] He returns to these memories ten years later:

Figure 14   Westermarck's office at LSE (ÅAU Library).

You know how deeply grateful I feel for all you have done in the past for your initial help, when I was quite alone & unbefriended in London; for your advice & assistance in bringing out my book & most of all, for your personal friendship with which you have honoured me.[87]

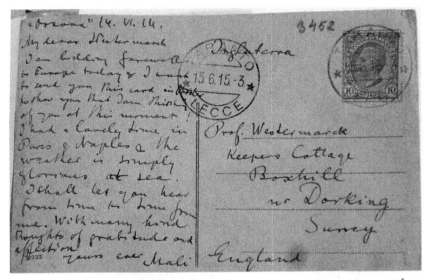

Figure 15　Malinowski's last postcard before sailing off to the South Seas (ÅAU Library).

In 1914, Malinowski set out for fieldwork in Melanesia. On 14 June, he sent one last postcard to Westermarck on leaving Europe.[88] His sojourn in the South Seas proved longer than expected.[89]

Malinowski's situation was precarious when he finally came back in the spring of 1920 with a pregnant wife. He was short of money and his health was frail. But he now had manuscript material that would last him through several books. A letter from September 1920 shows that Westermarck and Malinowski were planning to publish his book – the future *Argonauts* – in the Åbo Academy series.[90] Westermarck and C.G. Seligman helped Malinowski to a teaching position at LSE and organized money when ill health prevented him from teaching.[91] In his letters, the ex-pupil was keen to show his appreciation of his teacher.

> I am very conservative in my friendships & I value yours very highly for many reasons, not the least because our scientific & general ideas & aims are very much in harmony. The war has spoilt & distroyed [*sic*] many things & many personal relationships. But as we two have as similar ideas & feelings about almost everything, why should we be brought one inch apart?[92]

Here, as in many of his letters, Malinowski emphasizes his scientific agreement with Westermarck; never, however, going much into detail. He wrote in this way still when their differences of approach must have been quite

Figure 16　Shereef sîdi Abdessalam El-Baqqâli, Westermarck's main contact in Morocco, with Mrs Holland, a member of the British community in Tangier (ÅAU Library).

evident to both.[93] In 1926 he calls himself 'a "young" & unworthy adept of the "old" School (Frazer, Westermarck etc!)'.[94] When Westermarck's *Ritual and Belief in Morocco* appeared in 1926, Malinowski wrote a review full of praise (1927). His letter was even more profuse:

> I am genuinely & spontaneously glad when I realize & see how your personal vigour goes on undiminishing, how you are constantly making headway in your ideas, enlarging, adjusting, going wider & wider perspectives; how in your fieldwork you are showing always new aspects of your genius. I know that Ethical Relativity will be a masterpiece. I trust you will not delay it.[95]

Westermarck's book of two volumes on Morocco was no doubt impressive. But his approach to field reporting was hardly up to modern standards as Malinowski then understood them.

The contrast between 'old' and 'new' anthropology was to an extent a question of generation. Westermarck still had no difficulties in getting work published. His colleagues of the same age group, such as Haddon and Seligman, looked at the subject much in the same way as he did. But it must have been painful to him to watch the introduction of functionalist and Freudian ideas to the LSE seminars. It seems that Malinowski's conscious deference towards Westermarck prevented any conflict from coming to the fore. Malinowski's letters indicate a cordial relation throughout. In other cases he was accused of arrogance towards the old school. A.C. Haddon, who was not on equally good terms with Malinowski, wrote, 'I understand that he considers there are only three ethnologists: himself – A. Ra[d]cliffe Brown & Thurnwald. [The rest] are nowhere.'[96]

Westermarck would attend Malinowski's seminars in the capacity of an ordinary student, and Malinowski would return the compliment.[97] Many of the attendees later became well-known authorities in their fields. Ashley Montagu, who frequented the seminars through most of the 1920s, mentions the participation of Talcott Parsons, E.E. Evans-Pritchard, Raymond Firth, Lucy Mair, Isaac Schapera, Hortense Powdermaker and Ian Hogbin (Montagu 1982:65). Today they are usually described as Malinowski's rather than Westermarck's students.

Westermarck encouraged his Finnish students to visit the department at LSE. Karsten and Landtman had already lived in London in the early 1900s. In a letter to Lagerborg, Westermarck tells him that the Finns Karsten, Cid Tallqvist and Julio Reuter had attended his seminar in the summer term of 1929.[98] In a letter to Westermarck's sister that same summer, Hilma Granqvist writes,

> I am glad to have the occasion to participate in his [Westermarck's] seminars. As they are attended not only by young students, but also by the really advanced, as well as the really knowledgeable, such as Prof. Malinowski, they get quite a different value from what they have back home, where it was simply the professor instructing pupils. Prof. Westermarck, who has been very friendly and amiable, said to me at once he wanted to present me to said Prof. Malinowsky [*sic*]. 'If you can muster him on your side as well, you get a much greater authority to lean on', Prof. Westermarck pronounced.[99]

This paragraph is quite informative. It documents Granqvist's participation at the seminars – which Westermarck for some reason omits in his letter, while male participants are mentioned. Secondly, it shows Westermarck as a forthcoming supporter of a young researcher with an unorthodox approach. Thirdly, it indicates that Westermarck appreciated Malinowski at a time when theoretical differences between them were already obvious.

Karsten was also acquainted with Malinowski since the 1910s,[100] but he was not impressed. In a letter he writes,

> I must hold on to my judgment of Malinowski. M was an intelligent
> man, but there was something of a bluff and of a sensationalist about
> him – possibly having to do with his Slavic descent – with which I had
> no sympathy. And there is far too much generalizing and theoretizing in
> his works. Why would you, e.g., call a work Crime and Custom in Savage
> Society when all you are talking about are the Trobriands.[101]

Of Westermarck's surviving students, Karsten was the one to reject functionalism most militantly. Even in 1945, in his textbook *Grunddragen av Sociologiens Historia* ('Outlines of the History of Sociology'), Karsten dismissed Malinowski with a few lines:

> In contemporary England, a number of other ethnological schools may to be
> mentioned, e.g., those founded by A.R. Radcliffe-Brown and B. Malinowski,
> but they are of minor importance ... Lately, a lot of fuss has been made here
> [in Finland] of him and his 'school', but his real value is restricted to the fact
> that he has written a few good monographs on the customs of the natives of
> the Melanesian Trobriands, of their sexual life in particular.
>
> (Karsten 1945:166–7)

Karsten's formulations indicate frustration over a paradigm change. We find it somewhat surprising that many of Westermarck's Finnish students proved so resistant to new ideas. They were not many years older than Malinowski. In any case, their conservatism was not for want of international contacts.

Conclusion

Academically speaking, Westermarck's move to the Academy of Åbo did not imply a radical change of his life. His work in Morocco and London continued as earlier, and had fruitful results. His Finnish students took advantage of the international contacts he had established. Westermarck's existing Finnish network was partly transplanted from Helsingfors to the new university. Thus

Figure 17   Some of the main protagonists from Åbo (ÅAU Library). Left to right: Rolf Pipping, von Törne, Westermarck, Lindman and G.O. Rosenqvist (Dean of the Faculty of Theology), on Westermarcks 75th birthday.

he had people around him to lean on from the very start. He also managed to gain the support of the university Trustees for his academic vision.

The Academy of Åbo profited in many ways from this kind of continuity at its initial stage. Westermarck's status as an internationally recognized scholar contributed to its academic standing. He was able to strengthen the position of the humanities by inserting his students and friends in teaching positions and into the administration. The Academy was able immediately to start a high-quality series. On the other hand, Westermarck and his friends harboured certain attitudes – in particular, prejudices against theology and applied science – that may have been counterproductive in the new milieu. At Åbo, Westermarck never quite achieved the results that the initial stages of his engagement there seemed to promise. In particular, the failure to get the faculty of Politics properly started must have been a disappointment to him.[102] Nevertheless, he wielded an influence that went far beyond his somewhat frustrating spell as the first Rector of the fledgling university.

Westermarck published copiously in the 1920s and 1930s. His years at Åbo saw the completion of many long-term projects. His main works were translated into French and other major languages. However, he was unable and perhaps, at bottom, unwilling to stem the tide of theoretical development that eventually led to a paradigm shift in the social sciences, and in anthropology in particular.

Appendix: The Westermarck Archives at Åbo[103]

The bulk of Westermarck's papers are kept in Åbo Akademi University Library. The Westermarck collection was founded in 1956, when The Westermarck Society deposited Westermarck's manuscripts and letters in the library. The collection now extends almost 15 shelf metres, and includes 1,900 assorted and catalogued letters, as well as manuscripts, diaries and lecture notes. Fortunately, in many cases the library has the both ends of Westermarck's correspondence, as the papers of his colleagues at Åbo are also deposited there. Rolf Lagerborg's collection, in particular, contains many interesting letters by Westermarck's hand. In 1975, Professor Hugo E. Pipping donated *c.*500 photographs that had belonged to Westermarck to the Åbo Akademi University Library picture collection. The Westermarck collection of photos at the library now consists of around 1,000 pictures. Some of Westermarck's negatives, depicting fieldwork, everyday life and religious ceremonies in Morocco were restored and developed only in the 1990s.[104] Westermarck's field library for Morocco is kept in the Donner Institute Library (also part of Åbo Akademi University Library).

Since 2007, a selection of the material has being digitized under the auspices of the Finnish national Philosophy portal (www.filosofia.fi), to make them freely available to researchers. Yrsa Neuman, of the Department of Philosophy, is the coordinator of this digitizing work.

The digitized material does not include books. A representative selection of shorter papers, often difficult to find in print, are included. Lecture manuscripts, diary notes and letters with relevance for Westermarck's research interests have been selected for digitization. The manuscript material is reproduced in pdf, but most of it is also transcribed (retaining the original layout, including insertions, line breaks and page breaks) in a way that makes the documents searchable. Westermarck's letters are mostly in Swedish, but there is also English material.[105] The easiest way to find the site is by looking for filosofia.fi/Westermarck.[106]

Notes

1   In this chapter, proper names will be given in the forms that Westermarck would
     have used; hence, Helsingfors and Åbo (rather than Helsinki and Turku). The
     official English appellation *Åbo Akademi University* was introduced only in the
     1990s. Westermarck used *The Academy of Åbo* (in Westermarck 1932) and *Abo
     Academy* (in Westermarck 1929).

2   All quotes from contemporary sources in Swedish will be presented in our
     translation. For details about the Westermarck Archives, see the Appendix.

3   The early stages of the founding of Åbo Akademi University are described in detail
     in Nordström 1968:7–130.

4   It may be more correct to describe the supposedly ethnic division within the political elite as one of cultural orientation. Many members of the elite were bilingual. Important leaders of Finnish ethnic nationalism, such as Y.S. Yrjö-Koskinen (formerly, G.Z. Forsman, 1830–1903) had converted to Finnish in adult age.

5   See Rantanen, this volume.

6   Westermarck was turned down for the chair in philosophy in 1905 because he refused to sit an exam in Finnish. The chair went to a Finnish-speaker, although a new one was later created for Westermarck as compensation. The decision was generally construed as politically motivated (von Wendt 1922). In a passage of his memoirs not included in the English edition (Westermarck 1927:369), Westermarck regrets that 'political and social life' distracts 'the true scientist'. He assumes that 'a scientist of this type would find a more suited milieu in Åbo than in Helsingfors'.

7   Incidentally, analogous considerations gave rise to a parallel campaign to found a Finnish-speaking university at Turku/Åbo. The University of Turku was inaugurated shortly afterwards. Today, Åbo Akademi University and the University of Turku share the same campus.

8   Rindell to Westermarck, 18 January 1918; 28 December 1917, ÅAB: EW.

9   Most notably, Lagerborg (1951:156) mentions 'repeated' offers from Harvard. See also J. Martin White to Westermarck, 12 September 1910, ÅAB: EW. The offer from Harvard is discussed in this letter.

10   Rindell to Westermarck, 30 March 1918, ÅAB: EW.

11   Chancellor, Baron R.A. Wrede and Vice-Chancellor Arthur Rindell. Wrede was engaged on Westermarck's suggestion. Axel Wallensköld, who succeeded Wrede in 1931, was a close friend of Westermarck's (see Westermarck 1929:26).

12   *Stiftelsens för Åbo Akademi styrelse* (Board of the Åbo Academy Foundation).

13   The initial members were Westermarck (Philosophy), P.O. von Törne (Scandinavian History), Severin Johansson (Mathematics), Karl P. Lindman (Physics), Walter Wahl (Chemistry) and Helge Götrik Backlund (Geology and Mineralogy) (Nordström 1968:120). Olaf Homén (History of Swedish Literature) was added as the third humanist in October 1919. Erik Hägglund (Chemistry and Chemical Engineering of Wood Products) joined from the beginning of 1921 (Nordström 1968:144, 148).

14   The Swedish original of Westermarck's memoirs reproduces Westermarck's inauguration speech *in extenso* (Westermarck 1927:374–82), and it generally dwells more than the translation on the initial phase of the Academy. Also see Nordström 1968:132–3.

15   *Acta Academiae Aboensis* Ser. A, Humaniora, 1., 1920.

16   Edvard Westermarck, 1936, 'Boken om Severin Johansson', *Åbo Underrättelser*, 11 February 1936, quoted in Lagerborg 1948:144–8.

17   See Rantanen, this volume.

18 Per-Olof von Törne to Westermarck, 13 December 1920, ÅAB: EW. Referring to one of the main donors, the Dean of the Faculty of Arts writes, 'Finally the access to funds is now so meagre that I am not taking the risk even of going to beg from Jacobsson!'

19 Eli F. Heckscher to von Törne, 26 December 1921, ÅAB: POvT.

20 *'[B]ankruttmässig.'* Westermarck to Lagerborg, 22 April 1924, ÅAB: RL.

21 Johansson's inauguration speech of 15 September 1921, as reported by Huldén 1935:123–4.

22 Rindell to Westermarck, 2 December 1920, ÅAB: EW; Westermarck to Rindell, 10 January 1921, ÅAB: AR; See also Rindell to Westermarck, 9 October 1920, ÅAB: EW.

23 Some Swedish-speaking members of the clergy had floated the idea of creating a Faculty of Theology at Vasa, in a region where Åbo was hoping to recruit students. According to Arthur Montgomery, this stirred up 'instincts of self-preservation' at Åbo. Arthur Montgomery to Eli F. Heckscher, 26 April 1922. KB: EFH. Quoted in Hultberg 2013 (unpublished).

24 Montgomery to Heckscher, 26 April 1922. KB: EFH. Quoted in Hultberg 2013 (unpublished).

25 Westermarck to Svante Dahlström, 6 May 1922, ÅAB: SD.

26 Westermarck to Lagerborg, 22 April 1924, ÅAB: RL.

27 Rolf Pipping to Westermarck, 12 March 1924, ÅAB: EW.

28 In the event, Westermarck chose not to provoke a conflict with the theologians (Nordström 1968:191). Many of the theological faculty members came from Sweden. They represented liberal religious views and had no scores to settle with Westermarck.

29 Rindell to Westermarck, 2 December 1920, 8 February 1921, ÅAB: EW.

30 Lagerborg to Westermarck, 29 March 1921, ÅAB: EW. Quoted in Lagerborg 1948:129.

31 Westermarck to Rindell, 24 April 1921, ÅAB: AR. See also Nordström 1968:155. The appointments of Professors Gadolin, Nikander and Sundwall were cleared soon afterwards (Lagerborg 1948:130). Huldén (1935:139–40) claims, on the other hand, that the chair of Swedish had deliberately not been filled in order to leave Rolf Pipping (Westermarck's nephew) time to qualify for the post. The chair was advertised in 1920, during Westermarck's absence and against the wish of the faculty of Arts, outmanoeuvring Pipping (Nordström 1968:156).

32 Walter Wahl to Johansson, 12 May 1921, ÅAB: SJ. Also see Huldén 1935:116–17.

33 Huldén 1935:120. Ignacy Jan Paderewski was the Prime Minister of Poland from January to December 1919.

34 Rindell to Westermarck, 19 April 1921, ÅAB: EW.

35 Westermarck to Lagerborg, 24 April 1921, ÅAB: RL. Quoted in Lagerborg 1948:137. See also Westermarck to Rindell, 24 April 1921, ÅAB: AR.

36 Westermarck to Lagerborg, 24 April 1921, ÅAB: RL.

37 Westermarck to Lagerborg, 8 November 1921, ÅAB: RL.

38 The following account is mainly based on Westerlund 1985. Nordström 1968 has also been consulted.

39 Dahlström's salary was cut from 51,000 to 24,000 Marks per annum. Nordström 1968:176.

40 Svante Dahlström to Westermarck, 13 July 1923, ÅAB: EW. Quoted in Westerlund 1985:11.

41 R[olf] P[ipping] 1924.

42 Nils Pipping was Lecturer and later (1930) Professor of Mathematics.

43 'Åbo Akademi', *Åbo Underrättelser,* 12 September 1924, quoted in Westerlund 1985:21.

44 Arthur Rindell to R.A. Wrede, 27 October 1924, quoted in Westerlund 1985:22.

45 Hultberg 2013 (unpublished), Montgomery to Heckscher, 30 October 1924. KB: EFH.

46 Lagerborg (1951:156) reports that Carl Johan Dahlström, Severin Johansson and others approached Westermarck in the early summer (*vårsommaren*) of 1924 with the suggestion of sending him on a propaganda tour of the US for the benefit of the Academy. This might have attracted donations, although, conveniently for Johansson, it also would have removed Westermarck from Åbo at this critical point. Westermarck declined.

47 Westermarck to Lagerborg, 22 February 1927, ÅAB: RL. Also see Westermarck 1929:249.

48 Also see Westermarck 1927:372.

49 For an account of the entire debate, see Lagerborg 1948.

50 Nordström 1968:350. Rolf Pipping, professor of Swedish, was Rector from 1936 –42.

51 Westermarck to Lagerborg, 17 June 1929, ÅAB: RL.

52 On Westermarck's role in securing the Kiseleff legacy and hiring Gabriel Nikander (Ethnology), see Nordström 1968:213–14 and Edvard Westermarck, 1936, 'Boken om Severin Johansson', *Åbo underrättelser* 11 February, quoted in Lagerborg 1948:148. On Westermarck's role in hiring his student K. Rob. V. Wikman (Sociology), see Westermarck, loc.cit..

53 Arthur Montgomery to Westermarck, 13 June 1925, ÅAB: EW.

54 For Westermarck's teaching programmes at Åbo and LSE, see Ihanus 1999:314–18.

55 See, for example, Westermarck, *Föreläsningar i filosofins historia,* ÅAB: EW, Kapsel 78.

56 Westermarck to Lagerborg, 17 June 1929, ÅAB: RL; Westermarck to the Faculty of Arts, 4 May 1930, ÅAB: EW; P-O. von Törne to Westermarck, 9 February 1931, ÅAB: EW.

57 The two latter works were translated by Van Gennep.

58 Westermarck to Lagerborg, 2 May 1932, ÅAB: RL.

59 On Westermarck's ethics, see Bloch, in this volume.

60 On the Westermarck Hypothesis, see Wolf, this volume.

61 Westermarck to Helene Arrhenius, 18 June 1939. Quoted in Lagerborg 1951:446. See also Lagerborg 1951:366.

62 Westermarck to Lagerborg, 18 April 1939, ÅAB: RL.

63 See Shankland, this volume. On the general development of Westermarck's relations to functionalism and French sociology, see Lagerborg 1953.

64 On the other hand, Westermarck wrote of his work on Morocco: 'What had more than anything else preserved my interest unimpaired throughout all those many years was the hope that my detailed study of the popular religion and magic beliefs of the Moors might cast a light on questions of a more general character and not only form a monographic contribution to the science of religion.' (Westermarck 1929:303).

65 The statement is not strictly true, as the Moroccan groups that Westermarck studied were in many respects separate societies. But in his contribution to Seligman's Festschrift (Westermarck 1934b) he concentrated on blood feud among a single ethnic group (the Ait Yusi, south of Fez).

66 Westermarck to Lagerborg, 28 August 1928, ÅAB: RL.

67 Westermarck to Landtman, 3 March 1922, ÅAB: GL.

68 Westermarck to Lagerborg, 17 June 1929, ÅAB: RL.

69 Westermarck to Lagerborg, February 1901, ÅAB: RL. Quoted in Lagerborg 1951:428 (with the year misprinted as 1911). We are correcting Lagerborg's reading from '*blodskam*' [incest] to '*blodshämnd*' [blood feud]. The reference is possibly to Durkheim 1901. Another possibility would be Durkheim 1898 (retaining Lagerborg's reading).

70 'Karsten has been behaving so oddly that the task is all but inviting,' Edvard Westermarck to Helena Westermarck, 13 December 1925, ÅAB: HW.

71 According to Salomaa 2007, 'The first significant intellectual clash between Karsten and Westermarck already took place in 1919 when Karsten expressed his disapproval of Westermarck's theory about the function of primeval art. Then, Westermarck felt that Karsten's criticism on his concept of art was unfair and groundless.'

72 Karsten to Westermarck, 17 January 1926, ÅAB: EW.

73 'I am so sorry about that ... Karsten. He wrote to me, but I did not answer his letter, (I am writing him now that you <u>will</u> write the Preface), I had heared though, thorough the Alvens & Landtman that you <u>are</u> writing a Preface,' Malinowski to Westermarck, 1 January 1926, ÅAB: EW.

74 Malinowski to Westermarck, 1 January 1926, ÅAB: EW.

75 Westermarck to Lagerborg, 17 June 1929, ÅAB: RL.

76 The following presentation is mainly based on Widén 1989 and Suolinna 2000.

77 Quoted in Suolinna 2000:19.

78 Widén points out, however, that there is no evidence of Helena intervening on Granqvist's behalf.

79 Aapeli Saarisalo, professor of Oriental Literature, and Rafael Karsten, professor of Practical Philosophy, were members of the senate.

80 Granqvist to Westermarck, undated draft, ÅAB: HG. Quoted in Widén 1989:29.

81 Westermarck to Granqvist, 24 March 1929, ÅAB: HG. Quote in Suolinna 2000:19.

82 Granqvist to Helena Westermarck, 27 May 1929, ÅAB: HW.

83 On Granqvist, see Suolinna 2000 and Widén 1989.

84 See Dahrendorf 1995:245–7.

85 See Young 2004:166, 173. Westermarck was, according to Young, '[b]y far the most important academic friendship that Malinowski made during his first year at the School.... Malinowski developed an enormous liking for Westermarck, and the affection was mutual.' (Ibid.).

86 Malinowski to Westermarck, 14 September 1911, ÅAB: EW.

87 Malinowski to Westermarck, 18 July 1921, ÅAB: EW.

88 Malinowski to Westermarck, 14 June 1914, ÅAB: EW.

89 It is often said that Malinowski, an enemy alien, was prevented from going back to Europe during the Great War. However, Kuper (1997:12) points out that all enemy scientists who chose to do so were allowed to return. Malinowski had in any case been planning to do fieldwork in New Guinea or Melanesia (see Malinowski to Westermarck, 23 December 1913, ÅAB: EW). His return was further delayed by ill health and his involvement with Elsie Masson, his future wife.

90 Malinowski to Westermarck, 5 September 1920, ÅAB: EW.

91 Malinowski could not teach in the spring of 1923 because of illness. He asked Westermarck to contact J. Martin White for financial support: 'As I am still anticipating a deficit in my finances, may I still take advantage of your kind offer, so nicely & generously put, of tapping Martin White on my behalf?' (Malinowski to Westermarck, 22 June 1923). White obliged and wrote also to Seligman about him. Malinowski to Westermarck, 30 January 1923 and 22 June 1923; White to Westermarck, 8 July 1923 and 1 August 1923, ÅAB: EW.

92 Malinowski to Westermarck, 18 July 1921, ÅAB: EW.

93 'Have been reading your Marriage again & each time I look at it I like it better', Malinowski to Westermarck, 30 January 1923, ÅAB: EW

94 Malinowski to Westermarck, 1 January 1926, ÅAB: EW.

95 Malinowski to Westermarck, 9 September 1926, ÅAB: EW.

96 Haddon to Westermarck, 13 November 1929, ÅAB: EW.

97 See Montagu 1982:64–5. Westermarck mentions to Lagerborg that Malinowski has 'faithfully assisted him' through the seminar during the term. Westermarck to Lagerborg, 17 June 1929, ÅAB: RL.

98 Westermarck to Lagerborg, 17 June 1929, ÅAB: RL.

99 Granqvist to Helena Westermarck, 16 May 1929, ÅAB: HW.

100 Malinowski to Westermarck, 15 January 1914, ÅAB: EW.

101 Rafael Karsten to Ragnar Numelin, 28 July 1947, ÅAB: RN.

102 In 1931, the faculty of Politics had only 11 students. A turn to the better occurred only in the middle of the 1930s (Nordström 1968:320).

103 This section is mainly based on Neuman and Lahtinen 2011.

104 A selection has been published in Suolinna, af Hällström and Lahtinen 2000.

105 For some reason, possibly in order not to have his letters held by British war censorship, Westermarck was at one point in the habit of writing in English to friends in Finland.

106 The present chapter was written as part of the project *Westermarck and Beyond. Evolutionary Approaches to Morality and Their Critics*, financed by the Kone Foundation. The Westermarck digitizing process has also received funding from this project. Tommy Lahtinen, of the Åbo Akademi University Library picture collections, and the staff of the Manuscript Collection are gratefully acknowledged for their help.

References

Acta Academiae Aboensis (ser. A, Humaniora 1). Åbo: Åbo Akademi, 1920.

Dahrendorf, R. 1995. *LSE: A History of the London School of Economics and Political Science 1895–1995*. Oxford: Oxford University Press.

Durkheim, E. 1898. La prohibition de l'inceste et ses origines. *L'Année Sociologique* 1:1–70.

Durkheim, E. 1901. Deux lois de l'évolution pénale. *L'Année Sociologique* 4:65–95.

Granqvist, H. 1931. *Marriage Conditions in a Palestinian Village*. Helsingfors: Societas Scientiarum Fennica.

Huldén, J.J. 1935. *Severin Johansson: Ett amatörporträtt.* Stockholm: Bonnier.

Ihanus, J. 1999. *Multiple Origins: Edward Westermarck in Search of Mankind* (trans. M. Toivonen). European Studies in the History of Science and Ideas 6. Frankfurt am Main: Peter Lang.

Karsten, R. 1926. *The Civilization of the South American Indians, with Special reference to Magic and Religion; with a Preface by Edward Westermarck.* London: Kegan Paul, Trench, Trubner & Co.

Karsten, R. 1945. *Grunddragen av sociologiens historia*. Helsingfors: Söderström.

Kuper, A. 1997. *Anthropology and Anthropologists. The Modern British School* (3rd edn.). London: Routledge.

Lagerborg, R. 1945. *Ord och inga visor- andras och egna.* Helsingfors: Söderström.

Lagerborg, R. 1948. Ett rektorsval med efterspel. *Ajatus* 15:129–59.

Lagerborg, R. 1951. *Edvard Westermarck och verken från hans verkstad under hans tolv sista år 1927–1939.* Helsingfors: Schildt.

Lagerborg, R. 1953. The essence of morals. Fifty years (1895–1945) of rivalry between French and English sociology. *Transactions of the Westermarck Society* 2:9–25.

Malinowski, Bronislaw, 1922. *Argonauts of the Western Pacific: An Account of Native Enterprise and Adventure in the Archipelagoes of Melanesian New Guinea.* London: Routledge.

Malinowski, B. 1927. Anthropology of the westernmost Orient. [Review E. Westermarck, 1926, *Ritual and Belief in Morocco*]. *Nature* 120:867–8.

Montagu, A. 1982. Edward Westermarck: recollections of an old student in young age. In T. Stroup (ed.), *Edward Westermarck: Essays on his Life and Works. Acta Philosophica Fennica* 34:63–70.

Neuman, Y. and Lahtinen, T. 2011. Wmck goes Internet: Westermarcksamlingen i Filosofia.fi. *Laboratorium för folk och kultur* 1:27.

Nordström, W.E. 1968. *Academia aboensis rediviva 1918–1968*. Ekenäs: Ekenäs Tryckeri Aktiebolag.

Pipping, R. 1924. Åbo Akademi i en återvändsgränd. *Nya Argus* 1/8.

Söderhjelm, A. 1938. *Åbo tur och retur.* Stockholm: Bonniers.
Suolinna, K. 2000. Hilma Granqvist: a scholar of the Westermarck School in its decline. *Acta Sociologica* 43(4):317–23.
Suolinna, K., af Hällström, C. and Lahtinen, T. 2000. *Portraying Morocco. Edward Westermarck's Fieldwork and Photographs 1898–1913.* Åbo: Åbo Akademis förlag.
von Wendt, E. 1922. Filosofiska professurer och politiska utnämningar. Konturer under ett sekel. *Finsk Tidskrift* 4:60–74.
Westerlund, L. 1985. *Sammanslutningen Svältremmen. Åbo Akademis Lärare- och tjänstemannaförening 1923–27.* Åbo: Åbo Akademis kopieringscentral.
Westermarck, E. 1926. *Ritual and Belief in Morocco* (vols. I and II). London: Macmillan.
Westermarck, E. 1927. *Minnen ur mitt liv.* Helsingfors: Schildt.
Westermarck, E. 1929. *Memories of My Life.* London: Kegan Paul.
Westermarck, E. 1930. *Wit and Wisdom in Morocco: A Study of Native Proverbs* (with the assistance of Shereef `Abd-Es-Salam El-Baqqali). London: Routledge.
Westermarck, E. 1932. *Ethical Relativity.* London: Kegan Paul.
Westermarck, E. 1933. *Pagan Survivals in Mohammedan Civilization.* London: Macmillan.
Westermarck, E. 1934a. *Three Essays on Sex and Marriage.* London: Macmillan.
Westermarck, E. 1934b. The bloodfeud among some Berbers of Morocco. *Essays Presented to C.G. Seligman,* 361–8. London: Kegan Paul, Trench, Trubner & Co.
Westermarck, E. 1936. Methods in social anthropology. *Journal of the Royal Anthropological Institute* 66:133–248.
Westermarck, E. 1939. *Christianity and Morals.* London: Kegan Paul, Trench, Trubner & Co.
Widén, S. 1989. Hilma Granqvist – en forskande kvinna i en manlig värld. *Naistutkimus – Kvinnoforskning* 2(3):26–35.
Young, M. 2004. *Malinowski. Odyssey of an Anthropologist.* New Haven & London: Yale University Press.

Manuscript material

At Åbo Akademi University Library
ÅAB:AR. Åbo Akademis bibliotek, Arthur Rindells samling.
ÅAB:EW. Åbo Akademis bibliotek, Edvard Westermarcks samling.
ÅAB:GL. Åbo Akademis bibliotek, Gunnar Landtmans samling.
ÅAB:HG. Åbo Akademis bibliotek, Hilma Granqvists samling.
ÅAB:HW. Åbo Akademis bibliotek, Helena Westermarcks samling.
ÅAB:RL. Åbo Akademis bibliotek, Rolf Lagerborgs samling.
ÅAB:RN. Åbo Akademis bibliotek, Ragnar Numelins samling.
ÅAB:SD. Åbo Akademis bibliotek, Svante Dahlströms samling.
ÅAB:SJ. Åbo Akademis bibliotek, Severin Johanssons samling.
Åbo Akademi University (ÅAU) Library Picture Collections.

Other Material
KB: EFH Royal Library, Stockholm, Eli F. Heckschers samling.
Hultberg, Ralf, 2013 (unpublished). Vetenskap och politik. Vetenskapliga kontakter Sverige-Finland under en brydsam tid. Manuscript, the University of Stockholm, the Department of the History of Ideas.
Veronica Wirseen's family album.

Digital material

Salomaa, I. 2007. *Rafael Karsten (1879–1956), a Finnish Scholar of Religion (A short biography by Ilona Salomaa)*. Projekt Runeberg. Available at http://runeberg.org/authors/karstraf.html, accessed 1 July 2012.

The Edvard Westermarck Online Collection in Filosofia.fi, ed. Juhani Ihanus, Tommy Lahtinen and Yrsa Neuman 2011 (Eurooppalaisen filosofian seura ry). http://filosofia.fi/Westermarck.

3

Edward Westermarck as a Finnish patriot abroad

Pekka Rantanen

Introduction

Edward (Edvard) Alexander Westermarck was born on 20 November 1862 in Helsinki, Finland. He was the fourth child of Nils Christian Westermarck (1826–1904) and Constance Gustava Maria Westermarck (1830–1909), whose maiden name was Blomqvist. His father was a bursar at the University of Helsinki, and his mother's father had been a professor of the history of learning, also at the University of Helsinki. Edward's family background was therefore influenced by academic life and culture, and the family was part of the Swedish-speaking upper-middle class. He died at the age of 76 on 3 September 1939 in Tenhola, Finland, a few days after a severe asthmatic attack. His long-time friend, Professor Rolf Lagerborg, believed that the news of Nazi Germany invading Poland agitated Westermarck deeply and caused the fatal seizure. Edward was still very active just few days before. The last diary entry (29 August 1939) reveals a man in full-fledged activity:

> Reverend Ramdal on dinner. Finished Ethical Relativity [Swedish language proofs].
>
> Should go through the whole manuscript before it can be sent to the printing house.

According to his sister, Helena, Edward was a fragile child. He suffered from asthma in early life, and was not able to participate in children's sport or other physical activities (Lagerborg 1951; Numelin 1970:28; Stroup 1982; Westermarck 1941). In later life, Westermarck managed impressive hiking tours, for example to Norway, where he met English psychologist James Sully, and of course undertook extensive field work in Morocco under demanding circumstances (Hirn 1947:44; Pipping 1982:354). The time spent doing fieldwork would be an impressive accomplishment in current academic life. Westermarck was able to arrange his time between the University of London (Professor of Sociology), the University of Helsinki (Professor of Practical Philosophy) and investigations in Morocco (Liukkonen and Pesonen 2008; Lundberg-Kelly 2005:8–9).

Edward was very fond of his mother, but felt distant to his father, though he valued his hard-working spirit. His mother promoted an atmosphere for learning and high arts, especially music (Hirn 1947:41; Stroup 1982:13; Westermarck 1929). He was especially close to his sister Helena, who became a noted artist and a writer. She was also active in the Finnish women's movement at the time. Interest in political activism seems to have been something they shared, albeit with different approaches.

Westermarck's intellectual and scientific career is well documented, both in this volume and elsewhere (Pipping 1982; Stroup 1982). Needless to say, he was a prominent figure in social sciences both in Finland and internationally. This chapter aims to shed light on the political aspect to Edward Westermarck, the importance of which came to the fore on three occasions (Ginsberg 1982:4). These were, first, defending Finnish autonomy within the Russian empire, especially in 1899. Second, when the Russian empire re-enacted its integration policy towards Finland in 1910s, Westermarck took part in the Finnish underground movement whose purpose was to provide military training for Finnish youths. Third, when the Åland dispute between Finland and Sweden emerged in the aftermath of the independence 1918, Westermarck supported the view that Åland belonged to Finland both historically and culturally. This is not an exhaustive description of his involvement in a variety of political issues, but rather illustrate that he was not merely an academic intellectual, but one who took an active role in politics, especially in relation to Finland.

The early years

Westermarck recalls his time in school as a not particularly happy phase of life. He considered himself as a slow reader with a poor memory. (Westermarck 1929). Such an evaluation is surprising, as others would later describe him as a man whose 'knowledge was literally encyclopedic' (Montagu 1982:64).

Edward was seemingly active in his school's student association. In his notebooks he describes his roles in their activities, and from his list we can see that he was in the editorial team, the library committee, the album committee and the inspection committee. He was elected the head of the covenant in 1880, receiving 26 votes. At university he would later be active in the Nylands Nation (Lagerborg 1951; Numelin 1970:29), an association whose membership was based on provincial background. These 'nations' were hugely important places, where young intellectuals could promote scientific activities and be engaged with politics; many members were engaged in the formation of Finnish press, a politically important and growing medium at the time.

As noted, Westermarck showed at school that he liked writing, and he took part in the student association's activities. I know not whether these tasks were politically motivated or were directed to certain political issues, but one can say at least that organizing group activity was something that he had interest in (Westermarck's notebook 1878–1880). Ragnar Numelin (1970) notes that Westermarck was engaged to political activity many times over his lifetime.

In his time at the University of Helsinki he was politically liberal-minded (Numelin 1970:29), but he was also close to promoting Finnish nationalism within the circle of 'Young Finnish movement'. Current political debate circled around issues of language and nationalism; for example, which of the intellectual groups would have the right to represent the people. The people, however, were not yet asked about such important political questions. That would only happen later.

Politically, there was a 'Swedish Front' and, close to them, the 'Young Finnish', who were ridiculed by the more conservative 'Old Finnish' as 'a Finnish speaking tail of the Swedes'. The consolidation of political parties would take place later in the process of the first Finnish Parliament elections in 1907, and by then the Young Finnish Party, the Finnish Party and Swedish People's Party existed as distinctive political organizations. Liberalism was, in the late nineteenth century, one potential ideology, but its advocates had not formed into a coherent movement. However, it influenced many people, especially in the younger generations.

The first time Westermarck took part in public political debate was in a speech given in 1887 in Upsala, Sweden, where he had gone as a part of University of Helsinki students' delegation. His speech described Sweden more favorably than Finland, and was objected to by the 'Old Fennoman' press. A debate followed, and critics argued that Westermarck had deeply insulted Finland with his statements. Westermarck responded by giving more details from his speech to the press, and by defending his statements. (Lagerborg 1951:25–30). Westermarck himself thought that this incident was the reason he was appointed to be the superintendent of the Nylands Nation, the student association at the university (Lagerborg 1951; Numelin 1970:29). His views could be described as 'liberal nationalism', a stance that was common at the time in Finland, especially in relation to the Russian Empire. But these views developed and changed over the years. Minority issues became more prominent at around the turn of the century, and later, at the time of Finnish

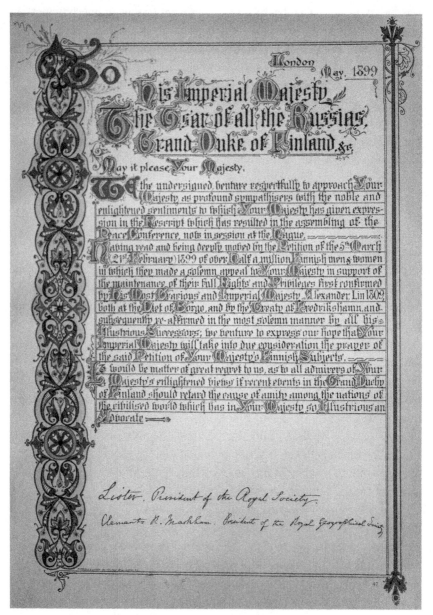

Figure 1   Pro Finlandia, 1899.

independence, it became an important topic in his political writing. Finnish independence, however, remained dear to him. His writings on the Åland question in 1920 clearly demonstrate this.

Nationalism, Westermarck and the father of 'The Radicals'

Perhaps the most notable political activity Westermarck was deeply involved with was the birth of the Europe-wide petition (1899) supporting Finland's constitutional rights as an autonomous Grand Duchy of the Russian Empire. The petition 'Pro Finlandia' had a long list of signatures from notable European academics and intellectuals. The Finnish politicians felt that Russia had violated 'constitutional rights' of Finland in its legislative measures during 1890s, especially in 1899, when the Finnish Diet was bypassed by Russian legislative measures. From the Russian perspective it was partly a process of unifying the state formation of the empire. This was something that was not easily accepted in Finland. The Finns even suggested such an activity to be a form of colonialism by the Russian Empire (Rantanen and Ruuska 2009).

The origin of the idea of a European petition to the Russian Tsar derives in part from Westermarck's discussions with Mrs Gertrud Coupland. She presented the Finnish question to her friend in Germany, who was married to Professor Rudolf Eucken. Eucken gave the initiative momentum, as his connections were wide and influential within European intellectuals, and his specific area of interest was nationalism and minority population rights. He later, in 1908, received Nobel Prize for Literature. Similar ideas of an international petition had been considered at around the same time by the journalist Konni Zilliacus (Gummerus 1933:63–4), and he took part in planning and organizing the petition with Westermarck, linguist Julio Reuter and other politically active Finns living in England.

The plan of action started to emerge, but, according Konni Zilliacus, the Finnish constitutionalists in Finland, along with their leader Leo Mechelin, then hesitated because of the potential political consequences (Gummerus 1933:65; Numelin 1970:47; Zilliacus 1920). Zilliacus, then a constitutionalist and later a more radical activist of the Finnish cause (Gummerus 1926), writes that it was Edward Westermarck that reacted first towards the news of the hesitation. Mechelin had informed them by telegram from Finland more or less to 'hold your horses'.

Konni Zilliacus (1920:18–19) wrote in his memoirs:

> The preparations for the petition had gone so far that we with great
> certainty could assume it to become a reality. Therefore we sent a telegram
> to the committee that had the task of leading resistance in which senator L.
> Mechelin was the chairman ... and informed them about the endeavour and
> what we had accomplished and about our hopes for its realization.

The answer from Finland was, to their surprise, that the endeavour should be given up. The explanation given was that it was 'far too grandiose and it had inherent and unpredictable political dangers to it'. They were shocked by the negative response from the committee in Finland, which advised them to bury the enterprise of the international petition altogether. According to Zilliacus, after a brief shocked silence, Westermarck said: 'We simply telegraph the answer back that we shall continue, and show the gentleman the devil.' Despite the resistance from Finland, the planning continued. This rather radical statement was supported by Zilliacus and Reuter. Zilliacus was later one of the key actors in the Finnish Active Resistance Party, which promoted even more direct measures of resistance towards Russian unification policy. Reuter was a member of the Kagaali organization, which had similar aims, but was more inclined towards passive forms of resistance.

Westermarck's European connections served well in getting signatures for the petition.

> [Anthropologist E.B.] Tylor was running around with me all yesterday
> morning, and we made up a list of about 20 names. Everyone so far has
> agreed to sign.... Forel [François-Alphonse Forel (1841–1912), limnologist,
> professor of medicine at Lausanne] wrote me a letter yesterday, full of
> sympathy. He is already collecting signatures in Switzerland.
>
> (Letter to Reuter from Westermarck, 18 May 1899)

His connections were important at other times as well, especially in acquiring legal backing for Finnish autonomy and support for claims that Finnish resistance to Russification measures were justified (Numelin 1970:45). Support was given, for example, from Professor John Westlake, who was at the time one of the leading figures in international jurisprudence (Estlander 1930:23; Numelin 1970). Questions of nationalism and minority rights were topical at the time. 'The age of Empires' was gradually losing its legitimacy, and nationalism was one of key themes of political debate concerning the rights of people and nations. Here names like Rudolf Eucken were important to Finland. He had written on the topic of 'the mission and aims of minor nations' (*De mindre nationernas uppgift och betydelser*, 1901). His views were known and cherished in Finland, as the country was easily considered as such a 'minor nation' by virtue, for example, of having its own particular constitutional forms and institutions. Eucken would again be active in the Finnish question when the second wave of Russification intensified from the 1910s (Estlander 1930:21).

Edward Westermarck wrote an article 'Finland and the Czar' for *The Contemporary Review* in 1899, describing Finland as a 'democratic nation' with 'strong national spirit' that had indeed been 'placed among the rank of nations' by an earlier Russian emperor, Alexander I, in 1809. Such a conception represented a common ideal for the upper strata of Finnish society, and the unity of the nation was often stated in its support in political writing (Huxley 1990:202). Westermarck lamented the unification policy of the Russian Empire towards Finland: 'We are treated as rebels, although there is not a slightest symptom of rebellion.' Further, he stated that no one wishes open rebellion in Finland against The Russian Empire, but nonetheless peaceful resistance was offered as a means to defend violated rights (Westermarck 1899:658). Westermarck did not believe in overtly careful political activity in this respect (*överdrivande försiktighetspolitiken*). He wrote to his friend in Finland that he was making wide variety of efforts to get support and media attention for the Finnish question in England. (Lagerborg 1951:211).

The Russian authorities often classified the Finnish constitutionalist movement as separatism and even as revolutionary. One of the key arguments the Russian press and government used was that Finland was not a nation, only a province (Pollari *et al.* 2008). This conception was something that Westermarck addressed, first refuting the idea and then lamenting that the Russian policy had the aim of turning Finland's Diet into a provincial assembly simply 'by the stroke of a pen' (Westermarck 1899:654).

In practice, what Westermarck and others were doing was building their arguments on European civic notion of justice, and claiming that it was in fact the Russian Tsar who was a rebel or revolutionary, or even an anarchist in destroying the previous order and stability of relations between The Russian Empire and The Grand Duchy of Finland (the emerging Finnish underground press would state the emperor to be a tyrant or such like, but other newspapers would be more cautious in their choice of words as strict rules of censorship existed). Westermarck would be in close connection with Kagaali, which continued to organize passive resistance up to 1905, when visiting Finland (Landtman 1940:157), and he was invited to take part to its meetings (Numelin 1970:45).

The Russification measures ceased with the Russian revolution of 1905 and the aftermath of the general strike in Finland few days later. Tsar Nikolai II was forced to sign a manifesto agreeing to stop integration measures and promised parliamentary reform for Finland. Changes were to include moving from the four estate diet to a single-chamber parliament, general suffrage and women's universal right to vote. The Finnish Active Resistance Party put up candidates for the general elections. Westermarck was in this context ridiculed as its intellectual father in the Finnish satirical journal *Velikulta*, which was politically allied with the Young Finnish party, whereas Westermarck was closer to The Swedish People's Party, although in the current political context he was indeed linked to the resistance movement.

Russification measures strengthened in 1910s, and in 1911 Westermarck became involved in the establishment in London of the Anglo-Finnish Society

Figure 1   'The Radicals: Westermarck, thy shall we follow', Velikulta 7, 1907.

to promote the case of Finland there. Then the political situation changed, especially with the start of the First World War. It was the Russo-Japanese war and its aftermath that primarily influenced Finland's relation to Russia by amplifying the notion of, and even need for, independence. There were many instances when the possibility of independence was imagined, especially if a favourable political situation was to come about in Russia. In 1905 the Finnish Active Resistance Party had drafted a proposed constitution for Finland (Castrén 1905) that had a strong democratic ethos, and included clauses that in practice would have mean that by the popular will of the people the path to independence could have been started (Rantanen and Ruuska, 2009). This constitutional draft remained just a draft, but it illustrates well the scope of political activities and imagination that these 'radicals' had, including Westermarck.

The First World War and its aftermath had huge impact on Finland. During the war the idea emerged that Finnish male youth should be educated to be military men. In brief, quite a number of men were sent to Germany for military training. This was highly risky practice, carried out with utmost secrecy, because Germany was at war with Russia, and therefore military laws were active also in Finland. However, the Russian government suspected something like this was underway and made constant house searches in Finland. Edward Westermarck was among the suspects, but was able to escape back to England. The men trained in Germany were called *Jääkärit* (infantry) and later took part in the Finnish Civil War in 1918, fighting against the Finnish socialist army. Westermarck took part in planning and in acquiring financial support to make military training possible for the Finns. It is clear that this military training was a preparation for a possible independence struggle, even though at that time, before the Russian revolution, the prospects of such were thin. Westermarck commented at one point that if the troops trained in Germany would prove to be useless for gaining independence from Russia, they might be needed against working-class revolutionary attempts if such internal hostilities were to break out. As we know, such a civil war did erupt after the collapse of the Russian Empire, and with the demise of the Finnish socialist army non-socialist independence was secured. One must be cautious in taking Westermarck's words concerning the use of *Jääkärit* too literally. Heikki Sarmaja reminds us that Westermarck's writings on the right of property and its future struggles (Westermarck 1926), and his relations to the Fabian Society, for example, show that he was not hostile towards working-class aspirations. As with many other 'radical cultural liberals', there was room for interaction with socialist intellectuals. Westermarck explains both the right of property based on labour and on ownership (possessing a thing) as deeply rooted in human nature. Here, according to Sarmaja, we can see an expression of Westermarck's evolutionary thinking (Sarmaja n.d.).

The Åland question and promotion of minority rights

When Finland became a sovereign state, and there was civil war going on with German troops taking part, a question concerning the Åland archipelago surfaced. In Sweden it was thought that the Åland should be returned to Sweden, but in Finland the issue was seen differently. The dispute became an issue for international law, and in the autumn of 1920 the League of Nations took on the task of arbitration. A diplomatic deputation from Finland would take part in the process. There in Geneva we can find Professor Edward Westermarck, once again actively taking part in politics. Again, Westermarck (1920) would write an article ('The Aaland Question') for *The Contemporary Review* supporting the Finnish viewpoint.

The debate between Finland and Sweden rested on empirical matters in many respects, on population, language, geography, strategic requirements, differences within the archipelago population itself. For Westermarck, the status of the Swedish-speaking minority was important, but he did not wish that Åland and its Swedish speaking population would join Sweden. For him, this would weaken the position of Swedish-speaking population of mainland Finland, and even create unnecessary hostility between Sweden and Finland. Secondly, he argued that Finland as an independent state could not allow part of its territory to be taken away, and therefore did not support the idea that a particular part of a nation would have rights to self-determination on such a question. Particular issues were brought up to defend this view; for example, that the Swedish-speaking population was not, by any means, oppressed by the Finnish. Westermarck was more or less appalled that on occasion three international jurists had described Finland as a province, and not necessarily as an internationally approved state. His shock derives from the background of the dispute between the Russian Empire and Finland a few decades earlier, in which the naming of Finland as a province was also used by the Russian Empire with regard to the Grand Duchy of Finland in order to delegitimize Finland's status as autonomous unit. As we can remember, Westermarck wrote about the issue in 1899. In the end, The League of Nations determined that the Åland Islands would remain under Finnish sovereignty, but also stressed that measures of autonomy should be given to the Åland; these the Finnish legislation has guaranteed.

The promotion of the rights of the Swedish minority was important to Westermarck, who himself belonged to the Swedish-speaking minority and considered education of the Swedish-speaking population important. He was the first rector of the Swedish-language university, Åbo Akademi University, which was founded in 1918. This was also nationalism, yes, but on the other hand he saw the question of minority rights as pivotal. Relations between Finnish- and Swedish-speaking groups and the regulation of the rights of minorities in relations to the majority population in Finland can be deemed, historically, as a rare success story. The tensions did not lead to violent conflict, as has happened in so many other cases. However, they have left some hidden antagonisms below the surface that can still be sensed around particular issues. Olli Lagerspetz (2013) points out that when Westermarck took a stand in Finnish politics, there was a strong likelihood for it to involve the defence of minority rights.

Conclusion: Westermarck , an engaged scholar and political activist

It is well known that Edward Westermarck was an excellent and hard-working scholar. In this chapter I have tried to demonstrate that he was also very engaged with, and active in, politics. One could even say that in terms of Finnish politics at the time he was important international actor. I suspect that further research may show his political activity to have been even more extensive than we now realize.

A few more examples can be provided. Westermarck took part in the Prometheus Association in Finland, which was anti-clerical and supported freedom of religion. He was openly agnostic. He was also one of the first to defend the rights of sexual minorities. He was also one of the founding members of the Anglo-Finnish society. He took a place on the board of the Finnish Tourism Association (*Finland*, 17 March 1892), perhaps prompted by his own interest in hiking and travel.

Westermarck was a child of his times. In his inaugural address he states that knowledge of social institutions would be useful to colonial officials if they were to go out to rule over non-European natives. However, in the lecture he also attacks the actions of Europeans towards such natives:

> I have sometimes been simply amazed, not only by the arrogance, but
> by criminal ignorance with which European residents have treated its
> [Moroccon] native inhabitants.

Westermarck supported ideas of empirical research. For him it was important to ground research on thorough empirical investigations (Stroup 1982:26). He was not just a Finnish patriot, nor a pure cosmopolitan intellectual, both sides were present and intertwined. His patriotism was connected to a wide variety of issues. In political action, when he decided to take part, he considered particular issue at hand pretty much along the lines of Realpolitik, and was ready to use his connections to promote the cause in question.

Finally, what ultimately proves his importance is that his political action and his scholarly work were an object of ridicule in the contemporary satirical journals, which were flourishing at the time. As shown above, a Finnish satirical journal made fun of his support for the Finnish Active Resistance

Party, as its intellectual father (the party, however, did not gain seats in the first parliamentary elections of 1907, nor later). For anyone apart from the politicians and celebrities, gaining attention from a satirical journal is no easy task. We can safely, therefore, on the basis of the concrete evidence from Finland above, and the final example from an acclaimed British counterpart below, deem Edward Westermarck as a highly important figure of his era.

> *Punch*, 1 January 1908:
> Dr Edward Westermarck, in an address on the evils of our present marriage
> system, spoke approvingly of a custom prevalent among various Bechuana
> and Kaffir tribes whereby a youth is prohibited from marrying until he
> has killed a rhinoceros. As a precautionary measure the specimen in the
> Zoological Gardens is now being guarded night and day by detectives.[1]

Notes

1   The details of this joke were taken from Westermarck's inaugural address 'Sociology as a university study', 1908. See Chapter 10, this volume.

References

Anon. 1892. Turistföreningens årsmöte. *Finland* 64 (17 March).

Estlander, B. 1930. *Elva årtionden ur Finlands historia.* Helsingfors: Söderström.

Eucken, R. 1901. *De mindre nationernas uppgift och betydelser.* Upsala: T:S Boktryckeri.

Ginsberg, M. 1982. Life and work of Edward Westermarck. In Stroup 1982:1–23.

Gummerus, H. 1926. *Aktiva kampår 1899–1910.* Helsingfors: Söderström & Co.

Gummerus, H. 1933. *Konni Zilliacus. Suomen itsenäisyyden esitaistelija.* Jyväskylä: Gummerus.

Hirn, Y. 1947. Edward Westermarck and his english friends. *Transactions of the Westermarck Society* I:39–51.

Huxley, S.D. 1990. *Constitutionalist insurgency in Finland: Finnish 'Passive Resistance' against Russification as a case of Nonmilitary Struggle in the European Resistance Tradition.* Helsinki: Suomen historiallinen seura.

Lagerborg, R. 1951. *Edvard Westermarck och verken från hans verkstad under hans tolv sista år 1927–39.* Helsingfors: Schildt.

Landtman, G. 1940. *Studenter under Finlands kampår 1898–1909.* Helsingfors: Svenska Litteratursällskapet.

Lundberg-Kelly, G. 2005. Född till resenär. Ett urval ur Edvard Westermarcks resebrev. *Historiska och litteraturhistoriska studier* 45:28–68.

Montagu, A. 1982. Edward Westermarck: recollections of an old student in young age. In Stroup 1982:63–70.

Numelin, R. 1970. Edv. Westermarck. Fjällvandrare – Fältforskare i Marocko – Politiska engagemang kring sekelskiftet – Under världskriget och Finlands frigörelsekamp – Ålandsfrågan. In T. Steinby (ed) *Historiska och litteraturhistoriska studier* 45:28–68. Helsingfors: Svenska litteratursällskapet i Finland.

Pipping, K. 1982. The first Finnish sociologist: a reappraisal of Edward Westermarck's work. *Acta Sociologica* 25(4):437–57.

Pollari, M., Ruuska, P., Anttila, A.-H., Kauranen, R., Löytty, O. and Rantanen, P. 2008. Alamaisjärjestyksen konkurssi ja avoin tulevaisuus. In P. Haapala, O. Löytty, K. Melkas and M. Tikka (eds) *Kansa kaikkivaltias. Suurlakko Suomessa 1905*, pp. 43–73. Helsinki: Teos.

Rantanen, P. and Ruuska, P. 2009. Alistetun viisaus. In Anttila, A.-H. *et al.* (eds.) *Kuriton kansa. Poliittinen mielikuvitus vuoden 1905 suurlakon ajan Suomessa*, pp. 33–56. Tampere: Vastapaino.

Sarmaja, H. n.d. Westermarckin suhde sosialismiin. Unpublished manuscript.

Stroup, T. (ed.) 1982. *Edward Westermarck: Essays on his Life and Works*. Helsinki: Acta Philosophica Fennica 34.

Westermarck, E. 1899. Finland and the Czar. *The Contemporary Review*, pp. 652–9.

Westermarck, E. 1920. The Aaland question. *The Contemporary Review*, pp. 790–4.

Westermarck, E. 1926 *The Origin and Development of the Moral Ideas* (vol. II). London: Macmillan and Co., Limited.

Westermarck, E. 1929. *Memories of My Life* (trans. A. Barwell). London: G. Allen & Unwin.

Westermarck, H. 1941. *Mina levnadsminnen*. Helsingfors: Söderström.

Zilliacus, K. 1920. *Sortovuosilta: Poliittisia Muistelmia*. Porvoo: WSOY.

Manuscript material

Castrén, G. 1905. Förslag för statsförfattning för Finland. Archives of the Finnish Active Resistance Party, National Archive, Helsinki.

Letter to Reuter from Westermarck. 18 May 1899. Åbo Akademi University archives, Turku.

Westermarck, Edward notebook 1878–1880. Åbo Akademi University archives, Turku.

Digital material

Lagerspetz, O. 2013. Westermarck, Edvard. http://filosofia.fi/node/2420.

Liukkonen, P, and Pesonen, A. 2008. Edvard (Alexander) Westermarck (1862–1939). http://www.kirjasto.sci.fi/ewester.htm. Kuusankosken kaupunginkirjasto.

4

Carl Starcke and Wilhelm Bolin on Edward Westermarck's dissertation, *The History of Human Marriage*

The question of plagiarism

Juhani Ihanus

Correspondence

In the autumn term of 1889, a young Finnish-born postgraduate student, Edward Westermarck (1862–1939), who was later to become a world-famous sociologist and social anthropologist, submitted his academic dissertation, *The History of Human Marriage. Part 1. The Origin of Human Marriage*, for examination at Imperial Alexander University (University of Helsinki). Wilhelm Bolin was nominated (6 November 1889) opponent of Westermarck's work; Hjalmar Neiglick, a gifted Finnish psychologist, who died earlier that year, was to have been the opponent.[1]

Bolin had himself written on the family (Bolin 1860 and 1864). His first academic dissertation submitted at the same university in 1860 had dealt with the development of the concept of the family down until the Reformation. In addition, in 1864 he published an enlarged and theoretically more advanced version of his dissertation. Bolin had a vague notion of the successive development of ethical standards towards higher levels – a notion which he also applied to the family. For him, unlike Snellman and Westermarck, the family formed, in principle, an unbroken ethical tie. Bolin's concept was of a kernel family, with husband, wife and children, in accordance with the bourgeois and middle-class family and the home cult of the nineteenth century.[2] In his early studies on the family, Bolin saw the basis of the family as moral, not primarily as economical. A well-balanced combination of reciprocal moral feelings and insights between husband and wife ensured the ethically enlightened and sound spiritual atmosphere of family life.

Bolin had not studied the family from an anthropological, biological or cultural-historical perspective. He was not very well prepared for Westermarck's Darwinian method, which cherished the natural history of human civilization and analyzed human social institutions on evolutionary and ethnographic grounds. Young Westermarck, with his comparative method, studied anthropological data on marriage from different nations, 'civilized' and 'uncivilized'. He defined marriage in evolutionary terms simply as 'a more or less durable connection between male and female, lasting beyond the mere act of propagation till after the birth of the offspring' (Westermarck 1891:110). Westermarck was in favour of the universality of monogamy and opposed to the hypothesis of primitive promiscuity.

Bolin had, however, already in 1884 been in contact with a Danish Feuerbach enthusiast and philosopher, later pedagogical reformer and politician, Carl Nicolai Starcke (1858–1926), who in 1888 published a book called *Die primitive Familie in ihrer Entstehung und Entwicklung* (The primitive family in its origin and development). This work dealt with the same kinds of questions as Westermarck's did. Consequently, it was natural that Starcke should become interested in Westermarck's dissertation, which was sent to him by Bolin. But this interest was in time to turn to indignation.

For Starcke (who was only four years senior to Westermarck), young Westermarck seemed too careless with, and oblivious of, his references, especially Starcke's own work. In correspondence with Bolin (between 8 December 1889 and 22 January 1890) he criticized Westermarck's dissertation; later, in 1893, he accused Westermarck more pointedly of plagiarism. Starcke felt that Westermarck should have given him credit for being the first to refute the hypothesis of the originally promiscuous union of the sexes. This must have hurt Starcke's pride.

This later accusation occurred two years after Westermarck had published the extension of his dissertation, *The History of Human Marriage* (1891), in England. This work became a best-seller, and was translated into several languages. Starcke's own *Die primitive Familie* was also translated into English (1889) and French (1891), as well as Italian, Russian and Hungarian. In spite of this, it was Westermarck's rather than Starcke's work that was widely reviewed in journals and newspapers. Westermarck achieved fame, at least for a while.

Nowadays, both Starcke and Westermarck are recognized as 'classical scholars' of late- and post-Victorian anthropological debates, and we can speak of them as figures in the history of ideas, where reputations have their own dramas.

When Starcke first received from Bolin a substantial part of Westermarck's dissertation, he wrote back that Westermarck defined marriage just like he had also done in *Die primitive Familie*.[3] This claim does not stand up to scrutiny, as Starcke had defined marriage as 'a connection between man and woman which is of more than momentary duration, and as long as it endures they seek for subsistence in common' (Starcke 1889[1976]:13). In Starcke's view a man linked himself to a woman who was subsequently supposed to keep house for him and rear his children (though he considered childless unions marriages too). Starcke maintained that the family was founded on marriage (Ibid.:12), while Westermarck, on the contrary, held firmly to the argument that marriage was rooted in the family, rather than the family in marriage.[4] Westermarck, unlike Starcke, stressed the birth of the offspring and the instinctual nature of the tie developed through the strong influence of natural selection between male and female.[5] Starcke had also noticed that for Westermarck 'tribal life may not have originally existed but the family may have existed', whereas Starcke himself stated that 'the tribe, the horde has existed as originally as the family'.[6]

When Starcke had received Westermarck's whole dissertation, he reported again to Bolin that Westermarck's results were like his own (Starcke's), but he also reminded Bolin of Westermarck's methodological shortcomings and was curious as to of Westermarck's age (Westermarck was then twenty-seven years old):

> If the work is written by a young man, I would say that it gives great
> promises for future achievements; but if the author is already of such age
> that his somewhat loosely surveying and reckless research method has
> become his habit, I do not know whether this part of the work can raise
> hopes.[7]

After Westermarck had presented his dissertation at Imperial Alexander University, Helsinki (20 December 1889), Starcke in his correspondence with Bolin still continued to comment on Westermarck's shortcomings and stressed his own contribution to the criticism of the theory (or hypothesis) of primitive promiscuity:

> 1) The theory of prom.[iscuity] is a hypothesis that cannot be verified
> through direct observation. It can only be concluded from it.
>   2) It is psychological, ... further it has to be discarded, as long as there
> are still other possibilities open.

3) Prom.[iscuity] will be deduced from the maternal line existing here and there. This conclusion is not wrong only because it is not necessary. One cannot prove that the maternal line is more original than the paternal line, that it is based on the unknown father....

However, there still remains the abstract possibility that in a time from which there are no more traces left prom.[iscuity] may have dominated. I may call this psychologically absurd, somebody else may propose it to be probable, this does not affect me; I will have no strife about that. The theory of prom.[iscuity], however, is not satisfied with this 'assured-faith conviction': it will see in prom.[iscuity] a situation that has set its traces in still discernible legal situations. This I have denied; the traces cannot without exception be interpreted in this way.

Our author, Westermarck, I believe, has missed his target especially because he, as I wrote, never allows himself to study the details of the phenomenon. That is why he manages only to show the possibility of another hypothesis than that of promiscuity.... That is why I have scolded the author about his reckless method.[8]

It seems that Bolin had in his letter (his letters to Starcke are not known to be extant) asked Starcke to assess Westermarck's merits as an academic scholar, as Starcke gave the following conclusion:

when you ask whether the man [Westermarck] is merited for a Docentur, I, not knowing him, can only point to the future. If he doses the ethnographical science in the way he has partly done in his book, his listeners will not be able to reach any independent assessment of the matter, because he will not give them any exact data. Nevertheless, many docents are certainly no better than he will be. I believe that the man will be helped by a stern critique, and so when he delivers a second, better work in the future, he will be able to present something really sound.[9]

Westermarck was soon to achieve even greater merit with the publication of his *History of Human Marriage*. What Starcke could not have anticipated at this time was the popular success Westermarck's work would achieve, overshadowing even Starcke's own work. In his correspondence with Bolin Starcke was quite generous in his assessment of Westermarck, and was not really overtly bothered by Westermarck's scanty references to his own work. After having received a book from Westermarck (presumably Westermarck's dissertation), Starcke was ready to accept Westermarck's 'Docentur': 'a Docentur should be cordially granted to him'.[10] He assured Bolin that he would not tell Westermarck about their relationship.[11] So, Westermarck was ignorant of the correspondence between his opponent Bolin and his public accuser to-be Starcke.

Bolin's statement

In his official statement, written for the University, on Westermarck's dissertation, Bolin inserted, partly in straight translation into Swedish, Starcke's arguments, cited above, against the unsubstantiated promiscuity theory. Bolin wrote the statement (dated 10 January 1890) shortly after he had received Starcke's letter. It should be noted that Starcke had in his published work interpreted marriage as an essentially economic institution. As a solid bourgeois of his time, Starcke even thought that it would be fatal to the bond of marriage if women were to be given legal independence with respect to property.[12]

In his statement, Bolin stressed heavily the property aspect, even more than he himself had done in his earlier studies of the family. Bolin asserted that Westermarck's arguments against the promiscuity theory would have been more convincing 'if he had paid more attention to the property relation that is significant in the relationship of the offspring to its natural provider in all primitive cultivation conditions.'[13] Bolin would also have liked to see Westermarck paying attention to property relations when analysing the system of appellations (the nomenclature), the matrilineal descent and phenomena induced by jealousy.[14] However, Bolin stated that Westermarck's dissertation undoubtedly had fulfilled its purpose and that he was ready to accept it. He did not, of course, mention anything about Starcke's role as a background critic. Their correspondence remained private.

Critique revived

In England (from October 1890 to June 1891), Westermarck expanded his dissertation into a book entitled *The History of Human Marriage*, which included new biological and anthropological sections. While this work was in progress he received valuable comments from Alfred Russel Wallace, the co-pioneer with Darwin of the theory of evolution. Wallace read the proofs of Westermarck's work and wrote a flattering introduction to it. In a letter to Westermarck, Wallace (4 May 1891) mentions having seen that a 'French writer' had 'anticipated' Westermarck's ideas. Wallace's 'French writer' is almost surely Starcke, whose work had just then been published in French. Wallace suggested that: 'It might be as well to refer to it, either in the concluding Chapter or in the Preface.'[15] This Westermarck never got around to doing, as his book was already at the printers. Later, in his fifth and rewritten edition (in three volumes) of *The History of Human Marriage*, Westermarck mentions Starcke in each volume, but is still reticent as to who should have priority for refuting the promiscuity theory.[16]

Irked by the popular success of Westermarck's book and by the relative neglect of his own work, Starcke in 1893 published an angry critique of Westermarck's work, as a reminder of his own contribution to the field, first in Danish (in *Tidsskrift for Retsvidenskab*, published in Norway) and then an English version (in the *International Journal of Ethics*).[17] By this time, Starcke had sharpened the critique that was already present in his correspondence with Bolin. Bolin, himself, in autumn 1893, wrote a short unpublished account in which he approved of Starcke's critique on Westermarck's 'puffed-up literary miracle'.[18]

Starcke's article repeated the shortcomings of the theory of primitive promiscuity. He concluded that the theory was based principally on three considerations (cf. Starcke 1893b:453–5). First, in 'modern' times certain customs and relations, in tribes that lacked 'all sense of sexual honor', were seen as relics of a former entirely promiscuous way of life. Secondly, the nomenclature for the degrees of relationship among many primitive tribes seemed to indicate the confusion of kinship relationships, typical of promiscuity. Thirdly, and most importantly, descent through the mother's line was taken to prove that originally a child's father was not known, as would be the case in states of unregulated sexual relations.

Starcke had picked holes in all these three arguments, and he tried to conclude that Westermarck's parallel criticism was fashioned after his previously published remarks and explanations: 'But as this [Westermarck's] criticism, in its methods and results, often entirely coincides with mine, it cannot be thought an unjustified desire to wish that fact had been mentioned. But this never happens, although Mr. Westermarck knows of the existence of my book, and quotes it here and there upon minor points.' (Ibid.:455).

In his desire to be justified as the *Urquelle* and originator, Starcke, however, had to admit that Westermarck was not totally in accordance with him. But the discrepancy was, according to Starcke, due to Westermarck's poor explanations, which lay too much stress on 'instinct' and were thus favouring 'biological points of view, to the exclusion of social and psychological' (Ibid.:464):[19]

> Biology must ally itself with psychology and sociology. Mr. Westermarck
> admits that this is so; but this necessity seems to mean for him that a mass
> of facts is to be heaped together from all three departments; and yet it
> cannot be otherwise understood that every fact is to be regarded from all
> three points of view. No problem of human life can find its perfect solution
> in such a conception as that of utility to the race and of an instinct resting

on this utility. These concepts are in themselves empty categories, well fitted
as such to afford the desired cloak for ignorance.

(Ibid.:459-60)

Westermarck's instinct-account of exogamy and especially of the universal
'horror of incest' (instinctive 'aversion to marriage between persons living
closely together')[20] was for Starcke unscientific and without proof. Again, he
thought that he himself had given a better hypothesis, which stated that 'the
prohibition of marriage was based upon the legal status the persons concerned
had in the body politic. The son could not marry his mother, nor the brother
his sister, nor the father his daughter, without upsetting the legal relations
which had hitherto obtained between them.' (Starcke 1893b:462–3). Curiously
enough, this purified social legitimation explanation of the 'body politic' has
become almost obsolete, while Westermarck's 'horror of incest' account is still
alive in recent anthropological and sexological discussions.

Westermarck's defence

Starcke failed to appreciate Westermarck's striving for a three-level model
concerning the history of marriage. Westermarck was not so oblivious of
social and psychological points of view as Starcke suggested. Westermarck
embedded the social 'facts' in the context of a continuous interplay
between biological foundations, psychological 'causes' and social processes.
Psychological explanations were mediators between biological and social
levels. In his early research period Westermarck was much more impressed
by Darwin's versatile empiricism, Spencer's large-scale biopsychological and
sociopsychological theories and Tylor's reform of the anthropological method
that contributed to the elimination of unilinear evolutionism than by Starcke's
'minor' arguments.

Westermarck, however, did not fail to counter, albeit succinctly, Starcke's
accusations. In the *International Journal of Ethics* Westermarck hit back, not
so politely either:

Dr. Starcke seems never to have suspected that if I do not refer to his book
so often as he would have liked, the explanation may be that I do not hold
the same high opinion of it as he does himself. We agree in thinking that
there is no truth in the hypothesis of promiscuity; but the ways in which he
and I have dealt with the problem are so different that it did not occur to
me that any talk of plagiarism would be even possible. Dr. Starcke's method
is nothing if not critical.... As a rule, his collection of facts is too scanty to
serve as a basis for trustworthy inductions.... If my conclusions happened
to coincide, in certain points, with another writer's unproved statements,

this was for me a matter of little consequence. I had conceived the whole
plan of my work, and written the larger part of it, before I had ever heard
Dr. Starcke's name. And I now 'openly and honestly' confess that I owe to
Dr. Starcke absolutely nothing but what I have acknowledged, and that,
when I have mentioned his name, I have done it, in most cases, merely for
politeness' sake.

(Westermarck 1893:95–6)

It should be remembered that Westermarck was at that time just over
thirty, and at the height of his youthful vigor after achieving surprising literary
fame. Westermarck came to be known as the defender of monogamous
marriage. Even in George Bernard Shaw's play (*Man and Superman*, 1903),
Westermarck's *The History of Human Marriage* was mentioned as necessary
reading for civilized discussion. At that time both Westermarck and Starcke
were 'armchair anthropologists'. They made their conclusions on the basis
of literary material. Later, beginning in 1898, Westermarck began to draw
away from simple armchair-theorizing by doing anthropological fieldwork in
Morocco and by gathering empirical data.

Even in his later, rewritten edition of *The History of Human Marriage*
(1921) Westermarck kept to his earlier formulations. He could find no evidence
for the hypothesis of primitive promiscuity. On the contrary, he tried to
show that: i) no known primitive people had been, or actually was, living in
complete promiscuity; ii) the arguments of earlier researchers were obscure
and untrustworthy; iii) in cases of some kind of group marriage formation, the
group marriage had developed as a combination of polygyny and polyandry;
iv) in some hypothesized cases of 'sexual communism', no single woman was
really married to more than one man, so that an individual marriage existed
alongside sexual (male) libertinism; and v) even in most early hunting and
gathering groups a family, consisting of man, woman and children, was a
significant social unit (see Ihanus 1999:207).

Monogamy, according to Westermarck's firm notion, was the earliest
form of marriage, whereas polygamy and group marriage were later and
insignificant deviations from the natural and universal monogamy. In the last
chapter of his dissertation, Westermarck had stated that he did not deny that
with some peoples 'intercourse between the sexes may have been on the whole
promiscuous', but he most decidedly denied 'the likelihood of promiscuity
having formed a general stage in the social history of mankind' (Westermarck
1889:143; see also Ihanus 1999:207).

From his reading of Darwin's *The Descent of Man* Westermarck had
come to doubt the hypothesis of primitive promiscuity and to realize that
further evidence was needed to substantiate it. Darwin was not sure about

how the various forms of marriage had developed and he demanded facts instead of loose speculations: 'The licentiousness of many savages is no doubt astonishing, but it seems to me that more evidence is requisite, before we fully admit that their intercourse is in any case promiscuous.' (Darwin 1871, vol. II:359). Along Darwinian lines Westermarck claimed that the strongest argument against primitive promiscuity could be deduced from 'the psychical nature of man and other mammals' (Westermarck 1889:142), namely from jealousy. As Darwin implied: 'from the strength of the feeling of jealousy all through the animal kingdom ... I cannot believe that absolutely promiscuous intercourse prevailed in times past' (Darwin 1871, vol. II:361).[21]

Westermarck's argument rested likewise on the fundamental feeling of jealousy: 'if jealousy could be proved to be universally prevalent in the human race of the present day, it is impossible to believe that there ever was a time when man was devoid of that powerful feeling' (Westermarck 1889:143).[22]

Thus, besides being biologically rooted in human history, monogamy was, for Westermarck, also psychologically deeply rooted in primeval times. He, like Starcke, was also opposed to the idea of primitive matriarchy, where the father would have had neither rights nor responsibilities to the family or to the clan. This idea of matriarchy had been deduced by Bachofen from the myths concerning the Amazons (Bachofen 1861). Westermarck, on the contrary, thought that, in the 'Archaic state', the paternal family ties had, for the most part, dominated over maternal family ties. The patriarchal family got stronger when the clan got weaker. In more developed 'States' the family and patriarchal ties, however, lost their importance (Westermarck 1908:223; 1921, vol. I:45–6).[23]

In *The History of Human Marriage* (1921) Westermarck crystallized his conception of the origin and development of the institution of marriage:

> As for the origin of the institution of marriage, I consider it probable that it has developed out of primeval habit. It was, I believe, even in primitive times, the habit for a man and a woman (or several women) to live together, to have sexual relations with one another, and to rear their offspring in common, the man being the protector and supporter of his family and the woman being his helpmate and the nurse of their children. This habit was sanctioned by custom, and afterwards by law, and was thus transformed into a social institution. In order to trace marriage in its legal sense to its ultimate source, we must therefore try to find out the origin of the habit from which it sprang.
>
> (Westermarck 1921, vol. I:27–8)

In its natural history meaning 'marriage' does not belong to man solely. That is why Westermarck called his study the history of *human* marriage. Human marriage has its counterparts in many other animal species. Westermarck's approach to sociological issues was similar to his approach to biological and psychological issues, namely he sought to study man (and his institutions) not as an isolated phenomenon, but in connection with other animal species and with the whole evolutionary process.

Starcke was surely earlier than Westermarck in criticizing the then prevailing theory of primitive promiscuity, but their way of approaching the subject was different. In retrospect, there can be no question of crude plagiarism on Westermarck's part. Nonetheless, he was familiar with Starcke's work when writing his dissertation and he perhaps did not quite give the due acknowledgement to his predecessor for fighting against the anthropological dogma of the day that he should have. Starcke can still justifiably be viewed as a forerunner in the sociological interpretation of descent systems and relationship terminologies (see Needham 1976:xi). He was also one of the first to mark the distinction between the sexual relations and marriage that escaped his contemporaries.[24] This distinction was also present in Westermarck's definition of marriage.[25]

In defence of Westermarck, it can be said that Starcke had not formulated his results very clearly; they tend to get lost among his many digressions into details and summaries of anthropological reports and theories. The same is partly true in Westermarck's case, but nonetheless he had an independent style of reasoning. It could be argued that Starcke's critique was actually of benefit to Westermarck. The production of scientific credibility (see, for example, Bourdieu 1984) rests on often dramatic (or dramatized) struggles between theories, methods and even speculative rhetoric. We could paraphrase the notion that a man is akin to his totem[26] so that a researcher is akin to his or her theory (totems) and method (emblems). The Victorian issue of primitive promiscuity faded by the turn of the century, and was replaced by new themes, totems, intellectual strategies and struggles for symbolic power.

Closing the case: revisiting primitive promiscuity as a Victorian theme

When John McLennan, the Scottish lawyer, published his *Primitive Marriage* in 1865, he introduced the concepts of exogamy and endogamy, and opened the gates for the concern, and fascination, with the origins of marriage regulations and the scenarios of primitive promiscuity, group marriage, sexual communism, primal hordes, incest and the like (cf. Arens 1986:34–7). For the Victorian imagination, generating and reconstructing these unobservable and unrecorded ancient and 'indecent' scenes became an attractive obsession. A primitive society was the 'time machine' of Victorian anthropologists. By using that time machine, a researcher made an imaginative leap to get a privileged view, through a primitive society, of the peoples of the past, and of the continuity of the social process.[27] Admittedly, the Victorian authors tried to construct rational theories of stage-by-stage social evolution, but at the same time, they fixated their gaze wistfully on conjured-up primal scenes. These primal scenes served, as Arens has suggested:

> in part, to afford an attractive antithesis of ideal Victorian social
> arrangements, rather than verifiable propositions.... These imagined
> alternatives from distant times and places imparted positive meaning to the
> relatively enviable condition of nineteenth-century advancement and may
> even have provided intellectual relief from the more oppressive norms of
> the day. The fact that these fabricated societies did not have an historical or
> ethnographic base was irrelevant.
>
> (Arens 1986:37)

That unbridled sexual behavior was no longer directly, rather only vaguely, perceptible (among the 'lower races') in the nineteenth century of advancement, suited Victorian moral codes extremely well.

The taboos and the cultural paraphernalia of Victorian sexual attitudes, values and repressions have been focused on by several writers. Stocking, for example, gives the following list: 'The renunciation of all sexual activity save the procreative intercourse of ["muscular"] Christian marriage; the education of both sexes in chastity and continence; the secrecy and cultivated ignorance surrounding sex; the bowdlerization of literature and euphemistic degradation of language; the general suppression of bodily functions and all the "coarser" aspects of life' (Stocking 1987:199–200).[28] The holy trinity of purity, prudery and propriety loomed as the guardian of marriage and morals. Of course, this guardian was not impartial: it was stricter for women. And, naturally enough, the evolutionary process was accepted as culminating in a monogamous family that incorporated features of mid-Victorian middle-class family structure and ethos. 'The pedestal of Victorian domesticity' was the peak of evolutionary and moral progress (Stocking 1987:204–5).

Starcke and Westermarck were both writing against the grammar and authority of Victorian anthropologists. Learned men like Bachofen, McLennan, Lubbock, L.H. Morgan, Giraud-Teulon, Lippert, Post, Wilken and Engels defended the hypothesis of primitive promiscuity, some of them spoke for the priority of matrilineal kinship, too. But Starcke and Westermarck were not, however, alone in reacting against the consensus of the day. In England, Charles Staniland Wake, who had outlined a 'science of comparative psychology' (Wake 1868), criticized, as early as 1878, in his *The Evolution of Morality* the hypothesis of primitive promiscuity. In his *The Development of Marriage and Kinship* (1889) he espoused, independently, similar kinds of sociological arguments on marriage and kinship as those of Starcke against McLennan, Lubbock and L.H. Morgan (see also Needham 1976:xxvii).[29]

In his dissertation Westermarck had already quoted Wake's *The Evolution of Morality* (1878) and one of his articles (1872).[30] So Starcke was not the only predecessor for Westermarck, and soon others, like Kohler, Crawley and Letourneau joined in to criticize the promiscuity hypothesis and the priority of matrilineal kinship. In 1896, Tylor found that a 'reaction' against primitive 'matrimonial anarchy' was well under way and likely to cause it 'to pass away altogether' (Tylor 1896:82). And a few years later, in 1902, Crawley remarked on the changed attitude: 'It is unscientific to have recourse to a hypothesis of primitive incest and promiscuity' (Crawley 1902, vol. II:205).[31]

Wake, Starcke, Westermarck and others had presented post-Victorian scenarios with new problems and new quarrels. In the esteemed and hierarchic successions of anthropological historiography, McLennan's and Morgan's ideas may seem to have survived better than those of Wake, Starcke or Westermarck, whose ideas have tended to become largely obscured in mist and so mostly unrecognized. This neglect is unfortunate and perhaps reflects the slow pace at which established histories are changed from their standardized (and at the same time marginalizing) orders. New research can make corrections with regard to marginalized and less-researched authors when it comes to the history of ideas. Wake, Starcke, Westermarck, Bolin and many others deserve to be reinterpreted and their ideas recontextualized more carefully than hitherto.

Notes

1 Minutebooks of the Historical-philological Section of the University of Helsinki (6 November 1889 §1 and §2).

2 See Knif 1985:168, 176 and 179; see also Trudgill 1976:44.

3 Starcke's letter to Bolin (dated 8 December 1889, received 16 December 1889). Starcke's point is repeated later in Starcke 1893a and b.

4 Westermarck 1889. Westermarck had in his references Starcke's work under the German name, but the publishing place was, however, London (while it should have been Leipzig). It may be that Westermarck had available the English edition (1889) of Starcke's work.

5 See also Westermarck's (1893:97–8) comments.

6 Starcke's letter to Bolin (dated 8 December 1889, received 16 December 1889). The original text is in German, translated by Juhani Ihanus.

7   Starcke's letter to Bolin (dated 16 December 1889, received 21 December 1889).
      Translated by J. I.

8   Starcke's letter to Bolin (dated 26 December 1889, received 2 January 1890).
      Translated by J. I.

9   Ibid. Translated by J. I.

10   Starcke's letter to Bolin (dated 12 January 1890). Westermarck got his 'Docentur' in
      Helsinki on 8 August 1890.

11   Starcke's letter to Bolin (dated 22 January 1890, received 2 January 1890).

12   See, for example, Starcke 1889[1976]:269; see also Needham 1976:xv.

13   Bolin's statement on Westermarck's dissertation (dated 10 January 1890; original in
      Swedish).

14   Ibid. – In his letter to Bolin (dated 26 December 1889, received 2 January 1890),
      Starcke was doubtful of the usefulness and value of the property argument in
      dealing with primitive conditions in primeval times: 'Now, the question is really
      so complex that by referring to a property condition nothing important can be
      gained, as long as it remains possible that this condition is a result of a relatively
      late culture.' Starcke (1893b:453–4) suggested that it is only in a 'later' culture,
      where possibly promiscuous relations might be found, that these relations arise
      from a 'particular phase of the idea of property': 'Promiscuous relations are an
      effect rather of the sharp separation of tribes into units with relations of property
      rather than of an indiscriminate treatment of individuals.'

15   Wallace's letter to Westermarck (dated 4 May 1891) is included in Wikman 1940:19.

16   See Westermarck 1921 (vol. I):296 seq.; (vol. II):190 seq., 364; (vol. III):217.

17   Starcke 1893a and b. Everything we know indicates Starcke's eagerness to get
      his critique of Westermarck published in English. In Westermarck 1893:95, the
      Managing Editor of the *International Journal of Ethics* explains that Starcke's
      article (1893b) was first received in March 1892 with a request that it be inserted
      in the April number in place of Starcke's other article. The request came too late
      and Starcke's critique was returned to him, but it was received again and finally
      published 'at his earnest request' in the July number.

18   Bolin's statement on Starcke 1893a. Bolin characterized Starcke's criticism as 'stern
      but earnest and matter of fact' (original in Swedish).

19   Starcke forgot to mention that he had himself (1889:9) spoken of 'social instincts'
      (see also Westermarck 1893:98–9).

20   See, for example, Westermarck 1891:334.

21   The same statement by Darwin had also been referred to by Starcke (1889[1976]:255–
      6), but not as the strongest argument against primitive promiscuity.

22   On this occasion Westermarck reminds that according to Thlinket [Tlinget] myth,
      man's jealousy is older than the whole world.

23   In 1894 Westermarck was called to the membership of Institut International de
      Sociologie. In its second congress in 1895, Westermarck's paper on matriarchy was
      discussed. The paper and the discussion were published (see Westermarck 1896).
      Westermarck stressed that the paternal family had been dominating, though he

did not argue that patriarchy would have been omnipresent. The omnipresence of matriarchy he denied most decidedly, and stated that monogamy had always existed, even more in the 'lower' states of culture. See also Lagerborg's (1951:217–18) reference to the discussion.

24 See, for example, Starcke 1889[1976]:256. See also Arens 1986:38.

25 Westermarck 1921, vol. I:71: 'This definition [of the term marriage] lays stress on the highly important fact, only too often overlooked by sociologists, that there is a vital difference between marriage and merely sexual relations, even though these be sanctioned by custom.'

26 See Westermarck 1908:603; see also Smith 1894:285.

27 See Gellner 1964:18 and Ingold 1986:94–6.

28 See also, for example, Gay 1984; Trudgill 1976:159–73, 204–18; Weeks 1981.

29 In Darwin's later editions of *The Descent of Man* there is reference to Wake's criticism against McLennan, Lubbock and L. H. Morgan.

30 This article is not in Westermarck's list of authorities quoted (while Wake 1878 is), but Westermarck (1889) actually refers to it on page 53. Westermarck has also written short passages of Wake 1878 to his early (undated) notebook (in Edward Westermarck's manuscript collection, Åbo Akademi Library, Box 33).

31 In accordance with the changed post-Victorian climate of values, Friedrich Jodl (1908/1917) criticized the ethnographical 'mosaic of facts' in Westermarck's *The Origin and Development of the Moral Ideas* (vol. 1, 1906; published in German translation in 1907), although he found it otherwise to be 'an inexhaustible gold mine' (Jodl 1908/1917:35).

References

Arens, W. 1986. *The Original Sin: Incest and its Meaning.* Oxford: Oxford University Press.

Bachofen, J.J. 1861. *Das Mutterrecht: Eine Untersuchung über die Gynaikokratie der alten Welt nach ihrer religiösen und rechtlichen Natur.* Stuttgart: von Krais & Hoffmann.

Bolin, W. 1860. Familjebegreppets utveckling ända till reformationen. Diss. Helsingfors.

Bolin, W. 1864. Familjen. Studier. Helsingfors.

Bourdieu, P. 1984. *Homo Academicus.* Paris: Les Éditions de Minuit.

Crawley, E. 1902. *The Mystic Rose: A Study of Primitive Marriage* (2 vols). London: Macmillan.

Darwin, C. 1871. *The Descent of Man, and Selection in Relation to Sex* (2 vols). London: John Murray.

Gay, P. 1984. *The Bourgeois Experience: Victoria to Freud* (vol. 1: *The education of the senses*). Oxford: Oxford University Press.

Gellner, E. 1964. *Thought and Change.* London: Weidenfeld & Nicolson.

Ihanus, J. 1999. *Multiple Origins: Edvard Westermarck in Search of Mankind.* Frankfurt am Main: Peter Lang.

Ingold, T. 1986. *Evolution and Social Life.* Cambridge: Cambridge University Press.

Jodl, F. 1908/1917 Ursprung und Entwicklung der Moralbegriffe [review of Westermarck 1906 in German translation 1907). In Friedrich Jodl, *Vom Lebenswege: Gesammelte Vorträge und Aufsätze* (Zweiter Band, Herausgegeben von Wilhelm Börner), 28–38. Stuttgart: Cotta.

Knif, H. 1985. Familjekult och filosofi. En kritisk läsning av Wilhelm Bolins bok Familjen (1864). *Historiska och Litteraturhistoriska Studier* 60:141–82.

Lagerborg, R. 1951. *Om Edvard Westermarck och verken från hans verkstad under hans tolv sista år 1927–1939.* Borgå: Holger Schildts Förlag.

McLennan, J.F. 1865. *Primitive Marriage: An Inquiry into the Origin of the Form of Capture in Marriage Ceremonies.* Edinburgh: Adam & Charles Black.

Needham, R. 1976. Editor's introduction. In Starcke 1889[1976]:ix–xxxi. Chicago: The University of Chicago Press.

Smith, W.R. 1894. *Lectures on the Religion of the Semites* (new [second] edition). London: Adam & Charles Black.

Starcke, C.N. 1888. *Die primitive Familie in ihrer Entstehung und Entwicklung.* Leipzig: Brockhaus.

Starcke, C.N. 1889[1976]. *The Primitive Family in its Origin and Development* (ed. and introd. R. Needham). Chicago: The University of Chicago Press.

Starcke, C.N.1893a. Nogle bemærkninger om menneskeligt ægteskab. *Tidsskrift for Retsvidenskab* 6:132–42.

Starcke, C.N. 1893b. On human marriage. *International Journal of Ethics* 3 (July):452–65.

Stocking, G.W., Jr. 1987. *Victorian Anthropology.* New York: The Free Press.

Trudgill, E. 1976. *Madonnas and Magdalens: The Origins and Development of Victorian Sexual Attitudes.* London: Heinemann.

Tylor, E.B. 1896. The matriarchal family system. *Nineteenth Century* 40:81–96.

Wake, C.S. 1868. *Chapters on Man, with the Outlines of a Science of Comparative Psychology.* London: Trübner & Co.

Wake, C.S. 1872. The mental characteristics of primitive man, as exemplified by the Australian Aborigines. *Journal of the Anthropological Institute* 1:74–84.

Wake, C.S. 1878. *The Evolution of Morality: Being a History of the Development of Moral Culture* (2 vols). London: Trübner & Co.

Wake, C.S. 1889. *The Development of Marriage and Kinship.* London: G. Redway.

Weeks, J. 1981. *Sex, Politics and Society: The Regulation of Sexuality since 1800.* London: Longman.

Westermarck, E. 1889. *The History of Human Marriage. Part I. The Origin of Human Marriage* (Diss.). Helsingfors: Frenckell & Son.

Westermarck, E. 1891. *The History of Human Marriage.* London: Macmillan & Co.

Westermarck E. 1893. 'On human marriage' – a reply to Dr. C.N. Starcke. *International Journal of Ethics* 4(1):94–101.

Westermarck, E. 1896. Le matriarcat. *Annales de l'Institut International de Sociologie,* pp. 114–51.

Westermarck, E. 1906. *The Origin and Development of the Moral Ideas* (vol. 1). London: Macmillan & Co.

Westermarck, E. 1908. *The Origin and Development of the Moral Ideas* (vol. 2). London: Macmillan & Co.

Westermarck, E. 1921. *The History of Human Marriage* (3 vols). London: Macmillan & Co.

Wikman, K. Rob. V. (ed.) 1940. Letters from Edward B. Tylor and Alfred Russel
     Wallace to Edward Westermarck. Edited with introductory remarks
     concerning the publication of 'The History of Human Marriage'. *Acta
     Academiae Aboensis Humaniora* XIII (7):1–22.

Manuscript sources
C. N. Starcke's letters to Wilhelm Bolin. Wilhelm Bolin Manuscripts, vol. IX. Helsinki
     University Library.
Wilhelm Bolin's statement on Edward Westermarck's dissertation (dated 10 January
     1890). The archives of the chancellor's office. University of Helsinki.
Wilhelm Bolin's statement on Starcke 1893a (dated 'autumn 1893'). Wilhelm Bolin
     Manuscripts, vol. XV. Helsinki University Library.
Minutebooks of the Historical-philological Section of the University of Helsinki (6
     November 1889).

5

Westermarck and the
Westermarck Hypothesis

Arthur P. Wolf

Among sociologists and anthropologists Edward Westermarck is best known for the hypothesis that bears his name, the claim that 'generally speaking, there is a remarkable absence of erotic feelings between persons living closely together from childhood' and that this is 'the fundamental cause of the exogamous prohibitions' (1922, vol. 2:vi). The argument that these prohibitions are universal, together with the fact that they are the camshaft of human kinship systems, guaranteed that the hypothesis would be queried as anthropology emerged as a discipline in the early twentieth century, taking the comparative study of kinship as its special domain. What was not to be expected is that the debate would develop into a vitriolic contest involving biologists, philosophers and political scientists, as well as sociologists and anthropologists.

My purpose in this chapter is to review the history of this controversy in an effort to discover why it attracted so many participants and became so contentious.

The History of Human Marriage was a large book and became larger with every edition. It covered every aspect of marriage, including the evolution of the family. It was, however, the Westermarck Hypothesis that caught the attention of most reviewers. And with one notable exception, they applauded the hypothesis. Edward Burnett Tylor singled out as 'the most valuable chapters' those dealing with 'the prohibition of marriage between kindred', and wrote to Westermarck saying that 'I should not be surprised to find [your hypothesis] or something like it the real solution.' (Wikman 1940:18). Alfred Wallace also called attention to the book's 'ingenious and philosophical explanation of the repugnance to marriage between near relatives', and, like

Tylor, wrote to Westermarck saying 'I think you have solved the problem.' (Ibid.:18).

The one exception to the applause that greeted the Westermarck Hypothesis was the review by W. Robertson Smith. He accused Westermarck of assuming that 'the laws of society are at bottom mere formulated instincts' (Robertson Smith 1891:271), and thereby anticipated a criticism that became one of the most common of the many directed at E.O. Wilson's *Sociobiology*. It could be argued that what is now called the 'socio-biology debate' was initiated in the 1890s by Edward Westermarck.

It was not until the early 1910s that the tide of scholarly opinion definitely turned against Westermarck. The first blow was struck by Sir James Frazer. Complaining that the Westermarck Hypothesis is 'too much under the influence of Darwin', he argued that Westermarck could not possibly be right because if he were, there would be no incest taboo.

> It is not easy to see why any deep human instinct should need to be reinforced by law. There is no law commanding men to eat and drink or forbidding them to put their hands in the fire. Men eat and drink and keep their hands out of the fire instinctively for fear of natural not legal penalties... The law only forbids men to do what their instincts incline them to do; what nature prohibits and punishes, it would be superfluous for the law to prohibit and punish. Accordingly, we may always safely assume that crimes forbidden by law are crimes which many men have a natural propensity to commit.
>
> ([1910]1968:98–9)

This criticism was repeated by Sigmund Freud in 1911, Leslie A. White in 1948, Claude Levi-Strauss in 1949, David Aberle, Urie Bronferbrenner, Eckhard H. Hess, Daniel Miller, David M. Schneider, and James Spuhler in 1963, and, without attribution, by Bernard Williams in 1983, Richard Lewontin, Steven Ross, and Leon Kamin in 1984, Maurice Godelier in 1989, and, most recently, by Allen Johnson and Douglas Price-Williams in 1996.[1] All argued that the prohibitions Westermarck was trying to explain disproved the explanation he offered.

An even more consequential criticism of Westermarck followed hard on Frazer's initial blow. In the third of the essays published as *Totem and Taboo* Freud quoted Frazer at length, and then went on to argue that 'the findings of psycho-analysis make the hypothesis of an innate aversions to incestuous intercourse totally untenable. They have shown, on the contrary, that the earliest sexual excitations of youthful human beings are invariably of an incestuous character and that such impulses when repressed play a part that can scarcely be over-estimated as motive forces of neuroses in later life.'

(Freud [1913]1950:97–8). This argument was repeated in even more emphatic language in two of the lectures published as *A General Introduction to Psychoanalysis* (Freud [1920]1953:220–1, 343–4). We must credit Freud with recognizing that if Westermarck was right, there is no Oedipus complex and thus no basis for Freudian psychology.

Freud is quoted against Westermarck as frequently as Frazer, and often by authors who cannot by any stretch of the term be considered Freudians. Levi-Strauss agreed that 'psychoanalysis … finds a universal phenomenon not in the repugnance towards incestuous relationships, but on the contrary in the pursuit of such relationships' ([1949]1969:17); Murdock argued that Westermarck's hypothesis 'flagrantly overlooks, and even inverts, that vast body of clinical evidence which shows that incestuous desires are regularly engendered within the nuclear family and are kept in restraint only through persistent social pressure and individual repression' (1949:291); and, as though he wanted upstage Murdock, Claude Meillassoux argued that far from arousing '"natural" feelings of revulsion among the majority of people', incest 'seems to have exercised such a powerful attraction that whenever social conditions facilitated its practice religious terrorism had to be enlisted to control it' (1981:12).

When the third edition of *The History* appeared in 1922, it was reviewed by Bronislaw Malinowski, who predicted that 'Prof. Westermarck's theory of exogamy … will come to be considered a model of sociological construction', though Malinowski had to admit that 'at present it seems to find favour with no one' (1922:504). Westermarck's reputation prospered, but the Westermarck Hypothesis did not. In 1958, when an eminent selection of biologists, psychologists and anthropologists met on the hill behind my house (the site of the Center for Advanced Studies in the Behavioral Sciences), the Westermarck Hypothesis was so out of favour that they did not feel it worth their while to discuss it. It is mentioned in their joint publication 'only for the sake of completeness'. Their reasons were Frazer's and Freud's. 'It is hard to see', they wrote, 'why what is naturally repugnant should be tabooed, and the evidence for sexual attraction among kinsmen is quite adequate for rejecting the theory.' (Aberle *et al.* 1963:258).

To understand why everyone agreed that Frazer and Freud's reasons for rejecting the Westermarck Hypothesis were 'quite adequate', we have to recognize that this judgement was made in an empirical vacuum. Freud's evidence evaporated if one questioned his methods, and Westermarck's was not much better. Although he spent a large part of his adult life in Morocco, he never took advantage of the opportunity offered by *bint'amm* marriage.[2] All he had to say on the subject was that 'a Berber from the Great Atlas once said to me, "How can a man love a woman with whom he has grown up from childhood."' (Westermarck 1914:55). The fate of the Westermarck Hypothesis was not decided by evidence. It was decided by social forces of the kind studied by cultural historians.

What these forces were is evident in the arguments that were preferred to the Westermarck Hypothesis. The most popular by far were those that began with Tylor's suggestion that incest taboos were invented when savage tribes discovered 'a fundamental difference between marrying in and marrying-out' (Tylor 1889:23). In the work of Leslie White and Claude Levi-Strauss the discovery of the advantages of marrying-out was an epiphany. In White's words, this was the point at which 'social evolution as a *human* affair was launched upon its career' (White 1950:425). Without this discovery, 'social evolution could have gone no further on the human level than among the anthropoids'. Levi-Strauss saw the incest taboos,

> as kind of remodelling of the biological conditions of marriage and
> procreation compelling them to be perpetuated only in an artificial
> framework of taboos and obligations. It is there, and only there, that we find
> a passage from nature to culture, from animal to human life, and that we are
> in a position to understand the very essence of their articulation.
>
> (Levi-Strauss 1960:278)

This language should not be read as rhetoric. It is so extravagant because the story told expresses deeply held views of the nature of our species. We are not just 'intrinsically talented apes' as Clifford Geertz once put it (1963:112–13). We have transcended nature and are capable of making of ourselves what we will. Westermarck's offense was to suggest that the incest taboos were like bipedal locomotion – the products of natural processes and not evidence of our transcendent intelligence. Freud was advanced as Westermarck's foil because if the 'earliest sexual excitations of human beings are invariably of an incestuous character', then the incest taboos can be seen as repressing rather than expressing human nature.

In 1958, when what I will call the Advanced Studies Group met on the hill behind my house, it appeared that the debate initiated by Frazer and Freud had run its course. Henceforth, the Westermarck Hypothesis would be mentioned 'only for the sake of completeness'. But unbeknownst to the Advanced Studies Group, the empirical vacuum in which this judgement was made was about to be punctured by evidence from three natural experiments – communal child rearing in Israel (Shepher 1971; Spiro 1958; Talmon 1964), *bint'amm* marriage in Lebanon and Morocco (MaCabe 1983; Walter 1997), and my own work on minor marriages in South China (Wolf 1995). The first documents the effects of early association on children reared together in communal nurseries; the second compares partner preferences and fertility among cousins who were and were not reared together; and the third compares the fertility, divorce and adultery rates of women who were adopted and raised by their husband's family with those who did not meet their husband until the day of their wedding. In all three cases, the consequences were as Westermarck would have predicted. The Israel children enrolled in the same nursery before age three never married and never engaged in pre-marital sex; cousins who were reared together said they would not marry if given a choice and when forced to marry were substantially less fertile than cousins who were reared apart; and comparisons of 14,200 marriages in Taiwan shows that when a wife joined her husband's family as a small child, fertility, divorce and adultery were all affected. Divorce was three times as likely, fertility only half as high, and adultery at least twice as frequent. Evidence I hope to publish soon also shows that the men who married girls with whom they were reared were more likely to take concubines than men who did not meet their wife until later.[3]

William Whewell argued that the surest path to truth was what he called 'a consilience of inductions'. When inductions from classes of facts altogether different 'leap to the same point', we may take that as 'the point where truth resides' (Whewell 1967:65). By Whewell's criteria, the three experiments indicate that the point indicated by Westermarck was 'the point where truth resides'. Evidence from three very different contexts all leap in the same direction. They all say that 'there is a remarkable absence of erotic feelings between persons living closely together from childhood'.

Anyone who doubts that the debate over the Westermarck Hypothesis is about something larger than the incest taboos should study the reaction to this evidence. It was not what we expect of our peers. My book appeared on Finnish television, but was not reviewed in the *American Anthropologist*. After the book was published, graduate students who applied to work with me were not admitted. Scholars as different in their interests as Marvin Harris, Melford Spiro, Sir Edmund Leach, Paul Erlich, Philip Kitcher and Jesse Prinz challenged my evidence with what were clearly ad hoc arguments. Kitcher suggested that minor marriages only failed more often than other marriages because the men were the 'lame duck sons of wealthy parents' (1985:374), and Leach dismissed my account of the consequences of minor marriages as based on 'hearsay evidence'. He cited as counter evidence a Burmese author's account of how her parents adopted impoverished female relatives who had 'the status of servants' and were 'eventually given a dowry and married off to some other servant'. 'Wolf,' he concludes, 'has apparently not realized that in the Taiwan context the *sim-pua* was a serf. No wonder such girls were not rated as the most desirable wives.' (1991:102).

What is really at issue here is evident in Bernard William's relatively careful critique of the Westermarck Hypothesis. Williams accepts that biological constraints 'can rule out, or make unrealistic, some practices and institutions,' but asks, 'Might biological considerations then go further and explain the human adoption of other practices, which are conformable to biological constraints?' This, he argues, is impossible because of what he terms 'the representation problem':

> The most ... that a genetically acquired character could yield would be an inhibition against behaviors of a certain kind: what relation could that have to a socially sanctioned prohibition? Indeed, if the inhibition exists what *need* could there be for such a prohibition? If the prohibitionary norm is to be part of the 'extended phenotype' of the species, how could we conceive, starting from an inhibition, that this should come about?
>
> (Williams 1983:560)

In a manuscript I hope to publish this spring I try to show how this could come about, but I cannot pursue that argument here. The important point for the moment is that in William's view no argument can get from an innate disposition to a norm. There is an impassable gulf between human nature and human institutions.

It is difficult to specify the source of the forces that reversed Tylor and Wallace's judgements favouring the Westermarck Hypothesis and that now deny the validity of evidence supporting the hypothesis. I think there are at least three. One is more or less openly acknowledged religious beliefs that deny that man is just another animal. Another is political values that see any argument for a substantial human nature as putting limits on our ability to improve ourselves. The third – rarely acknowledged but obvious to anyone who earns his living as I do – is the fear that a hypothesis that attributes a human institution to biology will give biologists a larger share of the budget. It is a formidable, but unstable, alliance that will eventually collapse. I am confident that, eventually, we will hear again the applause with which the Westermarck Hypothesis was greeted. The reason is simple – Westermarck was right!

Notes

1   Freud [1913]1950:123–4; White 1948:420; Levi-Strauss [1949] 1969):18; Aberle et al. 1963:258; Williams 1983:560; Lewontin et al. 1984:137; Godelier 1989:69; Johnson and Price-Williams 1996: 28.

2   A form of marriage found in many Arab communities typically uniting a man and one of his father's brother's daughters.

3   The work, tentatively entitled An Aspect of Human Nature: Incest Avoidance and the Incest Taboos, is under review by Stanford University Press.

References

Aberle, D.F., Bronfenbrenner, U., Hess, E.H., Miller, D.R., Schneider, D.M. and
    Spuhler, J.N. 1963. The incest taboo and mating patterns of animals.
    American Anthropologist 65:253–65.
Frazer, J.G. [1910] 1968. *Totemism and Exogamy* (vol. 4). London: Dassons.
Freud, S. [1913] 1950. *Totem and Taboo* (trans. J. Strachey). New York: W.W. Norton.
Freud, S. [1920] 1953. *A General Introduction to Psychoanalysis* (trans. J. Riviere).
    New York: Pocket Books.
Geertz, C. 1963 The impact of the concept of culture on the concept of man. In J.R.
    Platt (ed.) *New Views of Man.* Chicago: University of Chicago Press.
Godelier, M. 1989. Incest taboo and the evolution of society. In A. Grafen (ed.)
    Evolution and Its Influence. Oxford: Clarendon Press.
Johnson, A. and Price-Williams, D. 1996. *Oedipus Ubiquitous: The Family Complex
    in World Folk Literature.* Stanford, Calif.: Stanford University Press.
Kitcher, P. 1985. *Faulting Ambition.* Cambridge, Mass.: MIT Press.
Leach, E. 1991. The social anthropology of marriage and mating. In V. Reynolds and
    J. Kellet (eds) *Mating and Marriage.* Oxford: Oxford University Press.
Levi-Strauss, C. [1949] 1969. *The Elementary Structures of Kinship* (trans. J. Harle
    Bell, J.R. von Strumer and R. Needham). London: Eyre and Spottiswoode.
Levi-Strauss, C. 1960. The family. In H.L. Shapiro (ed.) *Man, Culture, and Society.*
    New York: Oxford University Press.
Lewontin, R., Ross, S. and Kamin, L.J. 1984. *Not in Our Genes.* New York: Pantheon
    Books.
MaCabe, J. 1983. FBD marriage: further support for the Westermarck hypothesis of
    the incest taboo. *American Anthropologist* 85:50–69.
Malinowski, B. 1922. Sexual life and marriage among primitive mankind [review of E.
    Westermarck, *The History of Human Marriage* (5th edn)]. *Nature* 2378.
Meillassoux, C. 1981. *Maidens, Meal, and Money: Capitalism and the Domestic
    Economy.* Cambridge: Cambridge University Press.
Murdock, G.P. 1949. *Social Structure.* New York: Macmillan.
Robertson Smith, W. 1891. Review of *The History of Human Marriage* by E.
    Westermarck. *Nature*, 23 July.
Shepher, J. 1971. Mate selection among second-generation kibbutz adolescents
    and adults: Incest avoidance and negative imprinting. *Archives of Sexual
    Behavior* 1:293–307.
Spiro, M.E. 1958. *Children of the Kibbutz.* Cambridge, Mass.: Harvard University
    Press.
Talmon, Y. 1964. Mate selection in collective settlements. *American Sociologial
    Review* 29:491–504.
Tylor, E.B. 1889. On a method of investigating the development of institutions;
    applied to laws of marriage and descent. *Journal of the Royal
    Anthropological Institute of Great Britain and Ireland* 18.
Walter, A. 1997. The evolutionary psychology of mate selection in Morocco. *Human
    Nature* 8:113–37.
Westermarck, E. 1914. *Marriage Ceremonies in Morocco.* London: Macmillan.
Westermarck, E. 1922. *The History of Human Marriage* (5th edn., vol. 2). New York:
    Allerton.
Whewell, W. 1967. *The Philosophy of the Inductive Sciences* (part 2). London: Frank
    Cass.
White, L.A. 1948. The definition and prohibition of incest. *American Anthropologist*
    50.

Wikman, K. Rob. V. 1940. Letter from Edward B. Tylor and Alfred Russell Wallace to Edward Westermarck. *Acta Academia Aboensis Humanoria* 13(8).

Williams, B. 1983. Evolution and ethics. In D.S. Bendall (ed.) *Evolution From Molecules to Men.* Cambridge: Cambridge University Press.

Wolf, A.P. 1995. *Sexual Attraction and Childhood Association: A Chinese Brief for Edward Westermarck.* Stanford, Calif.: Stanford University Press.

6

Westermarck might have been both right and wrong
A comment on Arthur P. Wolf's Chapter

JAN ANTFOLK

'Westermarck was right!' This is how Professor Wolf ended his chapter, highlighting anthropological findings that support Westermarck's hypothesis on the origin of the incest taboo. As pointed out by Professor Wolf, this hypothesis postulates that human incest avoidance is in its fundament a psychological predisposition activated by shared co-residence in childhood.

As scientists aware of evolutionary mechanisms and constraints and their bearing on human psychology steadily become more prominent within the social sciences, more and more research has been devoted to the understanding of psychological processes governing human incest avoidance. Yearly, a handful of empirical or theoretical papers on Westermarck and human incest avoidance are published in the scientific literature, and during international conferences on human behaviour and evolution it is not rare to find sessions devoted to this particular topic. While the question as to whether Westermarck was right or not could be regarded as open, it is certain that Westermarck, once again, is of great interest. This said, to the extent evolutionary psychology is debated and criticized, Westermarck's hypothesis also suffers blows. Much like a century ago, many of those opposing Westermarck simply do not understand his theoretical viewpoint. Freudian psychologists might fail to understand that alongside abnormality, normality also requires scientific scrutiny. Others might regard the Westermarck hypothesis as a biologism, and see in it no room for social interaction and learning – an odd claim as to most of us 'living together and shared co-residence' are exactly that: social interactions. As in science, uninformed debate should be regarded as a detrimental vice, and I think it is essential to dissect Westermarck's argument and thus allow for a more informed debate.

I argue that the Westermarck Hypothesis should not be regarded as one, uniform hypothesis. Rather it is a line of argumentation consisting of at least three different parts.

First, Westermarck argued that human incest avoidance was an adaptation due to the detrimental effects in offspring from incestuous unions. Westermarck clearly recognized already in 1889 that natural selection can be expected to have formed sexual inclinations so as to exclude close relatives. The genetic detriments of inbreeding are well known and later research has estimated inbred offspring to be notably less fit than outbred offspring. This should indeed result in a high selection pressure against incestuous inclinations.

Second, Westermarck argued that as we cannot have predisposed knowledge as to who our biological relatives are, we use environmental cues that have been stably associated with kinship over evolutionary time, such as childhood co-residence with another child providing fairly reliable information about this child being actual kin. This does not imply that this cue is never erroneous. It is enough that it is more often correct than incorrect, or rather that it leads to more avoided inbreedings than missed outbreedings. Childhood co-residence could then be regarded as the proximal mechanism activating an aversion between two individuals. This has been supported both by empirical anthropological, psychological and ethological evidence.

Finally, Westermarck argues that this psychological predisposition extends into social norms against incest. The exact mechanisms of how this comes about are somewhat obscure in Westermarck's writings, but a key element is sympathetic emotions. These sympathetic emotions allow us to feel what someone does as if we ourselves would do it. In more current scientific literature, this has been called egocentric empathy and it has gathered some support in quasi-experimental studies on aversive reactions to other people engaging in incest.

Itemizing the Westermarck Hypothesis allows at least two important things. First, it should inform the debaters about its true content and allow for more precise scientific and philosophical discussions. Secondly, it should be clear that even if one item in the argument is supported by evidence, another item is not necessarily supported; and the converse, if one item is falsified, the falsification does not necessarily extend into a falsification of another item. Hence, Westermarck may have been both right and wrong.

7

Looking backwards and forwards

Timothy Stroup

More than forty years ago, when I first started my research on Edward
Westermarck, I was mostly looking backwards. I looked backwards at
Westermarck, who himself looked backwards to the works of David Hume,
Adam Smith and Charles Darwin (Stroup 1976:73–82). I looked backwards
at Russian Finland and Victorian England, where Westermarck spent his
formative years (Westermarck 1927, 1929). I looked backwards at Westermarck's
pioneering field work in Morocco, his comparative method, his research in the
British Museum, his massive tomes on marriage and morality (Westermarck
1891, 1906, 1908, 1914, 1921, 1926, 1932). And particularly I looked backwards
at the intellectual climate in the first decades of the twentieth century, when
Westermarck was a leading figure in the social sciences and philosophy, engaging
in heated controversies with such diverse thinkers as Émile Durkheim, Sigmund
Freud and G. E. Moore (Durkheim 1907; Moore 1922; Westermarck 1934).

As a result of looking backwards, it became clear to me not only that
Westermarck had played an important historical role in several humanistic
disciplines, but also that his work had value in its own right. It also became
clear that, with such notable exceptions as Georg Henrik von Wright (1965),
J.L. Mackie (1967) and Arthur Wolf (1970), Westermarck's writings   no
longer were receiving the attention they deserved. Philosophy, sociology and
anthropology had moved in different directions from his. He was thought of,
if at all, as a noble fossil.

Fortunately, that climate has changed for the better in recent times.
Since the early 1980s, there has been a flurry of interest in Westermarck's
work that has testified both to its intrinsic merit and to its suggestiveness
for other research. Perhaps the anthropologists deserve the better part of

the credit. Their interest has been manifested in several different areas: the re-examination of Westermarck's fieldwork in Morocco (Brown 1982; Dwyer 1982); the testing of Westermarck's hypotheses in other cultures (McCabe 1983; Wolf 1995); the theoretical enquiry into Westermarck's analysis of incest (Fox 1983); and the assessment of Westermarck's place in the history of anthropology (Ihanus 1999; Stocking 1987, 1995).

But philosophers have made a contribution as well. Mackie, long a champion of Westermarck's ethical views, built an analysis of punishment around a Westermarckian notion of the retributive emotions (Mackie 1982). Abraham Edel (1982) sought to put Westermarck's ethics into the context of other twentieth-century relativisms, while Kai Nielsen (1982) defended Westermarck's subjectivism against eight distinct attacks. More recently, Larry Arnhart (1998) has profitably argued that Westermarck's focus on moral emotions resulting from a process of natural selection links him with Arnhart's own version of ethical naturalism, which is indebted to Darwin and Aristotle.

In the intervening years, my own view of Westermarck's moral philosophy has scarcely changed, and it has already been expressed elsewhere (1980, 1981, 1982b, 1982c, 1984, 1985a, 1985b, 2001, 2004). Thus I shall give only a brief account of my conclusions here.

For Westermarck, the central question of moral philosophy is of interest not just to moral philosophers, but to people from all walks of life: Do moral judgements have objective validity? Another way of asking this question is: Can the statements that express our moral beliefs be proved or conclusively established? Or, if we appeal by analogy to ordinary statements about the world, which are verified by their correspondence to empirical facts, we can ask the original question in still another way: Are there 'moral facts' that correspond or fail to correspond to the claims we make about what is right and wrong? By 'moral facts' I do not mean descriptive facts about the way people behave morally – of course there are those – but rather some sort of prescriptive facts existing independently of us that give truth value to moral utterances. For example, when people said 'apartheid is wrong', was there some real wrongness about apartheid that made that statement a true one? If so, then people who defended apartheid would not simply have been mouthing different opinions, they would have been making objectively false claims.

Many people profess to be relativists and shy away from proclaiming that there are real rights or wrongs. Morality, on this simple account, depends in a fundamental way on the moral practices of a particular society. We all recognize the psychological point that people's moral views are heavily influenced by their cultural upbringing, but this simple form of relativism usually goes beyond that insight to maintain that 'right' means nothing more than 'considered right in a society'.

If this account were correct, there would be no way of settling the apparent dispute that results when people in another society think 'right' something that we think 'wrong', because the two parties would not even be disagreeing: we would be making a claim about our society and they would be making a claim about theirs, and both claims could be true. Another awkward consequence of this relativist view would be that moral reformers, those who stand up against the settled views of their societies, would by definition always be wrong until such time as they were successful in changing the views of those societies.

Nonetheless, the simple relativist view is initially attractive, in part because it preaches tolerance and respect for other people. If there are no real rights and wrongs, then it would be arrogant for us to think that our ways of doing things are the best or to fail to appreciate the different ways that people in different cultures have developed to address their problems. Yet in my view, and this is an empirical observation, such apparent relativism operates mostly at the surface, and critics of its prevalence fail to note the shallowness with which it is held. People do, in fact, pay lip-service to relativism, but this initial outlook conflicts with their deeper beliefs about right and wrong: scratch a naive relativist and you get an ethical objectivist. Even a cursory glance at the deep-seated moral conflicts around the world confirms this discrepancy. People may sometimes talk about living and letting live, but when push comes to shove most people are prepared to defend their views with objectivist vehemence.

Similar musings about the diversity of moral beliefs, and the grounds on which such beliefs are held, sparked Westermarck's initial interest in philosophical ethics in 1889. Westermarck noted that, as a result of witnessing the intractability of his friends' differing opinions (specifically over the question of the extent to which bad people should be treated with kindness), he was 'aroused to a work on the origin and development of the moral ideas which was to occupy his thoughts for well-nigh twenty years' (1927:31, 1929:32–3). This curiosity took two forms. On the one hand, he pursued a detailed empirical analysis of human moral beliefs from his armchair in the British Museum. On the other hand, he wanted to know whether people, whatever they believe, are correct or incorrect in so believing. In the case of ethical beliefs, that enquiry is the one posed at the start of this chapter, about whether there are moral facts rather than just facts about morality.

Westermarck's two main books on ethics, *The Origin and Development of the Moral Ideas* and *Ethical Relativity*, illustrate both of these perspectives. His strategy in analysing the objectivity of morality was complex, and proceeded along two distinct lines. First, he assessed and found wanting the arguments that had been advanced by moral philosophers like Mill and Kant in support of an objectivist ethics. Mill propounded a utilitarian view of morality in which right actions are those that produce the greatest amount of happiness or pleasure, whereas Kant sought to ground morality in a categorical imperative that would generate impartial rules of duty.

The standard objections to these two main objectivist theories are well known to philosophers. For example, maximized overall pleasure does not seem justifiable to us if purchased at the expense of the undeserved suffering of a few people; and adherence to rules will become rule-fetishism if there is no restraining limit placed by the utilitarian calculation of consequences.

Westermarck's contribution to the debate, besides being the first to state some of the now classic objections, was to show in detail how these two objectivist views at the same time appeal to and violate our moral consciousness. Both objectivist views capture something fundamental to our moral thought – that morality must be related to human well-being and that it must be disinterested and impartial – but both take their insights too far.

What seems needed, therefore, is an overarching theory that can take a bit of one objective theory and combine it with a bit of another. But such a theory would, for Westermarck, be essentially subjective. It would, in effect, be prescribing a moral cocktail, and like any cocktail its composition would be a matter of taste: there are no objectively precise quantities of ingredients that give the 'only true' blend.

Having demonstrated the difficulties that face objectivist theories, Westermarck turned to the second half of his strategy. He examined the facts of moral behaviour – a task subsidiary to the main philosophical enterprise of determining the validity of that behaviour – in order to see what range of data a moral theory must explain and whether these facts about behaviour themselves suggest a theory.

Based on his vast compendium of moral practices and beliefs, Westermarck was able to conclude that morality is essentially based on feelings, or in more sophisticated terms on 'retributive emotions'. The theory he developed is a form of subjectivism I have called 'soft subjectivism' (by analogy to a philosophical view known as 'soft determinism', and because it seeks to avoid the extremes of either nihilism or objectivism) (1982b). Even the objectivist critic Brand Blanshard grudgingly conceded that Westermarck has propounded 'a theory that, without any need for objective moral truths, covers the facts completely' (Blanshard 1961:120).

Westermarck studied moral behaviour in its widest context, examining such phenomena as altruism, revenge, respect for others, and jealousy, as well as such social institutions as marriage, property and slavery. In recent times, however, moral philosophers have focused their attention on one category of human behaviour above all others – moral discourse. They have sought to analyse moral language, starting with such building blocks as 'right', 'wrong', 'good', 'bad' and 'duty', and then examining sentences about what kinds of actions are right, what kinds of duties we have, and so forth.

Subjectivist moral philosophers have also participated in this enquiry, but while all subjectivist theories are similar in viewing feelings rather than reason as central to morality, they differ in how they treat moral judgements. On some theories, moral judgements are reports of feelings: for me to say 'lying is wrong' is the same thing as saying 'I don't like lying'. On others, moral judgements are expressions of feeling, something like the sighs or groans we might utter when confronted by beautiful or ugly works of art.

This emphasis on moral language has caused serious distortions in the perception of Westermarck's ethics by his critics. Moore was the first offender, but I have elsewhere cited a dozen misinterpretations by notable philosophers who based their views of Westermarck on simplistic treatments of his account of moral judgements (Stroup 1982c:199–200). If, as I have claimed, most people are objectivists deep down, then the standard subjectivist accounts do not do justice to ordinary moral utterances, and attempts to depict Westermarck as having committed this obvious mistake do not do justice to him. Westermarck himself strongly protested against this distortion of his view. In the margin of his copy of Moore's *Ethics*, where Moore tries to reduce ordinary moral discourse to a simple subjectivism, Westermarck penned an emphatic 'not the ordinary or common view!' To most people, and to Westermarck as well, the statement 'X is wrong' is a statement about X, not merely about themselves and their feelings.

A soft subjectivism like Westermarck's can, however, account for this phenomenon of ordinary language by pointing to a tendency that Hume first noticed. To use Hume's elegant words, taste (which on the subjectivist view includes moral 'taste') 'has a productive faculty, and gilding or staining all natural objects with the colours, borrowed from internal sentiment, raises in a manner a new creation' (Hume 1962[1748]:294[App.I.v.]). That is, we tend to project our feelings onto things, to objectify those feelings as properties of the objects rather than as mere states of our minds.

Moral judgements, then, function as objective claims about what is right and wrong, but for the soft subjectivist these claims must all fail, because there are no objective values or 'moral facts' to which the claims correspond. What results on this form of scepticism is an error theory of moral discourse, in which ordinary moral language is objectivist in intent but unsuccessful in execution. Westermarck maintains that 'the subjective experience has been objectivized in the speech as a quality attributed to the object'. He also says that 'if the definition of a moral proposition implies the claim to objectivity, a judgement that does not express this quality cannot be a moral judgement; but this by no means proves that moral propositions so defined are true – the predicated objectivity may be a sheer illusion.' (1932:143–4, 47). While Westermarck thus propounded a form of error theory, its most sophisticated modern expositor was Mackie (1977) in his book *Ethics: Inventing Right and Wrong.*

The moral I wish to draw was succinctly stated more sixty years ago by von Wright: 'When one criticizes Westermarck's theory of the moral judgement, one should remember that Westermarck nowhere explicitly says that a sentence about moral value means the same as a sentence about a moral valuation.' (1954:54). With this anti-reductionist principle in mind – that our moral judgements cannot simply be equated with descriptions or expressions of our moral feelings – it is possible to appreciate the complexity and fecundity of Westermarck's actual analysis of morality.

Whether or not an error theory adequately accounts for moral discourse is a subject beyond the scope of this brief chapter. Instead, I want to turn to a more normative concern that any subjectivist theory must face, a problem hinted at in the very title of Mackie's book. By abandoning objectivism, subjectivists forgo any solace that moral values are real, independent, waiting to be discovered; by contrast, morality must be invented. But then the worry arises that morality, deprived of its objective anchor, with no real rights or wrongs to guide it, will be dangerously arbitrary and nihilistic.

To respond to this concern, it is useful to distinguish between fundamental and derived moral principles. Much of ordinary moral disagreement takes place at the level of derived moral principles and revolves around differences about empirical facts, careless assumptions, unclarity in stating and developing positions, and false applications of higher-level principles. Subjectivism is no impediment to settling disputes of this sort.

What is less often noted is that objectivism is of little help in settling disputes about fundamental moral principles. As Westermarck observed, 'Each founder of a new theory hopes that it is he who had discovered the unique jewel of moral truth, and is naturally anxious to show that other theories are only false stones.' (1932:4). Unfortunately, the possessors of the false stones will not recognize the unique jewel, and so the disputes rage on. We see in the world around us a clash of competing objectivisms – personal, social, national, religious, philosophical – with little prospect of rational resolution. The belief that morality is objective, if correct, still leaves us with the daunting task of discovering which candidate theory is the true one.

But what about the charge that morality is arbitrary or nihilistic if subjectivism is true? Consider, by analogy, the more obviously subjective kinds of taste, such as food preferences. Even when I am shown that my predilection for vanilla ice cream rather than (say) cayenne ice cream is purely subjective, I would not characterize that taste as 'arbitrary', nor would I be indifferent about which of the two flavours I am served for dessert; my taste is part of my psychological makeup and no doubt there are explanations of it that draw on facts about my personal biography as well as broader facts about how people behave.

The case with morality is even stronger. If subjectivism is true, morality, far from being a matter of unconcern, belongs to the deepest and probably most intractable part of our mental constitution: 'We approve and disapprove because we cannot do otherwise; our moral consciousness belongs to our mental constitution, which we cannot change as we please.' (1932:58–9; 1906:19). Or, as Bertrand Russell put it in another context (1928), there are Catholic and Protestant atheists: our basic world outlooks survive shifts in ontological commitments, whether those commitments be theological or moral. Yet these basic facts of moral consciousness can be explained, and that is one of the tasks of the social sciences.

Soft subjectivists also reject the fear that their theoretical analysis would harm the moral fabric of an individual or a society. Most likely, the consequences of adopting subjectivism would be minimal, because the theory itself assigns the predominant role in ethics to emotions, which, as just noted, are difficult to change. Reason, and in particular philosophical reasoning, would have a limited scope for influence.

But insofar as the acceptance of soft subjectivism did affect behaviour, Westermarck thought that the effect would be salutary. On the one hand, it would encourage us to replace the doctrinal dogmatism of objectivism with a more critical attitude towards our own views and those of others. On the other hand, it would counter the tendency of crude relativism to define right and wrong in terms of what a given society thinks is right and wrong, which makes the individual a moral hostage to his or her society.

Moral values would thus be neither discovered in the world outside us nor received from others, but rather created – created by acts of individual choice. In Westermarck's words: 'Far above the vulgar idea that the right is a settled something to which everybody has to adjust his opinions, rises the conviction that it has its existence in each individual mind, capable of any expansion, proclaiming its own right to exist, and, if need be, venturing to make a stand against the whole world.' (1906:20).

I have been able in this short chapter to do no more than sketch what I take to be the impetus behind Westermarck's conception of morality and to show that it survives the common objections to it and is far richer and more valuable than its critics suggest. It not only contains the elements of a sophisticated meta-ethics coupled with a meticulous and fully elaborated descriptive ethics, but it also avoids nihilism while being normatively exhilarating in its own right.

It thus is time to stop looking backwards and to apply the lessons of Westermarck's magnificent legacy to the multidisciplinary and interdisciplinary concerns that formed the core of his intellectual life. And the best way of looking forwards, as well as the best testimony to the continuing vigour and relevance of Westermarck's accomplishments, is this book itself. Bringing together scholars from a wide variety of disciplines and with a diverse range of research interests, it reveals again the truth behind Ronald Fletcher's challenge: 'Where is the study of the elements of men's moral consciousness which is more wide-ranging, contains a clearer theoretical basis, and brings together more empirical evidence, and more satisfactorily than this? Let the question be answered.' (1982:209–10).

References

Arnhart, L. 1998. *Darwinian Natural Right: The Biological Ethics of Human Nature.* Albany: State University of New York Press.

Blanshard, B. 1961. *Reason and Goodness.* London: George Allen & Unwin.

Brown, K. 1982. The 'curse' of Westermarck. In Stroup (ed.) 1982a:219–59.

Durkheim, É. 1907. Review of *The Origin and Development of the Moral Ideas* (vol. 1). *L'Année sociologique* 10:383–95.

Dwyer, D. 1982. Litigants' law and judicial tensions in Morocco: Westermarck's ethnography of law in a contemporary context. In Stroup (ed.) 1982a:260–73.

Edel, A. 1982. Westermarck's formulation of ethical relativity, in twentieth century perspective. In Stroup (ed.) 1982a:71–98.

Fletcher, R. 1982. On the contribution of Edward Westermarck: the process of institutionalization: a general theory. In Stroup (ed.) 1982a:195–217.

Fox, R. 1983. *The Red Lamp of Incest* (2nd edn.) Notre Dame: University of Notre Dame Press.

Hume, D. 1962 [1748]. An enquiry concerning the principles of morals. In *Enquiries Concerning the Human Understanding and Concerning the Principles of Morals* (2nd edn., ed. L.A. Selby-Bigge). Oxford: Clarendon Press.

Ihanus, J. 1999. *Multiple Origins: Edward Westermarck in Search of Mankind* (European Studies in the History of Science and Ideas 6). Frankfurt am Main: Peter Lang.

Mackie, J.L. 1967. Westermarck, Edward Alexander. In P. Edwards (ed.), *The Encyclopedia of Philosophy*, vol. 8, pp. 284–6. New York: The Macmillan Company and the Free Press.

Mackie, J.L. 1977. *Ethics: Inventing Right and Wrong.* Harmondsworth: Penguin Books.

Mackie, J.L. 1982. Morality and the Retributive Emotions. In Stroup (ed.) 1982a:144–57.

McCabe, J. 1983. FBD marriage: further support for the Westermarck hypothesis of the incest taboo. *American Anthropologist* 85:50–69.

Moore, G.E. 1922. The nature of moral philosophy. In *Philosophical Studies*, pp. 310–39. London: Kegan Paul, Trench, Trubner & Co.

Nielsen, K. 1982. Problems for Westermarck's subjectivism. In Stroup (ed.)
     1982a:122–43.
Russell, B. 1928. On Catholic and Protestant skeptics. In *Why I Am Not a Christian*
     [1957], pp. 117–26. London: George Allen & Unwin.
Stocking, Jr., G.W. 1987. *Victorian Anthropology*. New York: Free Press.
Stocking, Jr., G.W. 1995. *British Social Anthropology, 1888–1951*. Madison:
     University of Wisconsin Press.
Stroup, T. 1976. Westermarck's debt to Hume. In *Wright and Wrong: Mini Essays
     in Honor of Georg Henrik von Wright*, pp. 73–82. Åbo: Åbo Akademi
     Forskningsinstitut.
Stroup, T. 1980. Westermarck's ethical relativism. *Ajatus* 38:31–71.
Stroup, T. 1981. In defense of Westermarck. *Journal of the History of Philosophy*
     19(2): 213–34.
Stroup, T. (ed.) 1982a. *Edward Westermarck: Essays on his Life and Works*. Helsinki:
     Acta Philosophica Fennica 34.
Stroup, T. 1982b. Soft subjectivism. In Stroup (ed.) 1982a:99–121.
Stroup, T. 1982c. *Westermarck's Ethics*. Åbo: Publications of the Research Institute of
     the Åbo Akademi Foundation.
Stroup, T. 1984. Edward Westermarck: a reappraisal. *Man* 19(4):575–92.
Stroup, T. 1985a. Westermarck's ethical methodology. In E. Bulygin, J.-L. Gardies
     and I. Niiniluoto (eds), *Man, Law and Modern Forms of Life*, pp. 85–95.
     Dordrecht: D. Reidel Publishing Company.
Stroup, T. 1985b. Reply to Professor Airaksinen. In E. Bulygin, J.-L. Gardies and
     I. Niiniluoto (eds), *Man, Law and Modern Forms of Life*, pp. 103–5.
     Dordrecht: D. Reidel Publishing Company.
Stroup, T. 2001. Westermarck, Edward [Alexander]. In L.C. and C.B. Becker (eds),
     Encyclopedia of Ethics (3 vols), pp. 1798–9. New York: Garland Publishing.
Stroup, T. 2004. Westermarck, Edvard Alexander [Edward] (1862–1939). In *Oxford
     Dictionary of National Biography*. Oxford: Oxford University Press [http://
     www.oxforddnb.com/view/article/75491].
von Wright, G.H. 1954. Om moraliska föreställningars sanning. In *Vetenskapens
     funktion i samhället*. Copenhagen: Munksgaard.
von Wright, G.H. 1965. Edvard Westermarck och Filosofiska föreningen. *Ajatus*
     27:123–61 [trans. A. Landon as The origin and development of
     Westermarck's moral philosophy. In Stroup (ed.) 1982a:25–61.].
Westermarck, E. 1891. *The History of Human Marriage*. London: Macmillan and Co.
Westermarck, E. 1906, 1908. *The Origin and Development of the Moral Ideas* (2
     vols). London: Macmillan and Co.
Westermarck, E. 1914. *Marriage Ceremonies in Morocco*. London: Macmillan and
     Co.
Westermarck, E. 1921. *The History of Human Marriage* (5th edn., 3 vols). London:
     Macmillan and Co.
Westermarck, E. 1926. *Ritual and Belief in Morocco* (2 vols). London: Macmillan and
     Co.
Westermarck, E. 1927. *Minnen ur mitt liv*. Helsinki: Holger Schildts Förlag.
Westermarck, E. 1929. *Memories of My Life* (trans. A. Barwell). London: George
     Allen & Unwin.
Westermarck, E. 1932. *Ethical Relativity*. London: Kegan Paul, Trench, Trubner &
     Co.
Westermarck, E. 1934. *Three Essays on Sex and Marriage*. London: Macmillan and
     Co.

Wolf, A.P. 1970. Childhood association and sexual attraction: a further test of the Westermarck hypothesis. *American Anthropologist* 72:503–15.

Wolf, A.P. 1995. *Sexual Attraction and Childhood Association: A Chinese Brief for Edward Westermarck*. Stanford: Stanford University Press.

8

Westermarck's theory of
morality in his and our time

A perspective from the LSE
anthropology department

Maurice Bloch

Edward Westermarck is, with Seligman, one of the two founders of the anthropology department of the London School of Economics, and in this way one of the creators of the LSE as it has become. However, I am ashamed to say, that his and Seligman's contribution are now largely ignored. Ironically, this is in part because of their success and generosity in promoting their successor at the school, Bronislaw Malinowski, whose reputation has blinded us to their contribution. Malinowski can be considered as the founder of what has become modern British and European social and cultural anthropology. Westermarck, once said by Malinowski to be his best friend, promoted Malinowski's early career in many ways and wrote the preface to his first major work on the Australian Aborigines, but is much less well remembered in anthropology than his protégé. The anthropology department of the London School of Economics should be grateful for the role Westermarck played in helping his successor, but also should pay more attention to his scientific contribution.

Westermarck oscillated in his teaching career between the University of Helsinki (and then Åbo Akademi in Turku) and the London School of Economics. This bi-locality is actually uncannily coherent with an unresolved duality that seems to be strongly associated with so many aspects of his life and even his work. It still reappears to this day. I have been to Finland twice, both times for reasons connected with Westermarck. The first time was to give the Westermarck memorial lecture. This lecture is organized by Finnish social and cultural anthropologists, especially those from the department in Helsinki. The second time, a few years later, I was invited by the Westermarck Society, a more biologically and evolutionarily oriented group of scholars. I naively thought that on that second occasion I would be able to meet again my old acquaintances from the first trip, but this was not to be. There was clear distance, not to say hostility, between the two groups. I was nonetheless contacted by Jukka Siikala, my friend from the first occasion. He visited me for a drink on the island where the second meeting was held almost surreptitiously. Westermarck seems to be a very different type of ancestor to the two groups of his Finnish successors.

Such duality in his inheritance is the product of his complex theoretical position, which is particularly evident in his work on morality and which was central to his concerns. Here I concentrate exclusively on the two volumes of the book *The Origin and the Development of the Moral Ideas* published in 1905 and 1908.

Traditionally, the philosophers who have written on morality are divided into two camps, and Westermarck was well acquainted with the ideas of both. On the one hand, there are the realists who believe that moral rules exist in the world irrespective of human opinion. They may think that morality is just an essential characteristic of the species or they may believe that morality originates from a transcendental source like God. In either case, the realists are universalists. On the other hand, there are relativists who believe that morality is basically a matter of individual opinion or is the product of a particular culture or an epiphenomenon of the type of society in which people live. Theologians and politicians, in their public pronouncements at least, tend to be realists, and they like to talk of such things as universal human rights. Social scientists, especially anthropologists, tend to be relativists, because they are well aware of what is the apparently great variation that exists, and has existed, in what people consider to be right or wrong. However, like other relativists, they are ultimately ill at ease with such a position, as they, like everybody else, find unacceptable the apparent implication of such a stance that would imply that the wrongness of murdering little girls on their way home from school is merely a matter of opinion or culture. As a result of this dilemma, anthropologists attempt a number of compromises to anchor morality in non-arbitrary factors that, nonetheless, do not dismiss the differences in cultural rules as simply a matter of other people's immorality. This is also what Westermarck attempts. *The Origin and the Development of the Moral Ideas* is, therefore, in part, a typically nineteenth-century catalogue of what different people think is right or wrong, but it is also a more general explanation of the character of human morality.

Westermarck faces the problem posed by the fact of variation and the need for a general theory frontally. His first solution for dealing with the problem was a fairly standard one among the anthropologists who preceded him. They, for the most part, and he enthusiastically, were committed Darwinian evolutionists. However, they believed, quite wrongly, that such an evolutionist stance implies that mankind must necessarily pass through specific stages through which it 'raises' from lower states to higher ones. This conclusion is of course not Darwinian, even though Darwin himself was sometimes tempted to talk in these terms, since the theory of evolution is not about progress but about differentiation. Nevertheless, this was what Westermarck, like most anthropologists of his time, thought. Furthermore, they also believed that the contemporary peoples of the world represented different stages in the single and unified history of mankind. Human variation was explained by them as a kind of synchronic genealogy. Variation was thus not the roof of diversity, but merely an illustration of different degrees of advancement. When applied to morality, as it was by the hyper-liberal Hobhouse (1906), Westermarck's colleague at LSE, and by Ginsberg (1921), Hobhouse's pupil and successor, it produced a form of realism, since, for them, there was only one human history and therefore only one basic morality. Apparent differences were merely of the same order as the differences between children and adults, and therefore were not absolute.

Westermarck does adopt such a theory, but he also adopts another quite different theory which is much more interesting as it meshes so well with recent developments in anthropology, particularly in LSE anthropology.

In the book on morality Westermarck is strongly influenced by the great American psychologist William James, the brother of the novelist Henry James, who was, like Westermarck, an enthusiastic Darwinian. In particular, he follows James's theory about emotions, which became known as the James/Lange theory (1890). This stressed the automatic and non-reflexive nature of emotions. The key to his theory is that the inexplicit psycho/physiological experience of the emotion was the real thing; how it was to be labelled or explained or talked about by those who experienced the emotions was a subsequent and quite different phenomenon. James gives the example of meeting a bear in a forest. Our reaction involves physiological changes in our body and we run away. It is only afterwards that we can name our emotion as fear and reflect about whether it was legitimate or sensible to run away. We do not run away because we are afraid, we are afraid because we ran away. The emotion itself is not a matter of reflection, it is due to mental processes that we do not and cannot put into words.

Westermarck applies this theory to morality, which he identifies with our emotional reactions when we encounter some bad or good behaviour in ourselves or in others. What he is seeking is a characterization of that unique and fundamental aspect of our species, morality. In seeking a psychological, social and cultural characterization of the character of morality, he is shifting the discussion of origin away from evolutionary history, as it would have been undertaken by most of his contemporaries, to synchrony, an approach that was to characterize Malinowski's work.

Westermarck deals with two topics that have become central for bringing modern psychologists and anthropologists of morality into conversation. The first concerns the alleged psychological and cultural contrast between moral rules, such as not harming others for no reason, and conventions, such as not wearing bedroom slippers when one is giving a lecture. Whether this distinction is universal has been a subject of great controversy, and has led to much empirical research. Thus the realist psychologist E. Turiel (1983) argues for a sharp contrast between, on the one hand, moral rules, which, according to him, people believe are universal and unchangeable and, on the other, conventions which people believe could be changed. Against such a view, the anthropologist R. Shweder (Shweder *et al.* 1987) has sought to demonstrate that the distinction is inapplicable to a place like India . More recently R. Astuti, at the LSE, has redefined the debate in a way that can handle both sides (2007). She shows how people like the Vezo of Madagascar can consider taboos to be, in Turiel's terms, simultaneously conventional, in that they are the result of an arbitrary injunction by ancestors, and moral, in that ordinary Vezo believe that all human beings have an obligation and do obey unquestioningly their ancestors.

The second aspect of Westermarck's discussion that is uncannily modern concerns the relation of emotions and morality. Jonathan Haidt, following in the footsteps of Hume, James, Durkheim and Westermarck, argues strongly for the primacy of emotions, adding a good deal of experimental evidence in support. For all these writers the basis of morality is not reason, as Kant argued, but emotions. This means that people, ultimately, cannot produce satisfactory explanations for why morality is as it is, or if they do, this it is a matter of *post hoc* reflection or rationalization. An amusing experiment by the psychologist Haidt makes the point (2001). The experimenter tells a number of people a story about a brother and a sister, which I give here in simplified form. The sibling pair decide that because they are so fond of each other they will have sex. They promise each other to do it only once, not to tell anybody, and to take foolproof contraceptive protection. Afterwards they are very happy to have done it, and they carry on as blissfully as ever as brother and sister. Having told the story, the experimenter then asks his subjects whether they felt this had been a good thing to do. Most say no, it was bad and many express their horror with great emotion. Then the experimenter asks them why it was so bad, and the subjects then rush in with a whole lot of different explanations which have, in fact, been ruled out by the story. They say such things as: it was bad because the children of the couple would be deformed, but then it is pointed out that they have forgotten about the contraception; they say the pair would be traumatized for life, but that was to forget that the story tells that they were perfectly happy ever after; the subjects say their action would upset their parents or their elderly aunts, but this was to forget that they tell nobody... and so on. Confronted by these contradictions, the subjects then fall back, usually very annoyed, and often re-emphasizing their initial horror, that what had been done was wrong because it was wrong and would the experimenter please shut-up. In other words, the answers they declare to have been the cause of their horror could not have been. As Westermarck and James, and Hume for that matter, had argued, the emotion had come first, the explicit explanations were post hoc, not causal and beside the point. However, Westermarck goes on further than James and Haidt. Unlike them, he is an anthropologist, also interested in the variety of stories and rules which people express explicitly for morality. These too have to be studied, but distinguished from the foundational phenomena of morality itself. Once the distinction is clear, the relationship between the two can also become a central subject of the discipline.

The anchoring of anthropology in a naturalist understanding of the human species accompanied by a recognition of the variation caused by history forms the basis of Westermarck's reconciliation of his unversalist realist position with his recognition, even his emphasis, on the variability of moral rules and practices. He does this through a much deeper understanding of psychological issues than was common among anthropologists of his time, and this would still be true now. For him, the expressed rules are inevitably secondary phenomena; they are a kind of commentary by individuals and particular societies on their moral emotions and dilemmas. The examination of the relation of the implicit sub-linguistic foundations of action in the world and the explicit has, since Westermarck, been a particularly LSE theme, and was probably directly influenced by him. It is characteristic of the work of Malinowski and his pupils, Edmund Leach, and Malinowski's successor at LSE, Raymond Firth. More recently, Professor Astuti has again shown in a Westermarckian fashion how different are what people say about kinship and the concepts which organize their inferences and actions (2009).

There is, however, a further element to Westermarck's theory of morality which also links up with very recent developments in anthropology and other disciplines in the natural sciences. For Westermarck, morality is not simply an individual matter. Whether we are, or should be, theoretical realists or relativists is a philosophical question, but there is no doubt that, in our everyday lives, we act and think as though we were realists – we believe that we and others should act morally. As Durkheim and Kant stressed, moral obligation is experienced as being beyond question, as though coming from beyond or from above any particular member of the group. It is felt to apply to everyone and to be made by no one. How could that be explained by a Darwinian non-believer like Westermarck? More particularly, how can we explain the subjective centrality of morality for human action and, especially, the fact that we sometimes act against our own individual interest because of moral imperatives, and that we judge our own actions and the actions of others in terms of universal standards that can seem odd in the light of a certain interpretations of Darwinian theory. These would see natural selection as having bred in each one of us a form of categorical egoism often phrased as 'the survival of the fittest.' In this way, if that was all there was to Darwinian theory, the very existence of morality would be an argument against it. This could be a problem for a committed Darwinian such as Westermarck, and it is indeed a problem of which he, like many contemporary social scientists, who want to use Darwinism in their work, are well aware of. How could natural selection breed a moral attitude that goes beyond the interest of the immediate family? Westermarck's answer is surprisingly like that of many recent theorists. His answer to the problem is to be found the social nature of our species. I quote him 'The solution of this problem lies in the fact that society is the birth place of the moral consciousness; that the first moral judgements express not the private emotions of isolated individuals but emotions which are felt by the society at large.' (1906:117). He notes the degree of egoism that is indeed characteristic of our closest non-human relatives, the chimpanzees, and he explains the change that must have come about in humans' evolution away from our common ancestors as being innate characteristics of man: sympathy and empathy. These, according to him, were bred into humans so as to make the complex social within which we live possible. The modern theorists he reminds us of, such as the evolutionary anthropologist Michael Tomasello, have also stressed this innate cooperative character of our species, and have demonstrated its presence in surprisingly young infants (2009). Some evolutionists now talk of group selection, or of the importance, and moral reputation resultant, of being chosen as a trustworthy partner in shared enterprises. These would create the evolutionary fact of the creation of the subjective impartiality and the apparent externality of morality as a categorical rule (Baumard and Sperber 2012) . Westermarck's explanations are quite compatible with such recent theories, even though he naturally did not have the kind of knowledge about genetics and human evolution now at our disposal. In any case, it would be anachronistic to over- paraphrase him in such modern terms, though the convergence is nonetheless striking.

It is interesting how those aspects of his writing that I have chosen to stress seem modern; but it is not so much for these specific reasons that we should regret that his work has been so much forgotten by anthropologists. The reason is much more fundamental.

Westermarck may have been ahead of his time in certain respects, but in others he was behind. This is especially so in his adoption of the kind of unilineal anthropological theories that characterized the anthropologists of the end of the nineteenth century. Their work, and many aspects of Westermarck's ideas, were subsequently rejected because of the major errors contained in such theories, especially the illusion that mankind was moving in a single and predictable direction, as well as the idea that different peoples and cultures could be classed in terms of relative advancement or backwardness. But the rejection of these specific theories of evolution, and the ways in which they were demonstrated, led to a much more fundamental shift in the intellectual basis of anthropology than such corrections justified. It created in subsequent social and cultural anthropology a horror of any talk of evolution in general, which led to a total removal of anthropology from the kind of naturalist grounding that Westermarck understood as the very *raison d'etre* of the subject. As anthropologists fled in horror away from evolutionary discourse they lost interest in the natural phenomena that we are: our minds, our bodies, and our environment. Instead of seeking to connect with those such as William James or Darwin, or with the advances of psychology, physiology or biology, as Westermarck had done, they became uninterested and unable to communicate with such scientists. Philosophically, they knew what they were running away from, but they often were quite uncertain as to what kind of status they wanted to give their discipline. This, by and large, is what happened in Westermarck's old department in the LSE, and this is why he became forgotten. Admittedly, some scholars, usually outside social and cultural anthropology departments, continued the kind of work that Westermarck had done but, in a sense, they followed much too closely, as they were not benefiting from the help they might have gained from the by now absent anthropologists. These developments have been most harmful for both sides. It led to the strange situation I referred at the beginning of this chapter, where the two groups claiming themselves to be the heirs of Westermarck in Finland are unable to even speak to each other. A similar situation would occur in almost any other country. Westermarck, by contrast, in a book such as that on the origin of morality, as well as elsewhere, sees the value of anthropology in the attempt to anchor, in a non-reductionist way, the social, historical and cultural in a general evolutionist naturalist philosophy concerning human beings. He would refuse the feud that divides his heirs, and so, I believe, should we. If his general theoretical impetus had continued more strongly we would probably not be wasting our time with so much that is baroque and divisive in modern anthropology. But perhaps this an exaggerated picture that I draw, and the contemporary ghost of Westermarck returning to the battlements of Houghton Street should not be now as depressed as his Danish homolog. As he comes to haunt the LSE and other anthropology departments, I think he will be cheered by the fact that his stance is actually reviving in a variety of ways, and that the general epistemological position he advocated is regaining vigour and promises new fruits of a Westmarckian kind.

References

Astuti R. 2007. La moralité des conventions: tabous ancestraux à Madagascar. *Terrain* 48:101–12.

Astuti, R. 2009. Revealing and obscuring Rivers's natural pedigrees: biological inheritance and kinship in Madagascar. In J. Leach and S. Bamford (eds) *Kinship and Beyond: The Genealogical Model Reconsidered,* pp. 214–36. Oxford: Berghahn Books.

Baumard, N. and Sperber, D. 2012 Evolutionary and cognitive anthropology. In D. Fassin, *A Companion to Moral Anthropology,* pp. 611–27. Chichester: John Wiley & Sons.

Ginsberg, M. 1921. *The Psychology of Society.* London: Methuen & Co.

Haidt, J. 2001. The emotional dog and its rational tail: a social intuitionist approach to moral judgment. *Psychological Review* 108:814–34.

Hobhouse, L.T. 1906. *Morals in Evolution: A Study in Comparative Ethics* (2 vols). London: Chapman & Hall.

James, W. *1890. The Principles of Psychology* (2 vols). New York: Henry Holt and Co.

Shweder R.A., Mahapatra, M. and Miller, J.G. 1987. Culture and moral development. In J. Kagan and S. Lamb (eds), *The Emergence of Morality in Young Children,* pp. 1–90. Chicago, University of Chicago Press.

Turiel, E. 1983. *The Development of Social Knowledge: Morality and Convention.* Cambridge: Cambridge University Press.

Tomasello, M. 2009. *Why We Cooperate.* Cambridge, MA: MIT Press.

Westermarck, E. 1906, 1908. *The Origin and Development of the Moral Ideas* (2 vols). London: Macmillan and Co.

9

The relativity of Westermarck's moral relativism[1]

Camilla Kronqvist

The issue of moral relativism usually divides philosophers and anthropologists, at least in the Anglophone world, into two camps. Among anthropologists some form of cultural relativism, is widely accepted. It is even actively endorsed as a precept for anthropology, as it seems necessary to embrace what is called methodological relativism to avoid ethnocentrism and the colonizing tendencies that were part of early anthropology.[2] Morality is typically perceived as belonging to the aspects of culture that has to be understood in these terms. It is taken to be expressive of norms that are culturally formed, or that have to be accounted for within a cultural context. Among philosophers, at least of the analytical kind, on the other hand, moral relativism mainly surfaces as a very undesirable outcome of a discussion. Any moral account that ends in moral relativism, as it were, proves itself a failure in truly accounting for morality. It is, however, well worth noticing that the philosophers that anthropologists lean upon if formulating a theoretical basis for their methodological stance, when they do, are usually structuralist, post-structuralist and post-colonial thinkers belonging to the branches of philosophy that analytic philosophers call, somewhat pejoratively, continental philosophy.

In this respect alone, as a representative of both philosophy and anthropology, Westermarck's endorsement of moral relativism, or ethical relativity as one of his major works on the subject is titled,[3] is worthy of discussion. But his analysis of morality and ethics merits discussion in its own right as an ethical theory, as it presents a quite complex picture of the relationships between moral judgements, moral emotions and moral norms and of how they are culturally mediated. The simple picture of Westermarck's relativism is that he, by grounding moral judgements in emotions, is committing the *naturalistic fallacy*, so called by British philosopher G.E. Moore (Moore 1903). According to that view, Westermarck equates the judgement 'it is good' with the statement 'it feels good' or even 'I feel good', or more closely in line, but yet not completely, with what Westermarck is really saying, 'it has a tendency to make me feel good or bad'. In this, the criticism goes, he fails to show how 'good' is a predicate, and describes a property in an object, just as yellow describes a property of an object, and not just a property of a subject. He also fails to account for the possibility of disagreement in moral matters. According to this criticism, which I model closely on Moore's (1922) critique of Westermarck, based on *The Origin and Development of the Moral Ideas*, there cannot be disagreement, but simply divergence, between the feelings of two people. In other words, the mere bringing in of emotions and subjectivity into the moral debate, in this view, is enough to lead Westermarck's argument into a *reductio ad absurdum*. Taking this stance on his philosophy, however, fails to see that the relationships between moral judgements and moral emotions that Westermarck seeks to establish clearly differs from the form of emotivism that later philosophers such as A.J. Ayer and C.L. Stevenson presented.[4] These meta-ethicists took it upon themselves to explain the meaning and justification of moral language and regarded moral judgements as expressions of emotion. Furthermore, it does not give due attention to the role of a culture, society and religion in fostering moral norms, which to Westermarck is essential for understanding the notion of diverging moral views.

This recourse to culture, however, should not tempt us to think of Westermarck as an anthropologist or sociologist who only thinks of morality as socially constructed. There is an interesting question about just how Westermarck thinks of the process from moral emotions to moral norms, as well as of the relation of moral judgements to both moral norms and moral emotions, and how well he succeeds in describing this progress and their interrelations. In part, this discussion of his moral philosophy will also attempt to answer these questions. It is, however, worthy of noticing that the primordial place accorded to the emotions by Westermarck is expressive of an attempt to ground morality in our *nature* as living beings. In fact the aim of introducing examples of differences in moral views between different cultures, and sometimes also in comparison to animals, in Westermarck's works, is many times to present evidence for the prevalence of the retributive emotions that to him lie at the centre of moral life. Thus, one cannot consider the moral, or ethical,[5] relativism of Westermarck without in some way discussing how he views the old anthropological debate between aspects of human nature that are universal and aspects of human life that are culturally dependent.

The task of the following discussion is to bring these issues more clearly into view, and to present the philosophical and anthropological, or rather empirical, motivations driving Westermarck's account. Since I write this as a philosopher, the focus will in many cases be on the philosophical considerations underlying Westermarck's account and growing out of it. Considering Westermarck's role as both philosopher and anthropologist, however, I would claim that anyone taking an interest in his thought as an anthropologist should do justice to the philosophical side of his thinking. What is more, since any discipline that attempts to understand the conditions of human life will be concerned with philosophical questions taken broadly, the discussion also surpasses the subject of understanding Westermarck's thought, and reaches out towards the questions of how one is to perceive the relation between emotions and morality, the issue of moral relativism, and exactly what is taken to be relative to what by theorists claiming to be relativists.

In his entry on 'Relativism' in the *Stanford Encyclopedia of Philosophy*, Chris Swoyer (2010) suggests that the following general relativistic schema may be useful for thinking about what is claimed in a relativistic theory:

Relativistic Schema: Y is relative to X.

In this schema Y, the dependent variable, stands for that which is to be explained by its dependence on something else, X, whereas X, the independent variable, is something fixed that explains variation in Y. Swoyer also remarks that each form of normative relativism[6] has a realist element in it. In other words, once one relativizes Y to X, there are really facts about X that are not relative to anything else. From this schema follows three questions that any relativistic account should answer, although they do not always do so. 1) What is the dependent variable Y?; 2) What is the independent variable X?; 3) How does one describe the relation between X and Y? (Swoyer 2010).

If one takes this schema as the starting point for my following discussion, one could say that the first section is an examination of Westermarck's X, the moral emotions. The second section deals with the kind of relation that pertains between the X, the moral emotions, and how Y, or ethics, is perceived in the light of how Westermarck defines X. I conclude that in the scheme 'ethics is relative to emotion', Westermarck's main candidate for how to explicate ethics is, primarily, as moral concepts, and to some extent as ethical theories based on them. I do, however, take notice of the fact that Westermarck also presents a different relativistic schema, where moral judgements, beliefs or opinion are relative to cognition, superstition or religious beliefs. In the final section, I discuss the sense in which the moral emotions stand fast and serve as the independent variable, and follow Swoyer's suggestion with regard to Westermarck's account to point to something universally valid.

The moral emotions

Westermarck's moral theory is firmly rooted in the emotions. In *The Origin and Development of the Moral Ideas* he expresses the idea that moral judgements are grounded in emotions and attempts to prove this empirically with an abundance of supporting data; in *Ethical Relativity*, he constantly returns to, and attempts to spell out, the philosophical implications of the thought that moral judgements have their basis in feelings of disapproval and approval towards a living being perceived as the cause of pain or pleasure. In giving such an account of ethics, Westermarck is out to reject the notion that there are universal moral principles that philosophy, with the help of reasoning, could lay bare. In *Ethical Relativity* he reviews several of the attempts to appeal to such a principle made by previous philosophers, and concludes that the mere fact that there are so varying philosophical suggestions as to what the highest moral principle should be – the greatest happiness for all, duty and so on – should make us question whether the search for a universal principle is the place to start if we want to become clear about the grounds of morality.[7]

In attempting to create an ethics that does not propose normative principles, but rather emphasizes the psychological origin of morality, he returns to a line of thinking advanced by eighteenth-century Enlightenment thinkers, the philosophers David Hume and Adam Smith. Of these, it is particularly Adam Smith who receives favourable treatment. Westermarck maintains that

> Smith's Theory of Moral Sentiments is the most important contribution to moral psychology made by any British thinker, and that it is so in the first place on account of the emphasis it lays on the retributive character of the moral emotions. (*ER* 71)[8]

He also laments the fact that,

> though his book on the subject rapidly won popularity when it first appeared it was afterwards largely forgotten, save by historians of philosophy whose remarks on it, in England, were generally frigid and sometimes almost contemptuous. (*ER* 70)

It is also on the issue of retribution that Westermarck raises objections against the account of morality given by Hume. This disagreement with

Hume, however, presents us with an opportunity to appreciate the central tenets of Westermarck's own moral theory. In his lecture on Hume, deposited at Åbo Akademi University, he writes about Hume, 'as a thinker in the theory of knowledge he has not been surpassed. As a moral philosopher, on the contrary, he found his superior in Adam Smith' (1913:83 [my translation]). The reason for this is that '[h]e did not analyze the moral emotions with enough acumen and depth to find their retributive character' (ibid.).

> The core essential [in Swedish '*grundväsentligast*' which presents problems
> for translation] remark that can be made against the moral philosophy of
> Hume is [deletions] his flawed analysis of the nature of the moral emotions.
> They are not only desires and distastes, but emotions with strong elements
> of drives. They are retributive emotions, of approval or disapproval, and it is
> this characteristic that explains the puzzles that Hume could not solve from
> his perspective. [my translation] (Westermarck 1913: 82)

The first key feature of Westermarck´s moral theory then is the *retributive* character of moral emotions. By contrast to the priority Hume gave to feelings of desire and distaste, the important thing about these emotions is not their capacity to make us feel pleasure and pain, but their incitement to 'pay back in kind.' They are emotions that make us want to inflict the cause of our pain or pleasure with a similar emotion. The retributive emotions, as becomes clear in this quote, are also of two kinds, negative and positive ones. Moral disapproval, or indignation, the negative retributive emotion, 'is a form of resentment' (*ER* 89) that consists in 'a hostile attitude of mind towards a living being, or something taken as a living being, as a cause of pain' (*ER* 68). Moral approval, the positive retributive emotion, 'is a form of retributive kindly emotion' (*ER* 89), 'a friendly attitude towards such a being as a cause of pleasure' (*ER* 89). However, Westermarck also emphasizes that there are other retributive emotions than the moral emotions. These retributive emotions are akin to the moral emotions, but do not carry any moral weight themselves, such as wrath and vengeance on the negative side and gratitude on the positive side. In that way there are other causes for anger than the moral ones, and we can understand talk about justified anger by contrast to unjustified anger as a way of distinguishing the forms of anger that we consider as moral (*ER* 61).

The distinction between the moral retributive emotions and other non-moral retributive emotions leads us to a second key characteristic of the moral emotions. This is their *impartiality*. Here the influence of Adam Smith on Westermarck's thinking is made explicit. As Westermarck writes, 'Smith made the resentment and gratitude of the "impartial spectator" a corner stone of his theory of the moral sentiments.' (*ER* 70). So, too, is the impartiality of the moral emotions a cornerstone for Westermarck's thinking. It constitutes a different way of arguing for the general legitimacy of moral claims than the appeal to universal moral principles that can be recognized as true by all people.

Westermarck's explanation of the impartiality of emotions proceeds in two steps. First he recognizes the disinteredness that is always characteristic of moral judgement. 'When pronouncing an act good or bad, I mean that it is so quite independently of any reference it might have to me personally.' (*ER* 90). He also suggests that it is this disinterestedness of the moral emotions that underlies many moral philosophers' universalist formulations, as well as the injunction 'do not to others, what you do not want done to you', which, as Westermarck shows, is present in several different religions.[9] He adds, however, in his second step, that this disinteredness, 'is really a form of a more comprehensive quality of the moral emotions, namely, impartiality, real or apparent' (*ER* 93). The indignation we deem moral is so in virtue of the fact that it extends beyond the individual in him- or herself to that which happens to another person, independently of the relationship in which I stand to him or her. As Otto Piipatti writes, 'I recognize that *anybody* in my situation would feel the same kind of justified anger.' (Piipatti 2011:5 [my translation]).

This is not to say that we always react to all offences in the same way, be it toward friend or foe. In reality, Westermarck remarks, we are often influenced by the relationships in which we stand to someone, and this explains why we may attribute different rights to individuals and classes of individuals. This is the reason why Westermarck adds the refinement, 'real or apparent' in the previous quote. To recognize the inherent demand for impartiality in the moral emotions, however, it is enough for Westermarck that we 'assume that any impartial judge would share our view' (*ER* 93).

Society is also given an important role in Westermarck's explanation of the impartiality of the moral emotions. In one of the few places where he elaborates on the direct relation between the moral emotions and the moral rules of a society, he writes,

> society is the birth-place of the moral consciousness; ... the first moral judgements expressed, not the private emotions of isolated individuals, but emotions felt by the society at large; ... tribal custom was the earliest rule of duty. (*ER* 109)

He continues, 'Customs are not merely public habits ... but they are at the same time rules of conduct... And the rules of custom is conceived of as a moral rule, which decides what is right and wrong.' (*ER* 109). Westermarck, thus, latches onto the normative element of societal norms. In other words, whenever there *is* a customary way of doing something, there will also be ideas about how this something is to be done or how it *should be* done. Public disapproval ensues where a deviation from these norms occurs. So, too, with moral rules, the transgression of which will arouse public disapproval, which to Westermarck is the same as a moral emotion. Considering that the customs of a society are binding for all, and that they normally are also accepted as right by its members,[10] Westermarck suggests that we thereby see why moral emotions too should not admit of any exception to the rule based on my own preferences. I will return to how the connection between moral emotions and norms are established in Westermarck's writing, and what that tells us of the kind of philosophical work he is doing.

Thus Westermarck explains moral rules by reference to customs, which in turn are explained by the public expression of emotion; the public sentiment that anyone would be apt to disapprove or feel indignation at a certain form of conduct. In explaining moral rules, or duties, as becomes clear here, Westermarck gives priority to moral disapproval, which has the primary role of forming prohibitions, 'the minimum of morality' (*ER* 140). Moral approval, on the other hand, plays an important role in the formation of moral ideals and aspirations (*ER* 141). In that respect, it also seems to constitute the aspects of morality that Westermarck deems 'higher' (cf. e.g. *ER* 171).

These features, the retributive character or emotion, as well as the claim to impartiality, sum up the bulk of Westermarck's account of morality. Before I end this overview of his moral theory, however, I will quickly remark on the final central element in it. This is the 'whom' the moral emotion is a reaction against. Westermarck devotes a whole chapter to this issue and discusses it at great length, but a very brief summary would be to say that the object of the moral emotions is another person, and furthermore, another person perceived as acting wilfully.

Although this is not the place to elaborate on this aspect of Westermarck's thinking, it is to my mind significant. It is not so, primarily, in that it takes note of the difference in moral praise or blame, judging by whether someone has acted intentionally or not, which is a significant theme in many ethical theories. In particular, one may here think of theories of the deontological kind, beginning with the moral philosophy of Immanuel Kant. Rather, it distinguishes itself in that it focuses on the moral emotions as taking place within an interpersonal relationship. For a non-philosopher, the significance of such a viewpoint may be elusive, since it seems pretty self-evident that if I feel indignant at something you have done, my indignation is directed at you. If one, however, considers the meta-ethical debates that have taken place between realists, such as Moore, and anti-realists or non-cognitivists, of which the emotivism of Ayer and Stevenson is one form, it becomes clear that the interpersonal relationship does not take a primary role in the debates but rather what moral words such as 'good' or 'right' refer to. Are they facts, and how do we gain knowledge of them, etc.? Directing one's focus in this direction may well lead one to not appreciate the significance of personal relationships for understanding morality.

The relativity and variability of moral emotions and beliefs

We have now reviewed how Westermarck defined the characteristics of the moral emotions, and their role in shaping the ethical subjectivity he thought was fundamental to ethics. We have also slightly touched upon the contrast he draws to the attempts at objectivity made by most moral philosophers with a view to formulating universal moral principles. The next step is to consider what role this subjectivity has for the ethical relativity that forms the overarching theme of Westermarck's second book on the role of emotions for morality.

As I stated at the beginning, it is easy to assume that the relativity Westermarck suggests is a natural outgrowth of the moral subjectivity he describes, or rather that the suggested relativity simply consists in this subjectivity. In other words, morality and moral norms are relative because they are subject to the individual psychologies of different people. Timothy Stroup (1976:4) characterizes this view as plain subjectivism. However, in Westermarck's account of why there are varieties in moral norms, they are only in part an aspect of individual emotions. In fact, in the actual examples of differences between cultures he discusses, he includes questions about how different beliefs and cognitions, largely religious ones, underlie the differences. My concern in the following section is therefore to clarify just how Westermarck thinks that emotions and beliefs contribute to variability between different ethical systems. I also touch upon how Westermarck imagines that the formation of ethical norms takes place.

Many of Westermarck's critics, including Moore, take note of the fact that his thoughts cannot merely be written off as a version of plain subjectivism. Here they cite him as speaking of the tendency of certain actions to evoke feelings of approval or disapproval. This is in many ways a better description than the attribution of plain subjectivism to him, but as Stroup shows, it also has significant limitations. We will return to this formulation and how that adds to the understanding of what is relative to what in Westermarck's account. To begin with, it is however helpful to consider the ways in which Westermarck himself rejects the views of plain subjectivism, as well as the emotivism that equates the uttering of 'it is wrong!' with the expression of a feeling, such as saying 'that feels good!'. It is because the later emotivism, especially the one proposed by Ayer, suggested such an understanding of moral judgements, that one has called this theory the 'The Boo!/Hooray!'-theory.

For a first thing, Westermarck states that although there are cases in which saying 'it's good or bad' is expressive of an emotion, the meaning of saying this is different from saying 'I like that' or 'I didn't like that' (*ER* 114). This is true even if the said emotion is our reason for saying it. Thus, he recognizes that moral concepts are aimed at describing qualities in someone's conduct, rather than giving voice to qualities of one's emotion or a tendency among people to react in this way. They are predicates, Westermarck agrees, and he also suggests that they are predicates in which our emotions are objectivized (*ER* 49ff. See Stroup 1976 for a discussion of what objectivization can mean in Westermarck's thought). The question for him is rather to show how these perceived qualities originate in the emotions.

For a second thing, Westermarck rejects the notion that the intensity of one's emotion could be that which determines the greatness of a wrongdoing. Rather, Westermarck remarks that we are likely to feel more prone to react more intensely to a slighter wrong performed in our vicinity than to a greater wrong we read about in the papers (*ER* 419). The morally significant thing is how we would tend to feel about what was done if the circumstances were similar.

For a third thing, Westermarck from the beginning of *Ethical Relativity* makes it clear that moral judgements are not merely expressive of emotions, but are also shaped by thought, reasoning and cognition. In part, it also seems that it is on this path from unreflective to reflective that the development of moral consciousness takes place (*ER* 147), although Westermarck also speaks of the sympathetic or altruistic sentiment as playing an important part in the modification of moral judgements (see, for example, *ER* 95ff. and 207).

The sense in which morality is dependent on, or relative to, emotions, thus, again, brings us to the notion of an originator. But how should we think of this relation between emotions and morality? Furthermore, how does this contribute to the establishment of moral rules in a society? Now, Westermarck repeatedly speaks of the origin of the moral emotions, or the origin of their impartiality (*ER*109–10), but if one goes to Westermarck in search of the genesis of morality, formulated in terms of a psychological theory of how individual emotions are generalized, or of how expressed approval or disapproval are turned into customs that then take the shape of moral commandments, one will be heavily disappointed. Against possible expectations, Westermarck provides no theory of the process from the individual to the social and back again.

In my reading, it is more appropriate to say that his argument proceeds by way of internal definitions, or if one wants, stipulations. Returning to the role he gives to customs in accounting for the impartiality of emotions, his argument proceeds in the following manner: if we consider disapproval for the breaking of a moral rule a moral emotion, and we consider customs not only as habits but as such rules, then we can see how the disapproval of the transgression of what custom compels us to, is a moral emotion, and so on. Or he asks us to consider customs to be moral rules, and emotion that arise out of the transgression of custom to be moral emotions. Rather than explaining, or empirically proving, impartiality by telling us a story of how the feeling of it arises, he is offering us a way of looking at impartiality that ties it to what he regards as the moral in the moral emotions.

This kind of move is also present in his discussion of the moral concepts, and his attempt to show how they originate in the retributive kind of moral approval and disapproval that is central to his view. This discussion also seems significant for understanding the role of the social. For instance, he connects the concepts of 'duty', 'wrong' and 'right' with moral disapproval, and the concept of 'goodness' with moral approval. Therefore, it is also impossible, to him, to derive the second from the first and the other way around (*ER* 122). Such derivations have been attempted by Immanuel Kant, among others, who saw duty as the primary moral concept and goodness as doing one's duty, and by Moore, who regarded goodness as the central concept and attempted to derive the concept of duty from it. This identification of the concepts, to Westermarck, involves a failure to recognize that they have distinct meanings, as they originate in distinct emotions.[11] He also notes that disapproval is prior to approval (*ER* 122), or 'has played a far more important part in the moral consciousness of mankind than approval' (*ER* 122). The reason for this is that morality, to begin with, arises out of prohibitions expressive of disapproval, as our indignation is 'much more easily aroused by an action than by the absence of it' (*ER* 171). It is only at a later stage, 'the more scrutinizing the moral consciousness' (*ER* 171) is, that we find that the positive commandments to be the kind of person that merits moral approval or admiration gain greater weight. (*ER* 171, cf. also 134–8).

In trying to explicate how these moral concepts tie in with emotions, Westermarck speaks of the moral judgements we make in attributing the quality 'good' or 'bad' to the character or conduct of another person, as springing out of 'generalizations derived from approval or disapproval felt with regard to certain modes of conduct.... they are tendencies to feel one or the other of these emotions interpreted as qualities, as dynamic tendencies, in the phenomena which gave rise to the emotion' (*ER* 114). He also mentions the notion of a 'similar translation of emotional states into qualities', as in the case of calling something fearful because we fear it, or admirable because we admire it (*ER* 114). Further on, he says that the tendency among those who first established the use of the moral concepts to feel approval or disapproval in certain circumstances is part of the 'intrinsic meaning of the terms', adding, however, with reference to Bertrand Russell, that we do not have to think that the ones who use the concepts 'have ever thought out what the meaning is: the use of the word comes first and the meaning is to be distilled out of it by observation and analysis (*ER* 116, quoting from Russell 1922:127).

To a large extent, then, the sense in which ethics is considered as relative or subjective is in the relation that moral judgements and, particularly, the moral concepts have to moral emotions. This is also obvious in Westermarck's rejection of the possibility of applying the concepts of truth- or falsehood to an emotion. It can certainly be said to be true that someone has a certain emotion (*ER* 60), and Westermarck also concedes that 'the belief that gives rise to an emotion, the cognitive basis of it' can be said to be true or false (*ER* 60). Yet there are no other senses in which we can speak of some emotions as being more true than others. Therefore, it is also impossible for Westermarck to speak about moral truths, as they do not depend on sense-perceptions. He also rejects the notion that the introduction of a 'moral sense' or a 'moral intuition' (Moore 1903) that accounts for the perception of moral truths presents enough proof of the fact that there could be moral facts in the way there are intellectual truths. This becomes apparent, not least, in the difficulty of 'harmonizing conflicting moral convictions' and how different the difficulty is from harmonizing conflicting sense-perceptions (*ER* 216). Whereas there are settled ways in which we can correct a sense-perception and recognize our error, 'there often is conflict between the moral convictions of "thoughtful and well-educated people," nay, even between the moral "intuitions" of philosophers, which proves to be irreconcilable' (*ER* 216). This, however, is only what is to be expected if 'moral opinions are based on emotions', says Westermarck (*ER* 216). 'The moral emotions depend upon cognitions, but the same cognitions may give rise to emotions that differ, in quality or intensity, in different persons or in the same person on different occasions.' (*ER* 216). Westermarck also asks us to consider that moral judgements do not possess the kind of universality that is characteristic of intellectual truths. This becomes even more obvious, says Westermarck, if one considers that there are degrees of moral badness and goodness, 'virtues and merits may be greater or smaller, a duty may be more or less stringent' (*ER* 218), whereas an intellectual truth is either true or false.

Is it then, according to Westermarck, possible to derive all disagreement and diversity in moral beliefs from differences in the emotions of different persons? Certainly not. Westermarck notes that there are different causes for differences in moral opinion. Among these, he names insufficient knowledge of facts or insufficient reflection, in other words that we are not aware of all the relevant facts of a matter in order to respond to it in an appropriate way, or have not approached them in a thoughtful enough way. If a person, to give an example that Westermarck mentions a couple of times, lies to us, we may condemn the act until we come to know that he only did so to save our own or somebody else's life (cf. *ER* 147, 174). Making such mistakes is, of course, a constantly present risk in making rash moral judgements, as we do not always command a clear enough view of the background, consequences or motivations behind someone's conduct. He also discusses differences in moral ideas that grow out of very different 'external conditions of life' (*ER* 184) that have led people to think quite differently on a matter. The examples he discusses here, are the killing or abandoning of elderly parents and infants. Finally, he remarks that religious beliefs and superstition have fostered 'an extraordinary diversity of moral opinion' (*ER* 187). Here he gives the example of differences in the attitude taken to human sacrifice (*ER* 187–9), suicide (*ER* 189–92) and homosexual practices (*ER* 192–6).

In these respects, Westermarck suggests that morality, here taken in the sense of moral judgements, ideas and opinions that people make in a specific situation or in the context of a specific historical time, is not only dependent on emotion, but is also relative to a variety of beliefs and external circumstances. The crucial point in his discussion of these things as possible causes for variability in moral judgement, is that Westermarck does not regard the citing of these kinds of difference as sufficient reasons for denying that there is an objective standard of morality, or that one could muster up a universal moral truth.

His reasons for thinking thus are easy to make out in the first and the last case, that is in connection with a lack of factual knowledge and with religious belief. If we are really making a mistake in making a moral judgement because we do not command a clear view of the facts, then it should in principle be possible to get the judgement right if we had all the facts. Somewhat similarly, we can think of religious beliefs that foster hostile attitudes towards homosexuals as something of which we can rid ourselves with the recognition that the belief is expressive of prejudice. It is, however, not possible to discern whether Westermarck thinks that every religious belief is in fact a false belief, although his bringing religious belief together with superstition, in speaking of 'specific religious or superstitious beliefs' (*ER* 196), may be seen to indicate such an understanding. In pondering such questions, it is significant to remember that he also finds 'an echo' of the disinterestedness of the moral emotions in the religious maxims that in one way or another propagate the golden rule.

The sense in which Westermarck thinks that the second set of examples, that is, the cases in which external conditions give rise to 'different ideas relating to the objective nature of similar modes of conduct and their consequences' (*ER* 184), fails to deny the possibility of objectively valid moral statements, however, is more difficult to discern. One possible reading that one with good will may also gather out of Westermarck's remarks, is that here we are not confronted with a case that really proves the relativity of moral judgements in the sense that two people, set in different times and cultures, regard the *same* conduct in different ways, but rather that objectively the situations are different to such an extent that it is no longer possible for us to talk about what is done in the two situations as the same conduct, even if some features of the conduct in each situation bear similarity to the conduct in the other. All things considered, then, in these situations there might well be an objective description of what the conduct amounts to in the one and in the other particular historical situation, that makes us realize that they are not the same. John W. Cook calls the movement made by anthropologists who try to prove that there is moral relativism by citing evidence of different valuations of the same conduct in the way Westermarck deems impossible, the 'projection error' (Cook 1999:66, 69–70). In other words, the anthropologist, although his or her intention is to describe a piece of conduct as relative to a specific cultural context, takes him- or herself to recognize the same kind of conduct in another culture, not seeing that he or she thereby projects his or her own particular cultural understanding into the culture he or she wants to understand without appropriating it (Cook 1999:89–92).[12]

The only way in which Westermarck thinks it is possible to disprove the idea that moral judgements could be objectively valid is, understandably, to see how they are relative to emotions. He demonstrates this by asking his readers to consider that the 'moral rules laid down by the customs of savage peoples' (*ER* 197) in many ways resemble those of 'civilized nations' (*ER* 197).[13] The examples Westermarck gives of this is that they condemn homicide and theft, and praise charity and generosity. The only difference between the savage society and the civilized one is that in the first the moral rules only apply to members of the same group (*ER* 197). According to Westermarck, it is vain to think that we could widen the circle of people to which these people see their moral rules as applying through a process of reasoning. What has led the people of more 'civilized nations' to universalize morality, that is, to see moral rules as applying universally to everyone and not just the members of one's own clan or society, is, to him, a widening of the altruistic sentiment (*ER* 200). Such a widening has been occasioned by the fact that the social unit has grown, and that there has been more intercourse between people of different societies (*ER* 200).

In emphasizing the altruistic sentiment, we, of course, again see the significance given to emotions in Westermarck's thought, but also, as I mentioned in the beginning, the influence of Adam Smith. The altruistic sentiment

> induces us to take a kindly interest in the feelings of our neighbours. It
> involves a tendency, or willingness, and, when strongly developed, gives rise
> to an eager desire, to sympathize with their pains and pleasure. (*ER* 97)

It 'is not merely willingness to sympathize, it is above all a conative disposition to promote the welfare of its object' (*ER* 97). The altruistic sentiment also appears to be one of the clues to how Westermarck regards the development of moral consciousness. This sentiment is not a moral emotion in its own right, but it is that which explains the disinterested character of the moral retributive emotions. Furthermore, it appears to Westermarck that our moral consciousness is more developed in as far as it is expressive of the altruistic sentiment. It is, for instance, under the influence of the altruistic sentiment that the moral consciousness 'condemns any retributive infliction of pain that it regards as undeserved, and that forgiveness rather than revenge is preached as the moral norm' (*ER* 74).

The uniformity of the moral emotions

In the emphasis that the moral rules of savage societies resemble those of more civilized ones, we find another significant feature of Westermarck's moral thought. This is the great uniformity he recognizes in the moral lives of different people, and peoples, despite apparent differences. Thus, although Westermarck's main contribution to moral philosophy lies in his dissemination of how ethical concepts, as well as ethical theories that take their starting point in different moral concepts, are relative to emotions, his account of the moral emotions presupposes and builds on a large uniformity in our emotional reactions. This is true both on the level of our practical moral lives, as it is described by Westermarck, and in his attempt to delineate the general structure of the moral emotions.

In a remark that shows some of his subtle humour, Westermarck acutely states that 'it has often been remarked that there is much greater agreement among moralists on the question of moral practice than on the question of theory' (*ER* 45). Although the diversity among moral philosophers as to what is the highest moral principle is so great that it leads Westermarck to conclude that no universal principle is to be found, and that the field of moral philosophy as a normative science can never replicate the results of the natural sciences (*ER* 3), this degree of disagreement is not evident when these moral philosophers start to give more details on what their principles mean in moral practice. Here, there is suddenly much more agreement about how we should live our life. We should be kind to our neighbour, respect their life and property, speak the truth, be monogamous and faithful to our spouses, be sober and temperate (*ER* 45). This, to Westermarck, is a sign that these practical rules are rather expressive of our common sense, which in turn is grounded in certain natural moral reactions.

Westermarck's pleas for relativism do not in this way extend to the nature of the moral emotions. This can be read in relation to the anthropological debates about emotions, where one side of the discussion urges us to recognize that emotions too form part of the practices that have to be explained by reference to their cultural contexts.[14] Westermarck would probably side with the opposite camp, which sees emotion as belonging to our universal nature. (I was inclined to write human nature, but it should be noted that Westermarck also takes note of retributive emotions and reactions in the animal world in *The Origin and Development of the Moral Ideas*.) In his discussion of the nature of the moral emotions, Westermarck again and again tries to bring out the general structure of moral emotions. They are retributive emotions with a claim to impartiality, directed at the character or conduct of another person whose will is conceived as the cause of one's pleasure of pain. This formulation of what the moral emotions are is expected to apply universally.

Seeing morality as grounded in our nature also provides him with the means of securing morality against those critics who see the ethical subjectivity he proposes as a 'danger to morality' (*ER* 58). He writes,

My moral judgements spring from my own moral consciousness; they judge of the conduct of other men not from their point of view but from mine, not in accordance with their feelings and opinions about right or wrong but according to my own. We approve and disapprove because we cannot do otherwise; our moral consciousness belongs to our mental constitution, which we cannot change as we please. Can we help feeling pain, when the fire burns us? Can we help sympathizing with our friends? Are these facts less necessary or less powerful in their consequences, because they fall within the subjective sphere of our experience? So also, why should the moral law command less obedience because it forms a part of ourselves? (*ER* 58–9)

To the critics who think that it is inconsistent for him to speak of one morality as higher than another, he responds: 'my denial of objective moral standards does not prevent my pronouncing moral judgements which are expressions of my own moral feelings, and whatever terms I use they have to be interpreted accordingly' (*ER* 146). When he says this, it is not because he, as Timothy Stroup describes one of the fears of his opponents, is 'inconsistent in his denial of moral objectivity because he could not altogether shed his personal convictions' (Stroup 1976:24). He is saying it because this is in his mind the only thing he can do as a moral philosopher, because moral judgements in the end have to be traced back to emotions. In effect it is what every moral philosopher does, according to Westermarck, although the ones with a rationalistic bent are under the illusion that they are doing something else.

Nevertheless, he thinks that the origin of our moral concepts and theories that he has uncovered is available to anyone who considers his argument through rational analysis, and that the meaning of our moral concepts really has this logically coherent structure. He is also convinced that he, even more than any other philosopher, has provided empirical support for the fact that this is indeed an aspect of our universal nature as sentient beings. His aim is thus to persuade his reader through rational argumentation that things stand as he says. In these respects, he is not alien to the notion that reflection about morality takes the form of rational reflection, although the judgements we make, also in our role as moral philosophers, ultimately can be brought back to our emotion.

Through the roles Westermarck gives to reflection, both in the development of morality and in respect to emotions, he also suggests a different way of understanding the form of criticism we may make use of in the case of moral disagreement. Against the picture of a universal wrong and right that we as philosophers need to discover to settle moral disputes, he opens the way for a more nuanced understanding of different perceptions of what in a particular situation is wrong or right. Rather than seeing ethical subjectivity as a danger, he argues that recognizing this ethical subjectivity could be an 'advantage to morality'. If we trace back our moral opinions to their source, and see that they originate in 'ignorance and superstition or in sentimental likes and dislikes' (*ER* 59) we cannot, if we are thoughtful and unprejudiced, but help changing our views (*ER* 59–60). Or as he puts it in a telling footnote, 'if it could be brought home to people that there is no absolute standard in morality they would perhaps be more apt to listen to the voice of reason' (*ER* 147).

Westermarck, in this way, gives us a different ground for understanding the kind of critique that can be directed at moral judgements, as well as the kind of reflection that can be involved in the practice of moral philosophy. The focus of the philosopher trying to provide a rational justification of morality, and to articulate the highest moral principle, as it were, is on moving others to what the philosopher takes to be the only rational position. They are to be thus moved in virtue of being rational beings responsive to reasoning. The appeal to reason, however, as is indicated in Westermarck's display of how very differently the highest moral principle has been formulated by ethicists, carries with it the risk that what is presented as the only rationally available alternative harbours the philosopher's own moral intuitions that have not been put to sufficient scrutiny. Westermarck's account, on the other hand, suggests that moral reflection and criticism, in large part, have to entail an element of self-reflection and self-criticism. This is so, even if it is the public disapproval and approval of other people's conduct that lies at the heart of Westermarck's moral theory.

Conclusion

In my discussion I have presented Westermarck's views on the emotional background of morality, and the role the recognition of it has in the creation of ethical theories. Thereby, I have attempted to show what a re-reading of Westermarck may offer philosophers and anthropologists who are interested in what his notion of ethical relativism has to give to contemporary debates about the origins of morality. I have worked with the assumption that it is worthwhile to look beyond the schematic pictures that critics of Westermarck have used to deliver their critique, so as to recognize the complexity of his thought and his attentiveness to details in his response to criticisms. Therefore, the aim of the discussion has not been to offer a critical analysis of his ideas myself. Nevertheless, there are points with which I find myself in disagreement, and open questions that are not resolved by a reading of him. In conclusion, I will vent some of these concerns in the hope that it may take the reader who is interested in engaging in Westermarck's thought further in his or her own reflections.

On the whole I am sympathetic to the general thrust of Westermarck's argument, if one takes this to entail the recognition of the need to attend to how moral concepts cannot be given a merely rational justification but depend on our sensibilities as emotive beings. As a general remark, I would also suggest that Westermarck is at his best in the deflationary work he engages in, trying to steer our interest away from the notion of universalizable moral principles. In his positive account of the dependence of morality on emotions, however, there is considerably more unclarity than my account, for the sake of clarity, has shown. Yet, I have more deeply seated worries about the account of the meaning of concepts that is implicit in his writing.

This applies first to Westermarck's tendency to only define meaning as a matter of the emotional origin of a moral concept, or as a generalization of tendencies to feel. Here I am inclined to agree with Timothy Stroup that Westemarck's account would have prospered with the outspoken admission that moral words can be used in a variety of ways, which are also significant for understanding what is meant by them.[15] This would, for one thing, have lessened the tensions that ensue when he in his writings first admits that moral judgements serve as expressions of emotion or as prescriptions, but then repeats that their meaning is ultimately to be found in the emotions in which the concepts used originated.

A second more problematic tendency is the empiricist leaning in fashioning meaning as a matter of making generalizations. Westermarck treats questions of meaning as if they could be determined by factual considerations, and treats his data as evidence for his view, as if coming to see something as a fact or as proof would not in itself depend on an understanding that cannot solely be attributed to the facts. As I have indicated, what he is doing is not merely letting the facts speak for themselves, but rather lining them up in a specific manner to persuade us into thinking as he does, when he is not simply redefining what we should think of as morality or as moral emotions. This of course raises a different question about what is relative to what, namely, whether we can regard concepts as relative to facts about our nature, or whether what we come to consider as facts itself is relative to our conceptual frameworks?

Notes

1   The work on this article was made possible by support from the research project Westermarck and Beyond: Evolutionary Approaches to Morality and Their Critics, funded by Kone Foundation.

2   In making this claim I am leaning on Tove Österman's very lucid presentation of the issue (2007:97ff.).

3   Timothy Stroup raises the question whether the term 'relativity' is more ambiguous than the term 'relativism'. Relativism, he thinks, stands for 'a philosophical theory which denies absolute, objective moral values', whereas relativity can entail both a 'descriptive sociological use and an evaluative philosophical use' (Stroup 1976:23). This distinction is similar to that between descriptive and normative relativism, where the first 'is a family of empirical claims to the effect that certain groups in fact have different modes of thought, standards of reasoning, or the like. Such claims are meant to describe (but not evaluate) the principles and practices of the two groups', while the second 'is a family of non-empirical normative or evaluative claims to the effect that modes of thought, standards of reasoning, or the like are only right or wrong, correct or incorrect, veridical or non-veridical, relative to a framework'. (Swoyer 2010).

4   Westermarck's *The Origin and Development of the Moral Ideas* was published in 1906 and *Ethical Relativity* in 1932. Ayer's *Language, Truth and Logic*, in which one chapter is dedicated to his emotivism, came out in 1936, and C.L. Stevenson published seminal articles on his emotivism in 1937 (see Stevenson 1963), before his book *Ethics and Language* came out in 1944.

5   There is also an ambiguity in the choice of the word ethical. Many times ethics is used interchangably with morality, but at times ethics may also be used to denote

the study of morality or moral philosophy. It will become clear that both uses apply to Westermarck's discussion. He tries to show both how morality, and especially the moral concepts, depend on moral emotions, but also how this dependence extends to the concepts being favoured by different ethical theories.

6   I give a description of normative relativism in note 3.

7   In one of his many letters to his friend Rolf Lagerborg, who later became professor of philosophy at Åbo Akademi University, written on 2 May 1932, now available in the Westermarck online collection on www.filosofia.fi, Edward Westermarck describes his book *Ethical Relativity* that he was working on then as 'his dearest book'. This book, according to Westermarck, is 'at odds with almost everything that has been written in ethics in England during this century'. What it is at odds with, it should be clear, is the search for normative principles.

8   From here on I refer to *Ethical Relativity* as *ER*.

9   Westermarck cites the Christian Bible, the Indian Mahabharata and Confucius (*ER* 92).

10   Again dwelling on the difference between the ideals we commit to in society, and the actual form society takes, Westermarck notes that even though the members of a society recognizes its norms as rights of the individuals, the norms of a society do not have to press for impartiality for all. This is the case e.g. in societies where slavery is accepted. (Cf Westermarck 1900, 192)

11   In another place he mentions Hutcheson, Clifford, Fowler and Wilson, and Alexander as writers that have attempted similar identifications (Westermarck 1900:188).

12   Cook's original book is a rewarding read for anyone interested in anthropological and philosophical discussions about moral relativism.

13   The choice of the words 'savage' and 'civilization' is of course Westermarck's and expressive of an evaluation that later anthropologists have wanted to free anthropology from by, for example, relativizing our claims to knowledge and understanding to our particular historical and cultural context. The introduction of the term 'Orientalism' after Edward Said, and the post-colonialism of Franz Fanon, here come to mind. I leave the wording as it stands as an expression of Westermarck's views, which of course express that he too was a child of his time, and to provide an example of how he clarifies the notion that one morality can be seen as higher than another. This is a question that has been raised quite frequently in discussions of Westermarck (Moore 1922; Segerberg 1971–2), as the notion that one morality is higher than another seems to have no ground in a framework that analyses moral judgements as psychological statements. As Moore (1922) states, it seems that the only way of saying 'A's morality is higher than B's' is when A's morality is my morality. I hope that my discussion should have made clear that the description of Westermarck's relativism that sees it as a reduction of moral predicates to psychological statements is flawed. Yet there is a question of how he frames the notion of one morality as higher than another. Setting the question in relation to the moralities of different cultures may be controversial, but

at least within a culture it should be relevant to see what sense we can give to the idea that one moral idea is better than the other.

14 See, for example, Jean L. Brigg's *Never in Anger*, which is frequently cited in the philosophical literature (see, for example, Solomon 2007) as showing that a group of Eskimos in Canada are not angered in the ways Westerners are. See also Lutz and Abu-Lughod (1990) and Russell *et al* (1995) for more contributions to the debate.

15 'Among categorical ethical judgements', Stroup writes, 'we can recognize ... the imperative (including requests, orders, pleas, etc.), the interjective of expressive, the prescriptive, the reportive ... , the persuasive and the purportedly objective.' (Stroup 1976:19).

References

Ayer, A.J. [1936] 1946. *Language, Truth and Logic*. London: Victor Gollancz Ltd.

Briggs, J.L. 1970. *Never in Anger: Portrait of an Eskimo Family*. Cambridge. Harvard University Press.

Cook, J.W. 1999. *Morality and Cultural Differences*. Oxford: Oxford University Press.

Lutz, C.A. and Abu-Lughod, L. 1990. *Language and the Politics of Emotion*. Cambridge: Cambridge University Press.

Moore, G.E. 1903. *Principia Ethica*. Cambridge: Cambridge University Press.

Moore, G.E. 1922. The nature of moral philosophy. *Philosophical Studies*: 310–39.

Österman, T. 2007. *Rationality and Cultural Understanding*. Uppsala University: Doctoral dissertation.

Piipatti, O. 2011. Att känna med och att ge igen: Adam Smith och Westermarck om moralkänslorna. *Laboratorium för folk och kultur* 1:3–6.

Russell, B. 1922. *The Analysis of Mind*. London: George Allen & Unwin.

Russell J.A., Fernández-Dols, J.-M. and Manstead, A.S.R. (eds) 1995. *Everyday Conceptions of Emotion: An Introduction to the Psychology, Anthropology and Linguistics of Emotion*. Dordrecht: Kluwer Academic Publishers.

Segerberg, K.1971–72. Moores kritik av Westermarck. *Årsskrift* 56:74–80.

Solomon, R.C. 2007. *True to Our Feelings*. Oxford: Oxford University Press.

Stevenson, C.L. 1944. *Ethics and Language*. New Haven: Yale University Press.

Stevenson, C.L. 1963. The emotive meaning of ethical terms. In C.L. Stevenson, *Facts and Values*. New Haven: Yale University Press [originally published 1937].

Westermarck, E. 1900. Remarks on the predicates of moral judgments. *Mind* 9(34):184-204.

Westermarck, E. 1906, 1908. *The Origin and Development of the Moral Ideas* (2 vols). London: Macmillan.

Westermarck, E. 1932. *Ethical Relativity*. London: Kegan Paul, Trench, Trubner & Co.

Manuscript material

Stroup, T. 1976. In defence of Westermarck. Paper read at Helsinki University. [A revised version appears in *Journal of the History of Philosophy* 19(2):213–34.]

Westermarck, Edvard. Lecture 1913: Hume. pp. 44–83. Capsule 78: Lectures. Edvard Westermarck's fonds (ÅAB:EW). Manuscript Collection, Åbo Akademi University Library.

Digital material

Swoyer, C. Relativism, *The Stanford Encyclopedia of Philosophy* (Winter 2010 Edition), E.N. Zalta (ed.), http://plato.stanford.edu/archives/win2010/ entries/relativism/.

Part ii – By Westermarck

10

Implications of the theory of selection[1]

(1889)

EDITED AND TRANSLATED BY JAN ANTFOLK

Alfred R. Wallace wrote in his foreword to Westermarck's 1891 book, *The History of Human Marriage*, that, with 'an array of authority on the one side and a hitherto unknown student on the other', reason was clearly in favour of the latter (Westermarck 1891). Westermarck, the 'hitherto unknown student', gained immediate recognition among contemporary scientists for *The History of Human Marriage*, in which he made criticisms of such authorities as Herbert Spencer, John Lubbock and even Charles Darwin. With this book, Westermarck seems to have impressed Wallace and many other contemporary scientists with his clarity of style and his painstaking efforts to support his arguments with observations.

Darwin, whom Westermarck considered one of the most important scientists in history, and Wallace, with whom Westermarck later would correspond and who would write the foreword to *The History of Human Marriage*, influenced Westermarck greatly. Westermarck, who seemed to have recognized and appreciated the ingenious simplicity of the idea of natural selection and its capacity to explain the origin and the development of the organic world, held that the theory of selection was of importance not only to the sciences of physical life, but also to the sciences of psychological and social life. When twenty-seven years old, two years before the first publication of *The History of Human Marriage*, Westermarck delivered a speech to his fellow students. In his speech to the members of the student union Nyländska Afdelningen at The University of Helsinki (Helsingfors), Westermarck, who was currently writing his dissertation *The History of Human Marriage*, sums up the evolutionary perspective underlying much of his future work. Perhaps more concisely and lucidly than elsewhere in his work, Westermarck conscientiously explains the premises underlying the theory of selection, the evidence in favour of their validity, and their implications for the understanding of human psychology and behaviour. Here, he delivers his explanation of the almost universal fact that humans generally feel no sexual attraction towards close kin. The explanation, later often called 'the Westermarck Hypothesis', would be included in *The History of Human Marriage* and was instantly acknowledged by contemporary scholars as solving the question of the origins of incest avoidance and taboo. With this explanation Westermarck aimed to explain both our psychological aversion towards sexual relationships with individuals with whom we have co-resided in early youth, who generally are our relatives, and the social norm prohibiting such relationships, that is, the incest taboo. Arguing that the ultimate cause of this aversion was the increased mortality in offspring from incestuous relationships, Westermarck argued that the predisposition to this aversive feeling was shaped by natural selection. However, the other important point in Westermarck's explanation was that the individual aversion has then been generalized into a social norm against incest. Thus, Westermarck attempted to explain the contents and functions of social norms by evolutionary principles. (For more on the pertinence of this speech to Westermarck's explanation of human incest avoidance, see Antfolk, this volume).

His speech at Nyländska Afdelningen is likely one of the first recorded examples of his desire to subsume sociology and psychology under the theory of selection. He has been called the first sociobiologist (e.g. Sanderson, 2006), and Westermarck's reasoning in this case seems to have been a quite important preview of what would later become an independent field of science. Understandably, in his speech, Westermarck underlines the importance of the theory of selection to the social sciences. The timing of his speech is historically interesting, as it occurs midway between the presentation of Darwin's and Wallace's ideas around 1860 and their synthesis with Mendel's theories on heredity in the 1930s. From this perspective, the reader may find it interesting to read Westermarck's speculations about the nature of the laws of heredity, referring to Weismann, the well-known biologist, who almost simultaneously published his *Essays upon Heredity* (1889) and *Germ-Plasm: A Theory on Heredity* (1893), in which he presents his germ-plasm theory, according to which heritable information passes from parents to offspring in germ cells or gametes. The somatic cells do not function as agents of heredity and information cannot pass from somatic to germ cells (i.e. the Weismann Barrier), which rules out inheritance of acquired traits. Being part of the beginning of a new era in biology, Westermarck was simultaneously living at the end of an era in sociology. Westermarck's own student, Bronislaw Malinowski, would later be one of the most important scientists in the development of anthropology, leading it to abandon its evolutionary perspective and concentrate on sociological and psychological fields of enquiry. With this in mind, the enthusiasm with which Westermarck argued for the importance of the theory of selection for the sciences of the social and psychological life leaves a somewhat bittersweet taste.

The theory of selection and its importance for the sciences of the physical, psychological, and social life[2]

Gentlemen!

The 1st of July 1858 was a noteworthy day in the annals of science and modern civilization. On this day, two essays, about which one can unreservedly say that they launched a new era in the understanding of the history of organic nature, were read for the Linnean Society of London. One of these was authored by Mr Alfred Russel Wallace, the other by Mr Charles Darwin. Both delivered a new answer to the important question concerning the development of the species, and both answered this question – remarkably enough – in the very same way.

Nevertheless, these two naturalists had, completely independent of one another, arrived at these identical results. Mr Wallace had from the Malayan archipelago, where he was currently residing, sent his essay to Darwin, to Darwin's surprise expressing the very views to which he had been led by his own research several years earlier.

Darwin had, however, only announced his theory to some of his most intimate friends. And it was now, due to their insistence, albeit only after the kind of long hesitation typical of Darwin's noble character, he decided to, alongside Wallace's essay, submit an already completed résumé of his own theory to the society.

The two essays did not receive any particular attention. In his autobiography, Darwin says that the only published announcement they received, as far as he could remember, was one by Professor Haughton in Dublin, whose verdict was: 'What is true is not new, and what is new is not true.'[3]

But when, the following year, Darwin developed his ideas in detail in his work, *On the Origin of Species*,[4] the attention that they attracted was instead tremendous. A couple of editions sold out in days. The book was later translated into most European languages, including Spanish, Polish and Czech. It spread not only to scientists *ex professo*, but, due to its popular style, Darwinism soon became a catchword on the lips also of the general reader. Moreover, one can safely say that Darwin attained a more widespread reputation than any other scientist before or after him.

However, it has to be admitted that Darwin was often credited with merits that were not rightfully due to him, such as being the founder of the theory of descent or heredity. This theory, which claims that all the different species of animals and plants that at any point have lived or still live on earth are the gradually modified descendants of a single life form, or of only a few, originally very simple, spontaneously arisen primary forms, belongs mainly to the Frenchman Lamarck, and it was, at the time when Darwin published his work on the origin of the species, already recognized by many outstanding scholars. It is true that Darwin, in a much more comprehensive way than any of his predecessors, had pursued the theory of descent in detail, and had completed it in a much more rigorous context, but what was truly novel in his and Wallace's teachings consisted in showing why this continuous evolution has taken place, that is, the efficient causes of the changes, which in the theory of heredity were only presented as facts. These causes they found in natural choice or selection; and that is why only the theory of selection, but not the theory of descent, should be considered Darwinian.

The theory of selection is, in its main characteristics, utterly simple – so simple that many of those who have speculated over these questions, at their first reading of the *On the Origin of Species*, in the manner of Professor Huxley, have exclaimed: 'How extremely stupid of me not to have thought of this idea!'[5] It is mainly based on four categories of facts.

Firstly, it is an everyday observation that all individuals of one and the same species are never exactly the same. Should you look around, for example, in a birch forest, you will not find two trees that completely correspond with each other in their offshoots, in the number of their branches and leaves, flowers and fruits. A shepherd effortlessly recognizes each beast in his herd. And there are no two humans absolutely identical, completely similar in stature and size, in facial shape, skin colour, the number of the hairs, temperament, character etc. In the lower animals and plants, it is admittedly very difficult, often quite impossible, for us to discover individual differences; but this is no doubt due to the inadequacy of our senses and certainly not to the actual nonexistence of differences.

Secondly, it is a well-known fact that the number of eggs or seeds that organisms produce, out of each of which an individual under favourable circumstances could come into existence, is much larger than the number of individuals that really develop from these seeds, enter life and procreate. It has been said that if a fish were to develop from each corn of roe that is released and fertilized, the sea would soon be too small to harbour all these individuals. There are fowl who lay numerous eggs but still belong to the rarest of birds, while, on the other hand, one of the most common birds, the fulmar, lays only one egg. And if all the humans that are born were to live long enough to reproduce, the earth would soon be overpopulated. Hence, it is obvious that it is not the actual number of seeds or newly born individuals that decides the number of individuals that subsequently come into life and survive. Rather, the number of the latter is contingent upon completely different circumstances, in particular of the interaction of the organism with its organic, as well as its inorganic, environment.

This is because, thirdly, each organism must from the beginning of its existence fight several hostile influences. It struggles against inorganic influences of many sorts, against temperature, weather and other circumstances. It fights animals, who live off this organism and for whom he is their natural nutrition. Finally, and above all, he fights similar organisms, those most related to him, for each individual is engaged in a most severe competition with other individuals of its own kind living in the same location. The means to sustain life are in fact as a whole very limited, and are far from sufficient for the abundance of individuals that could develop from existing seeds or eggs. But now it is clear that, as all individuals of a species are never exactly identical, some of them will have more favourable prospects than others to prevail in this struggle for existence. The most favoured individuals will be victorious, stay alive and reproduce, while the less fortunate will succumb sooner or later without offspring. Suppose, for instance, that a number of plants of one and the same kind all grow together in a very dry habitat. As hairy leaves are particularly useful for the absorption of moisture in the air, and as there are strong variations in the growth of hair, the individuals with the most dense growth of hair will be the most favoured in this unfavourable place, where plants must both struggle directly for water and prevail, in addition, in the internal competition for water. Only these plants prevail, while the others with smoother leaves perish. This is now what Darwin called natural selection, as opposed to artificial selection, which is what man performs in raising domestic animals and cultivated plants.

Fourthly, we have the important law of heredity. That like begets like is an old truth, although the offspring of an organism are admittedly never exactly the same as the parent. According to this law, those most favourably equipped individuals who prevail and reproduce generally pass on their favourable qualities to their offspring, and thereby the individuals of this second generation, or at least some thereof, should through heritage have obtained those particular advantages through which their parents achieved their superiority over their competitors. Thus – sticking to the example just mentioned – the offspring of the plants with densely haired leaves should be characterized by denser and stronger growth of hair than generally was the case with the individuals of the first generation. Should this process continue over generations in one and the same locality, finally this particular trait, the increase of surface hair on the plant's leaves, is amplified to the degree that a wholly new species will appear.

Thus, the theory of selection does not rest on vague suppositions, but on a solid foundation of generally recognized facts. It is not merely a hypothesis that organisms vary in different directions; that there is and always has been a continuous struggle for existence in the organic world, a competition for the necessities for life; that in such a struggle the stronger win and the weaker die; and that the law of heredity is a law of nature. We know all this with the same certainty that we know that the earth orbits the sun. If we then concede that the only scientifically possible hypothesis concerning the origin of the organic world is the theory of descent, which tells us that all the currently living species have not appeared independently, but rather developed gradually from a common ancestral form – and this virtually all contemporary naturalists not restricted by theological presuppositions, admit – then we also have to concede at least this much, that it is utterly likely that natural selection has played a major role in the evolution of species. Day by day, opinion on this becomes more settled.

When Darwin published his work on the origin of species, he won barely half-a-dozen important adherents to his views. That the theologians would hurl their anathema over this new heresy was to be expected. Bishop Wilberforce wrote an article in *Quarterly Review*, in which he called Darwin a casual writer, whose miserable mishmash was a stain on all true science[6] – the same Bishop Wilberforce, who himself was so utterly ignorant about the theory he was criticizing that he seriously asked if any sensible person really believed that all good varieties of turnip had a tendency to become men. However, there was a barely less persevering resistance among scientists. There can be no doubt thereof, says Professor Huxley, that if a scientific synod were held at this time, the Darwinists would have been excommunicated with a crushing majority; but it is similarly certain, he adds, that if one were to be held now, the situation would be the opposite. All those objections that had been raised against Darwinism have in fact been demonstrated to be unfounded. It has been said that the time period that species would have needed to originate through natural selection cannot be estimated to be less than a few millennia. But geology allows us to suppose the existence of such vast stretches of time. It has been objected that no transitional forms between species have been found, although, according to the theory of selection, such life forms should exist in abundance. But, in fact, such transitional life forms exist everywhere that we are able to scrutinize a large number of individuals from related species; though they, for obvious reasons, are lacking among species close to extinction, such as the ostrich among the birds, and the elephant and the giraffe among the mammals. It has been said that there is a deep, impassable gorge between a species and a subspecies, so much that two really separate species never possess the capacity to create bastards that could successfully interbreed with one or the other of their parental species; while races, or varieties of on and the same species, are capable of creating bastards. But the fact that this is normally the case does not really prove anything else save that the more two species differ from each other, the harder or more impossible will the creation of bastards become. On the other hand there are numerous cases of bastards, which have been created from the interbreeding of two completely different species and who can procreate, while there are races of the same species that cannot mate with each other. This proves that the fundamental difference that has been assumed between a species and variety does not exist. As far as our knowledge extends, all the learned opponents of Darwin have not been able to present so much as a single fact that would contradict Darwin's hypotheses. And when Nägeli[7] a few years ago famously attacked the theory of selection, he was unable to provide any reasonable explanation to the organisms' suitability, which precisely through the theory of selection becomes understandable. It should not be too much to claim that Darwin's work on the origin of the species has exercised a wider and more thorough influence on science than any other work since the days of Newton. The theory of selection has shed light on such an immense amount of phenomena, previously enveloped in riddles, to the extent that it has reformed our understanding of nature. The progress of science is synonymous with a widening of our knowledge of the natural causes, available to reason, of the phenomena. It is the bitterest enemy of a theology that tries to explain everything as the direct product of a divine will. Have we not become used to marvelling at God's grace in the excellence of nature's order! Have we not praised him for creating so many useful animals and plants to serve man his nutrition and for decorating the fields with beautiful, fragrant flowers to delight our senses! Darwinism rejects such fantasies. It teaches us that each species is constituted thus not for the sake of anyone else, but for its own sake, and that its purpose in nature is at least not directly an act of divine benevolence and wisdom, but completely dependent on that general law of nature that says: the stronger live, the weaker die. With this I do not wish to declare that Darwinism would lead to irreligiosity in the broadest sense of the word. It does not deride the religious feeling, and neither denies nor supports the hypothesis of a personal God as the author of everything. It neither leads to materialism, pantheism, nor to any other teaching about the inner essence or origin of things, since it does not venture at all to explain what life is. It only states the laws under which life evolves, and the conditions for its continuation. In short, Darwinism is nothing more than a hypothesis in the natural sciences.

But, as such, it is one with truly incalculable implications. When we say that the theory of selection sheds light on the origin of species, we mean that it at least partly explains the various differences that separate the diverse species of the same or different families, whether these differences are of morphological, psychological or any other nature. For it is by no means only within the organism's physiological life that the conditions for a natural selection exist. Also individual psychology and the phenomena of social life vary in different directions, of which some, those most favourable for the species, are preserved, while others are doomed to succumb. The theory of selection has thus been crucial to the development of three of the main branches of science: biology, or the science of the physiological phenomena; psychology, or the science of the inner life; and sociology, or the science of society.

Among the numerous biological phenomena that, by the utmost likelihood, have arisen under the influence of natural selection, I wish, as one of the most illuminating examples, to call attention to the colours of animals. Mr Wallace has shown in detail what a remarkable harmony prevails between the colours of the animals and the colour of its environment. Arctic animals are white, desert animals are sand coloured, those that live among grass and leaves are green, and nocturnal animals are dark. This law is not without exceptions, but it is very general. I only have to remind you of the polar bear, which is white around the year; of the arctic fox, the ermine, the hare and the snowcock, which turn white for the winter; about the lion, the antelope and the camel, which are the same colour as the fields of sand on which they live; about a number of tropical birds who are as green as the evergreen forests of the tropics; about the nocturnal bat and the moles with their dark colours. Other animals are spotted or striped, so that it is virtually impossible to discern them from the rocks, the thicket or the flowers, among which they live. All these facts can now be easily explained by the principles of natural selection. It is useful – yes, indubitably necessary – for many animals to be coloured in accordance with their environment, both because they, thanks to this, more easily avoid their enemies, and because they can more imperceptibly attack other animals, who serve as their nutrition. The individuals whose colour offers the best protection stay alive and procreate, the others die. To the same extent as the morphological characters, the phenomena of the inner life have been subjected to natural selection. The animals' instincts, so carefully adapted to the needs of the various species, offer the best evidence hereof. But I will now choose an example from the history of man. Our legislation features a prohibition against marriage between the nearest kin. And such a prohibition not only exists among us in Europe, but one can say that among all, even the most primitive, peoples; among a large amount of savages it indeed does not only apply to the closest relatives but even to all persons of the same tribe, and the violation thereof is sometimes punishable by death. Mr Herbert Spencer, Sir John Lubbock and many other anthropologists have tried to explain this custom in different ways. But none of these explanations can, according to me, stand up to scientific scrutiny. Mr Morgan and Sir Henry Maine believe that the prohibition against marriage between close kin stems from the gradually acquired knowledge of the harm in such liaisons. That they really bring about defects in the offspring has admittedly been disputed, but, as it appears to me, on false grounds. Several experiments conducted on animals, as well as several facts drawn from the field of anthropology, seem to demonstrate that offspring from very closely related parents are relatively weaker than others. Even if this probably is the case, we cannot believe that the prohibition of incest is founded on experience. Even if we could assume that the savage had sufficient abilities to observe the detrimental effects of incest, he would hardly have allowed such knowledge to bridle his passions. Even a civilized man, in the case that he suffers from a congenital susceptibility to disease that probably would be inherited by his offspring, will only rarely abstain from marriage for this reason. But even if we were to assume that man originally, by wise reckoning, avoided marriage with relatives, and that he has done so over many generations, so that the custom has gradually become law, we would not have got one step further. Custom and law can prevent our passions being expressed in actions, but it cannot smother their silent existence in our souls. The law can prohibit a brother from marrying his sister, but it cannot prohibit him from being ignited by carnal love of his sister. Yet, where is this love? It is not laws, nor customs, nor nurture that keeps the home pure of criminal liaisons, but an *instinct*, which under normal circumstances makes carnal love between close relatives a psychological impossibility. The abstinence from the pleasures of passion between parents and their children, as well as between siblings, Plato says, belong to the unwritten laws inherent in the human breast. And it is probable that this instinct developed through natural selection. We cannot give away to carnal love with those with whom since our earliest childhood we have lived in propinquity, to whom we generally stand as siblings, parents or children; since each such passion must have gone extinct in our species' childhood through the increased mortality to which offspring from closely related parents are subjected.

Marriage between close kin is to us something immoral. Why? Because there is an innate aversion toward sexual relationships between persons that since early childhood have lived together on a daily basis; in consequence of such liaisons going against our natural instincts. It seems to be the same with other acts that we label immoral.

Darwin has, in one of the most ingenious chapters he has ever written, tried to show how even the moral sense can be explained by the theory of selection. There is no doubt, he says, that if humans were to be raised under the exact same conditions as bees, our unmarried women should like worker bees consider it a holy duty to kill their brothers, that mothers would try to kill their fertile daughters, and that no one would even consider opposing this. But man owns an inborn instinct-like love and sympathy for his companions; even the most brutish savage is helpful and loyal to his tribal fellows. Now it is hardly doubtful, as I will soon show, that such social instincts have been acquired through natural selection; and that from these social urges a vast amount of the acts we call moral originate. But why, says Darwin, should a human feel that they should obey one instinct-like wish rather than another? Why does he feel bitter regret if he has followed the strong urge of self-preservation and not, for example, risked his life to save a fellow human, or why does he feel regret if he has stolen food to satisfy his hunger? Darwin has not overlooked this circumstance, on which the entire question of the moral sentiment depends. The social instincts are constantly present and persistent in those animals that live continuously together, but, on the other hand, the longing to satisfy hunger or a passion, for example, revenge, is in its essence of a passing character and can be satisfied completely for a short time. As man, as a consequence of the workings of his faculties, neither can avoid reflexive thought nor hinder the perpetual passing of past impressions and images through his soul with complete clarity, he will be driven to compare the weaker impressions of, for example, surmounted hunger or of satisfied vengeance, or of a danger he has avoided on the expense of others, with the instinct-like sympathy and benevolence to his fellowmen, which is still present and unremittingly active within him. He will then in his mind feel that a stronger instinct gave way for another, as it now appears, relatively weak one, and since a feeling of discontent always follows upon a not satisfied instinct – a feeling with which man, as well as every other animal, is endowed in order for his instincts to be obeyed – he will even now experience discontent with his actions. Discontent is, according to Darwin, what we call remorse, and remorse generally constitutes a criterion that shows that our moral sentiment has been offended. I am not saying that Darwin's explanation is the absolutely correct one; I have given this example to show the way in which psychology and even ethics must take the principles of natural selection into account.

Moral sentiment and the social instincts lead us directly to the area of sociology. Also here the theory of selection has played a crucial role. One can safely say that the progress of the human race, as well as the development of the forms of social life on the whole, are necessary consequences of natural selection through the struggle for existence. It seems very likely that the earliest traces of human society, marriage and family owe their existence to this powerful process. Among many mammals, interaction between the sexes is limited to the mere act of procreation, and if one by 'marriage' means a more or less permanent liaison that extends beyond that, then marriage is a fairly rare phenomenon among those animals. Among the monkeys, however, and in particular among the highest standing of them, it generally exists. The chimpanzee and the gorilla live in families consisting of a grown-up male, almost always one female and one or more young. And here, as well as everywhere where the sexes enter into more permanent relations, the father contributes to the sustenance of the family. The manlike apes build their nests in high trees, the female and the young spend their night in the nest while the male sits on a lower branch or at the roots of the tree, guarding against night-time attacks. Even among the primitive human races, the father has the task of protecting the family against enemies and distress. Now it is very likely that such instincts, as well as marriage itself, at least to a considerable extent, arose through natural selection. For it is an established truth, as far as I can understand, only explainable through the theory of selection, that the number of eggs laid and the number of offspring born of a species is proportional to the number of those who succumb prematurely. Among the higher apes and among primitive men, the father's help is quite certainly indispensable for the continuation of the species due to the small number of offspring and the extended duration that the young are more or less helpless. More than one offspring is seldom born at once and puberty sets in only after the fifteenth year. When man ceased to be an exclusively frugivorous animal, the father became an even more central member of the family than he had been before. The hunt always falls on the man's part, and a family consisting of only mother and child would surely succumb sooner or later. A careful authority on Australia's utterly primitive aborigines says that among some of them the father's assistance is considered so necessary that if he dies, the newborn child is also killed, as it no longer has anyone to support and protect it.

The origin of society in a broader sense must also, I believe, be explained in terms of the theory of selection. Mr. Herbert Spencer has pointed out the extent to which the animals' social or non-social way of living is dependent on the kind of food on which they live. If the food is of such a quality that it exists in abundance in one place, such as grass and the like, it is advantageous for the animal to live in herds; in the opposite case it is more advantageous to live alone or in pairs. The highest apes are usually found in families, and only at the time when fruits are ripe do they gather in greater crowds. Thus it seems that it is the quantity of food, not some inherent antisocial instinct, that conditions their solitary living. The same would probably have been the case with primitive man to the extent he was a frugivorous animal. And it is also likely that later, when man commenced living on animal food, he continued to live in families, or that the family at least was the core of society; for almost all meat-eating animals are non-social, surely because a social life would be positively harmful to them. Even in our days, the Australians, the Fuegians, and the Bushmen dissolve their tribes, consisting of a few families, when food is scarce. But since man is a relatively weak animal and short of natural weapons, it was useful for him to combine into crowds or tribes for protection against common enemies, as soon as there was food in larger quantities and owing to the invention of numerous weapons, tools or traps, for killing and catching his pray, as well as the art of making fire, which allows hard and woody roots to be made edible and poisonous roots and herbs made harmless. Thus, I believe that human society in its basic forms is a product of natural selection.

Despite the abundance of facts that can be explained by the theory of selection, it must be admitted that there remains much that has not been solved by this theory. But we have to remember that the explanatory range of the theory of selection has been shown to be wider and wider, day by day, and it is to be assumed that in future we will manage to subsume many more phenomena under it, phenomena the survival value of which is currently unknown to us. But, in no case may we believe that the great question of the origin of species and the different phenomena of life are solved at source. Natural selection is the ultimate effect; the elimination of the weaker is the immediate cause. But what is it that makes one individual of a species stronger and the other weaker, one more suited for certain existential circumstances and the other less, or that there are no two individuals who are exactly the same? Natural selection works under the condition that there is variation between organisms, but why is there variation amongst organisms? Gentlemen, here we face one of science's highest and most difficult problems, which future generations perhaps will manage to solve, but to us it is shrouded in darkness.

Lamarck assumed that the proximate cause of the continuous transformation of organic forms is adaptation, which consists in the continuous gradual change of the environment, causing a corresponding change in the activity of the organisms, and thereby also in their shapes. He attached the greatest importance to the influence of habit on the use and non-use of organs. He stated, for example, that the giraffe's long neck has developed through the continuous stretch of ditto to the high trees and through the strife to pick the leaves of their branches; when the giraffe mostly lives in dry areas, where only tree leaves provide nutrition, he was thus forced to stretch his neck. This habit was manifested through heredity in its descendants, whereby the giraffes that best stretched their necks left offspring with the longest necks. In this manner, according to Lamarck, the giraffe finally achieved this curiously long neck.

Darwin and his followers combined this theory about direct adaptation with the theory of selection, and assumed that the use and non-use of the organism indeed was not the only, though it was in any case an important, cause of the transformation and variation of forms. Professor Weismann has, however, directed attention to the fact that this theory, which looks so probable, rests on a hypothesis, the truthfulness of which has hardly has been questioned until recent years, though it is in fact is completely unsupported. It is undeniable that if the giraffe continuously stretches his neck, it will gradually grow a bit longer, and that if I exercise my muscles, they get bigger and stronger; but it is not certain that these advantages, achieved through exercise are heritable.

Whether the characteristics that a living creature has achieved during its own lifetime, that is, characteristics that are not congenital, can be passed on to her offspring, is nowadays the greatest issue in biology. Weismann answers this question in the negative. He explains that to this date there is no evidence of a well-known case of acquired characteristics that really have been passed on, and that as long as no such evidence exists we are of course not entitled to assume their heritability. It would be too large a digression to enter into the physiological explanation Weismann provides to the problem of heredity, and into how he refutes all evidence from experiments with inoculation of diseases carried out on animals. He tries to show that we only inherit such characteristics from our parents and ancestors that they possess as natural tendencies, while everything that the individual himself has acquired, everything added through external influences during his lifetime, dies with him. In this way, children of highly civilized parents, who have grown up completely isolated from human company, show no signs of articulated language. We know that wild and civilized peoples, since the beginning of time, have performed mutilations of all sorts on their bodies: pulling out teeth, chopping off fingers, piercing their ears and so on, but never as yet have these mutilations been inherited by their offspring. Further, we know that changes in the colour of the skin, depending on sun and air, are completely temporary, that the children of a tanned farmer or a weather-beaten sailor are born just as white as the children of a pale town dweller, and that the Moors, who twelve-hundred years ago moved to Africa, themselves are brown, but that their children are as white as Europeans and stay so all their life, unless they are exposed to burning sun of Africa. Such facts do not speak for the correctness of the theory of adaptation, but the question must thus far be considered moot. We should therefore not take for granted that the variations, through which natural selection gives rise to new species, that is, the variations that are inherited, are even to a small part the result of such external influences.

But there is no doubt that different individuals of one and the same species are born with different natural predispositions, and that these predispositions or characteristics are inherited by their descendants. For lack of a better term, Darwin called such variations 'spontaneous'. But on what do these spontaneous variations depend? Why are the individuals already at birth different from one another? Weismann believes that this is due to sexual or amphigonous reproduction, that is, that the individual arises through the combination of two elements, a male and a female element, and is thus a result of two different heritable tendencies, whose combinations with one another are the cause to these variations. This is, however, just a hypothesis, a guess. Finally, one may ask whether these combinations are unlimited – or whether they occur in one direction only; and if so, by which laws this direction is determined. All of these are questions into which the theory of selection does not venture.

For all that, naturalists by no means sit with their arms crossed in the belief that all of life's mysteries have been solved by Darwinism. It is important to investigate the positive causes of the origin and development of the phenomena of life, as natural selection needs material to select from. The social sciences are from this perspective standing one step above the sciences of physical life, because it has already for a long time been incumbent on the historian to find the direct causes to the course of human development. But even if the theory of selection is nowhere near capable of revealing all the mysteries of organic nature, no one will have reason to deny that the theory of natural selection has been one of man's most epoch-making flashes of genius.

Notes

1   Westermarck's paper was delivered to the Student Union on 9 April 1889 and transcribed and published as a text in the student union's proceedings: E., Westermarck. 1891. Selektionsteorin och dess betydelse för vetenskaperna om det fysiska, psykiska och sociala lifvet. *Almbum utgifvet av Nyländningar* 10:218–40.

2   In this translation, effort has been made to stay as close to the Swedish original as possible. Written as a speech, not as scientific prose, the aim has been to maintain the speech's rhetorical momentum. However, whenever necessary, priority has been given to what the translator has found to be a correct representation of the meaning of Westermarck's argument. On three occasions, Westermarck paraphrases comments on Darwin's work. The first is a comment on Professor Haughton's statement about the novelty and correctness of Darwin's theory. The second is his comment on Huxley's famous statement about the simplicity of the theory of selection. The third and last is a comment on Bishop Wilberforce's verdict on Darwin's theory. In all three cases, this translation mirrors Westermarck's Swedish formulations, and, therefore, these paraphrases do not necessarily appear as in their English original.

3   'All that was new in them was false, and what was true was old.' (Darwin 1958:122).

4   Westermarck uses the Swedish title *Om arternas uppkomst.*

5   'How extremely stupid of me not to have thought of that!' (Darwin 1887:197).

6   In his article, Bishop Wilberforce writes that Darwin's argument is 'loose' and 'unphilosophical' and that his 'unfounded speculations' are '[u]tterly dishonourable to all natural science' and 'most dishonourable and injourous to science' (Wilberforce 1860).

7   von Nägeli (1865) criticized Darwin's theory of selection in favour of his own theory of perfectibility (*Vervollkommnung*). von Nägeli argued that natural selection would only work on functional characteristics, while the theory of perfectibility would also explain morphological differences. However, this criticism is based on the unwarranted distinction of function and morphology and was later dismissed by Darwin in later editions of *The Origin of Species*.

References

Darwin, C. 1958. *The Autobiography of Charles Darwin*. London: Collins.

Darwin, F. 1887. *The Life and Letters of Charles Darwin Including an Autobiographical Chapter* (vol. 2). London: John Murray.

Von Nägeli, C.W. 1865. *Entstehung und Begriff der Naturhistorischen Art*. Munich: Königl. Akademia.

Sanderson, S.K. 2006. Reforming theoretical work in sociology: a brief reply to my critics. *Perspectives: ASA Theory Section Newsletter* 28(3):9–11.

Weismann, A. 1889. *Essays Upon Heredity* (vols 1 and 2). Oxford: Clarendon Press.

Weismann, A. 1893. *The Germ-Plasm: A Theory of Heredity*. London: Charles Scribner's Sons.

Westermarck, E. 1891. Selektionsteorin och dess betydelse för vetenskaperna om det fysiska, psykiska och sociala lifvet. *Album utgifvet av Nyländningar* 10:218–40.

Westermarck, E. 1891. *The History of Human Marriage*. London: Macmillan.

Wilberforce, S. 1860. [Review of] On the Origin of Species. *Quarterly Review*: 225–64.

11

Sociology as a university study[1]

Professor Edward Westermarck's inaugural lecture

as Martin White Professor in Sociology (1908)

Mr. Vice-Chancellor, ladies and gentlemen,

Some days ago I heard a remark which I would like to repeat on this occasion, as I think it may interest you. A professor of an American university, who has been staying in England for some time, said that nothing in this country had impressed him so much as the exceedingly keen interest at present taken in sociology. If the same professor had visited England some four or five years ago he would perhaps have been equally struck by the almost complete absence of any traces of such interest. We all know that the change which has come about is in the first place due to the enthusiasm of Mr. Martin White, which has led to the establishment of chairs in sociology at the University of London, and, in conjunction with the incessant energy and fervour of Mr. Branford, to the formation of the Sociological Society. But a question which calls for an answer is : Why has sociology had to wait so long for a place in English universities ? To this problem I shall at first devote a few minutes' consideration.

The slow recognition of sociology as a university study is by no means peculiar to England; we meet with exactly the same case in continental countries. The main reason for it must therefore be sought in circumstances which are independent of any national characteristics. It simply lies in the nature of sociology itself. Sociology is a young science, because it is a difficult science. The object of every science is not only to describe, but to explain the facts with which it is concerned; and the object of sociology is to explain the social phenomena, to find their causes, to show how and why they have come into existence. Now, a social phenomenon is often exceedingly complex, and its causes are often so hidden that they can be detected only with the greatest difficulty or very incompletely. And these impediments in the way of sociology, which are due to the nature of its facts, are much increased by the circumstance that the interpretation of those facts is extremely apt to be influenced by the personal feelings of the inquirer. The sociologist occupies a quite peculiar position in respect to the facts with which he deals: he has to investigate phenomena many of which very vividly affect his sentiments, arousing either sympathy or antipathy, either approval or indignation. The sociologist must, so far as possible, cut himself off in thought from his relationships of race, country, and citizenship; must get rid of those interests, likings, prejudices, and superstitions which have been generated in him by the life of his own society and his own time; must look on the changes which social phenomena have undergone and are undergoing, without reference to nationality, or creed, or personal welfare; and all this, as Herbert Spencer truly remarks in his admirable book on *The Study of Sociology*, is what the average man cannot do at all, and what the exceptional man can do very imperfectly.

These difficulties will always be serious obstacles in the way of sociological research. They will, I fear, forever prevent sociology, or at least various branches of it, from attaining the same degree of exactness as is attained by most other sciences. Even the most careful, impartial, and unprejudiced student of social phenomena will very often have to be content with hypotheses and more or less doubtful presumptions instead of well established truths. Yet it must be admitted that hypotheses are legitimate in every science, and that exactness is, after all, a question of degree. By applying to the data of social life a strictly scientific method, investigators of such data have at last raised the study of them to such a level that sociology can justly claim a place in the list of sciences side by side with biology and psychology. But it can be no matter of surprise that the development of this science has been so late and slow. Nor is it difficult to explain the opposition which sociology has aroused, and still arouses, in certain quarters.

Whatever may be said about Auguste Comte's law of the three stages in reference to other sciences, it certainly holds true of the study of social phenomena. This study has passed both through a theological and a metaphysical stage. Genesis was once regarded as the sole authority for primitive society. The metaphysical stage, again, is typically represented by what the Germans call *Naturrecht*, by the idea that there are 'natural rights' inherent in human beings, and that their social relationships are governed by certain principles of 'natural law'. By entering into the third or positive stage, the study of social facts finally rose to the modern science of sociology, which is based neither on authority nor on any metaphysical principle, but on the data of our experience alone.

This development from one stage into another has naturally been accompanied by resistance. But in the present day the existence of an independent science of sociology is hardly denied either by theologians or metaphysicians, even though they claim that there *are* social phenomena which cannot be solved without the aid of either theology or metaphysics. The opposition to sociology rather comes from another quarter. It is not infrequently looked upon with suspicion, or barely veiled contempt, by students of other sciences. It is considered too vague, too constructive, too full of far-reaching but unproved generalisations, to deserve the name of science in the proper sense of the term. Look into one of those books called the 'Outlines of Sociology', or the 'Principles of Sociology', or the 'Elements of Sociology', of which there is at present a great abundance – look into one of these books, and you will find an astonishing amount of broad generalisations often enough stated in very positive terms, but combined with an even more astonishing absence of facts. If this is what is meant by sociology, it is said, then sociology can certainly not be regarded as a science in the same sense as physics, or chemistry, or physiology, or psychology. Before laws are formulated or generalisations made, there must be a careful examination of details – this is the rule in every science. But the students of modern sociology seem to think that they can dispense with the troublesome process of minute induction, and are consequently building castles in the air.

For my own part, I must confess that I consider these objections to contain a great deal of truth. If by sociology is meant the widest generalisations of social facts and nothing else, its pretensions to be a science are as yet premature. But I see no reason whatever why the term sociology should be reserved for such generalisations. They may or may not be the ultimate aim of sociology, but before any such aim can be attained the social phenomena must be studied in detail. And this study of details is a part of sociology itself, not only a preparation for it. In my opinion, sociology is not merely the philosophy of the social sciences, but these various sciences form branches of sociology. Sociology is the science of social phenomena in the widest sense of the word. What we want at present is not textbooks on sociology as a whole, but sociological monographs. Anyone who takes up the study of sociology must not expect to come to an exhibition, where every article may be had ready and finished. On the contrary, he will find that he has entered a workshop, where everything is in the making – and he will have to take part in the work.

If we define sociology as the science of social phenomena, we must admit that some branches of this science have now for a considerable time had their place in both British and continental universities – for instance, economics and the history of law. But at the same time, the introduction of the subject and name of sociology into the university curriculum implies a novelty of the highest importance; for there are various branches of sociology which have previously had no place in it: among others, the comparative study of social institutions and social anthropology. And the very name of sociology is a great gain, first, because it expressly co-ordinates phenomena which intrinsically form parts of one and the same group, and, secondly, because it emphasises the fact that these phenomena should be made subject to a thoroughly scientific treatment.

The term 'sociology' itself has also met with much opposition, which in some measure explains the long delay in establishing the first chairs in sociology. This term had the disadvantage of being introduced into the English language by Herbert Spencer, who was connected with no university, and whose philosophy was not accepted in the academic circles of his own country. If it had originated in the brain of some German philosopher, it would long ago have become a catchword in the older universities, and some insight into its mysteries would have become, the hallmark of a well-educated gentleman. As it then happened, it gave offence to purists, as being a word half Latin, half Greek; and it was also said that if there could be such a word at all, it would mean not the science of social facts but the science of partnerships or alliances, 'socius' denoting a partner or 'ally'. This opposition has been met by the argument that 'sociology' is not the only word against which similar objections might be raised. Many other words have been formed from heterogeneous roots, or mean something else than what the old Romans would have meant by them. Thus, the word 'suicidium', or suicide, would, if it had existed at all in classical Latin, have meant not self-murder, but the killing of pigs. Finally, it has been argued that sociology suggests socialism, and in fact sociology and socialism are even now frequently confounded with one another. Such a confusion is quite human. I am told that the Sultan of Turkey has prohibited the importation of dynamos into his country, because he is afraid of dynamite.

What benefits, then, may we expect from the study of sociology at the universities? In answering this question I shall restrict myself to the comparative study of social institutions and social anthropology, not because I underrate the importance of other branches of sociology, but because these are most closely connected with my own teaching. As to the purely scientific value of these studies I shall say nothing. It is obvious that if sociology is studied in the universities there will be an increasing number of professional sociologists, and sociology will consequently make a more rapid progress. But this argument would carry no weight with persons – and there are many such persons – who are doubtful whether sociology itself is good for anything, or simply a fad. I think we have every reason to believe that a study of the new branches of sociology which have been introduced into this university should prove very useful to certain classes of people, as also to the community at large. Legislators and lawyers ought certainly to profit by a comparative study of social institutions. Such a study must help to broaden and deepen their views on the subjects of their professions. It shows what a deep foundation the general principles of law have in human nature; how laws should differ in different cases, so as to suit the social environment; how laws, as a matter of fact, have an inveterate tendency to survive the conditions under which they were established, and how all kinds of sophistical arguments are often brought in to support laws that owe their origin to circumstances and ideas which have long ceased to prevail. By tracing a law to its ultimate source it may be found that it really has no longer any right to exist, and therefore should be repealed or altered; and nobody who has had the slightest experience in the matter can deny that the comparative study of legal institutions often throws entirely fresh light upon the history of laws which are still in force. It may be shown that there are laws which have their roots in sheer superstition or in primitive thoughtlessness, and yet continue to figure in the statute-book. On the other hand, the comparative study may also give direct hints to the legislator how the laws of his country should be improved. In spite of our own notorious excellence, we may even have to learn a few things from the customs of savages. For instance, when the suggestion has been made that the law should step in and prevent unfit individuals from contracting marriage, the objection has at once been raised that any such measure would be impracticable. Now we find that many savages have tried the experiment and succeeded. Mr. Im Thurn tells us that among the wild Indians of Guiana a man before he is allowed to choose a wife must prove that he can do a man's work and is able to support himself and his family. In various Bechuana and Kaffir tribes, according to Livingstone, the youth is prohibited from marrying until he has killed a rhinoceros. Among the Dyaks of Borneo no one can marry unless he has in his possession a certain number of human skulls. Among the Arabs of Upper Egypt the man must undergo an ordeal of whipping by the relatives of his bride, in order to test his courage; and if he wishes to be considered worth having, he must receive the chastisement, which is sometimes exceedingly severe, with an expression of enjoyment. I do not say that these particular methods are worthy of slavish imitation. But the principle underlying them is certainly excellent; and especially the fact that they are recognised and enforced by custom, shows that it has been quite possible among many peoples to prohibit certain unfit individuals from marrying. The question would naturally arise, whether, after all, something of the same kind might not be possible among ourselves.

Another class of persons to whom the comparative study of social institutions, and especially social anthropology, should be most useful, are colonial officials and, in general, everybody who has anything at all to do with races different from his own. I hope that you will not consider the remark I am going to make inappropriate, though it comes from a foreigner; for I have never felt myself as a foreigner in this country. I cannot help saying that it seems to me a perfect riddle how it is that no knowledge whatever of the native customs and ideas of non-European peoples is required of those who go out to rule over such peoples. The only solution I can possibly imagine is that colonial officials are supposed to acquire the necessary knowledge after they have settled down on the spot. But no error could be greater than this. It is no exaggeration to say that the large majority never learn to understand the natives. A few, no doubt, take an interest in their customs, and even write books on them; but these very books only too often show what an irreparable loss it was that their authors should have gone out to the colonies without having a previous training for their work. It is not necessary for the purpose to acquire a very comprehensive knowledge of social anthropology; the chief thing is that the interest should be stimulated, that attention should be drawn to subjects which otherwise would probably escape the notice of the European resident, and that he should be informed of the literature which might be useful to him. I cannot conceive how anybody can go to live among uncivilised or semi-civilised peoples without having in his portmanteau books like Prof. Tylor's *Primitive Culture*, and Prof. Frazer's *Golden Bough*. Now I am not merely thinking of the benefits which sociology would derive from an increased number of well-trained field-anthropologists; I am here in the first place concerned with the value which sociological studies would have for the ordinary work a colonial official has to perform, and for his intercourse with the natives. Ignorance has always been the main cause of the troubles which have followed upon the contact between different races. The Indian mutiny might in all probability have been prevented by a little greater insight into native ideas and beliefs; and the same may be said of many of those deplorable events which in recent years have taken place in Morocco. I have sometimes been simply amazed, not only by the arrogance, but by the criminal ignorance with which European residents in that country have treated its native inhabitants. I am convinced that in our dealings with non-European races some sociological knowledge, well applied, would generally be a more satisfactory weapon than gunpowder. It would be more humane – and cheaper too.

But even to the ordinary citizen sociology ought to commend itself as a study well worth his while. You can hardly be said to have a thorough knowledge of the society or country in which you live, unless you are in a position to compare it with other societies or other countries. Ignorance is particularly apt to make us over-estimate our own peculiarities, and this hardly makes for progress. Sociology reveals to us the interesting fact that people generally consider their own nation or tribe to be the best, however miserable and uncultured it really may be. In their intercourse with white men, savages have often with astonishment noticed the arrogant air of superiority adopted by the latter; in their own opinion they are themselves vastly superior to the whites. According to Eskimo beliefs, the first man, though made by the Great Being, was a failure, and was consequently cast aside and called *kob-lu-na*, which means 'white man', but a second attempt of the Great Being resulted in the formation of a perfect man, and he was called *in-nu*, the name which the Eskimo give to themselves. Australian natives, on being asked to work, have often replied, 'White fellow works, not black fellow; black fellow gentleman.' When anything foolish is done the Chippewa Indians use an expression which means, 'As stupid as a white man.' The Japanese imitate our inventions and utilise our knowledge, but have no admiration for our civilisation as a whole or our views of life. Muhammedans envy us our weapons of destruction, but in their hearts they regard us as their inferiors. When we carefully scrutinise what other people think of us, we come to the somewhat disappointing but not altogether unwholesome conclusion, that the belief in the extreme superiority of our Western civilisation really only exists in the Western mind itself.

Ladies and gentlemen, I am sorry that the shortness of the time at my disposal has enabled me to give only a very fragmentary sketch of the practical importance of the study of sociology. Should anybody among you still entertain doubts as to its usefulness, I must humbly invite him or her to come and attend the lectures on the subject which are delivered at this school, whether he or she be an ordinary citizen, a colonial official, or a future member of Parliament.

Notes

1   From *Inauguration of the Martin White Professorships of Sociology. December 17, 1907. Addresses by L.T. Hobhouse on "The Roots of Modern Sociology" and by Professor E.A. Westermarck on "Sociology as a University Study"*. London: John Murray for the University of London, 1908.

12

Survival in ritual

Delivered to the International Congress of Ethnological and Anthropological Sciences (1934)

Preliminary note

The chapter by Westermarck below is found in typescript in the RAI archives, with corrections by Westermarck himself. The transcript below incorporates his corrections, which are mainly minor deletions or clarifications. It was written by him for the International Congress of Ethnological and Anthropological Sciences, which was organized by the RAI and held at University College London in 1934. This congress had been planned already before the First World War by Marett, but owing to the conflict had to be postponed. Marett handed over the project after the war to Myres, an Oxford classicist and anthropologist, who became President of the RAI. Myres attempted with great vigour to put together a truly international programme. After many complications, the Congress finally was held, and drew together a significant range of anthropologists from around the world. The 'Congress' became the IUAES, the International Union of Anthropological and Ethnological Sciences, which still exists to this day.

In organizing the conference, Myres was influenced by his being General Secretary to the British Association for the Advancement of Science (BAAS). His publication of the conference volume, grandly titled, presumably to stress its international credentials, *Congres International des Sciences Anthropologiques et Ethnologique. Compte-rendu de la premiere Session, Londres, 1934, Londres: Institut Royal d'Anthropologie* mirrors the BAAS very closely in its format. Likewise, just as at the BAAS, Myres divided the Congress into academic 'sections'. Westermarck spoke in Section F, Sociology.

Seligman was the chair of the section, Firth its secretary. Westermarck's paper came after Evans-Pritchard speaking on 'What is ritual' and Hocart on

'The purpose of ritual', and before Levy-Bruhl on 'Ancestor Worship'. Clearly, Westermarck is still at the heart of anthropological debate, even as he comes toward the end of his career. His paper to the congress is not published in the conference book, but the abstract is (page 269). It reads as follows:

The object of this paper is to warn against interpreting without sufficient reason existing rites as survivals of something else in the past. The tendency to do so is instanced by the hypotheses of an early stage of promiscuity or of group-marriage (recently revived by Dr Briffault), and by Freud's theory of the Oedipus complex. In support of this theory various customs and rites are interpreted as vestiges of former incest; the fierce laws against it are regarded as evidence of a general incest desire; the repression of the original incestuous tendencies are accounted for by a primeval parricide followed by remorse and 'subsequent obedience' on the part of the guilty sons. Totemism is supposed to be a particularly important survival of that act, the totem animal being said to be a father substitute and the ritual killing of it to symbolise the killing of the father. This conclusion – like some others mentioned in the paper – is a transgression of the very obvious rule, often transgressed, that it must not be interpreted as a survival of something of which it cannot be a survival. Another fundamental rule, often transgressed, is that it must not be interpreted as a survival of something which is not known to have existed, or the earlier existence of which may not be assumed, or does not seem probable, for some other reason. There are other cases for which no general rules can be laid down. Although the present wants or beliefs of the people seem to afford a satisfactory explanation of a rite, it may nevertheless be a survival; instances of this are afforded by the marriage ritual. But though in this ritual new motives have often been substituted for old ones, the large bulk of marriage rites has undoubtedly originated in magical ideas intimately connected with the welfare of individuals, families, or whole communities; while their importance as means of studying earlier forms of marriage has been grossly exaggerated.

D.S.

Survival in ritual

In a paper to the Sociological Society Dr. Rivers described a social survival as a custom the nature of which cannot be explained by its present utility but only becomes intelligible through its past history.[1] This can be accepted as a definition on the presumption that utility means supposed utility, since a custom can be quite intelligible through existing conditions if it is merely regarded as useful by those who practice it. Ritual, again, I take to be an established practice the essence of which lies in its formal character, irrespective of either motive or purpose. A ritual may thus be a social survival;

but on the other hand it may also be a practice that can be explained by its present supposed utility.

That rituals very frequently consist of social survivals is so generally recognised that there is no need to emphasise it. The object of my paper is, on the contrary, to warn against interpreting without sufficient reason existing rites as vestiges of something else in the past. The tendency to do so was rampant towards the end of the last century, in those days when I first took up Anthropology for the guidance of my study of the early history of marriage. Many leading anthropologists then believed that mankind originally lived in a state of promiscuity, where individual marriage did not exist but all the men in a horde or tribe had indiscriminately access to all the women; and this hypothesis was principally based in the interpretation of various customs as survivals of such a state. It subsequently lost much of its earlier popularity, and the theory of group-marriage, according to which all the men of one clan or intermarrying group are married to all the women of another clan or intermarrying group, became in certain quarters its residuary legatee, or group-marriage was proclaimed the earliest form of marriage out of which the others have gradually developed; and here again the chief evidence was derived from the interpretation of certain customs as survivals. A detailed examination of all those customs which have been represented as survivals of promiscuity or of group-marriage has convinced me that they can be quite satisfactory explained by existing conditions; whereas no authentic case of either promiscuity or of marriage group-marriage of the type in question has been found anywhere. Dr. Briffault, the latest exponent of the group-marriage theory, says that 'in those societies which have preserved their primitive organisation in clans or intermarrying groups, recognised freedom of access between any male of the one group and any female of the other is, in fact, the rule rather than the exception'.[2] In a book published this summer I have criticised his evidence, and come to the conclusion that such unlimited freedom has not been proved to exist even among a single people.[3] Individual marriage is a universal institution in mankind, and it is the more likely to have prevailed among primitive men as the family consisting of male, female or females, and young exists among the anthropoid apes[4] and apparently among all monkeys.[5]

The interpretation of customs or rites as survivals play a very prominent part in Freud's theory of the Oedipus complex, according to which every heterosexual person cherishes in the unconscious part of his or her mind a desire for sexual intimacy with the parent of the opposite sex, accompanied by jealousy towards the parent of the same sex and by the wish to remove him or her by death. This theory owes its origin to analytic investigation of adults who have become neurotics, every one of them said to be himself an Oedipus. But while the Oedipus complex is represented as 'the nuclear complex of the neuroses', it is also said to be a universal human characteristic.[6] This statement requires, of course, a great deal of confirmation from other sources than psycho-analysis. Various customs are made out to be the vestiges of the occurrence of incest in the past, such as the brother and sister marriage in some reigning families,[7] the levirate, the sororate,[8] group-marriage,[9] and the so-called jus primate noctis, the defloration of a woman being said to be performed originally by her father.[10] And to the evidence from anthropology psycho-analysis has added facts from mythology, arguing that when incest was repressed among men, the incest wishes found a vent in the fanciful creations of myth and legends.[11] In my recent book *Three Essays on Sex and Marriage* I have examined the evidential value of the supposed survivals of an original incest desire and found it to be none.[12] They are perfectly explicable without the assumption that there was any such desire; while the psycho-analytic foundation for this assumption consists in a certain number of Freudian findings, the accuracy of which has even been disputed by psycho-analysis of other schools, Adler's[13] and Jung's.[14]

In his discussion of the repression of the original incestuous tendencies Freud has again in a large measure relied on customs as social survivals. He took up the conjecture made by Darwin and further developed by Atkinson, to the effect that man lived originally in small family groups like the gorilla, consisting of an adult male, a number of wives, and immature individuals. When the younger males became old enough to evoke the father's jealousy they were driven off by him.[15] This is the starting point of Freud's theory of the origin of exogamy; what then follows is his invention. One day the expelled brothers joined forces, slew and ate the father. But though the brothers hated the father who stood in the way of their sexual demands and their desire for power, they also loved and admired him. Hence, after they had satisfied their hate by his removal their suppressed tender impulses asserted themselves in the form of remorse; and 'in the psychic situation of subsequent obedience, they renounced the fruits of their deed by denying themselves the liberated women'.[16] Now the hypothesis of a primeval parricide due to jealousy and hate is not substantiated by anything we know about either apes or savages. The many reports we have of solitary old male gorillas and chimpanzees[17] do not support the assumption of patricidal tendencies among those apes; and in the ethnological literature I have found extremely few instances of parricide, except in quite particular circumstances that have led to the killing of parents of either sex – when they are worn out with age or disease or otherwise become a burden to the tribe.[18] But the murder of the primeval father is alleged to have left vestiges in various customs and institutions, bearing testimony to its reality in the past.

Foremost among these is totemism. Freud maintains that the totem animal was a father substitute, and that the ritual killing of it symbolizes the killing of the father. But his assumption that the totems were originally only animals[19] is a mere conjecture, and the ritual killing of the totem animal is no general characteristics of totemism. Freud falls back upon Robertson Smith's theory of a totem sacrament, according to which the totem animal, whose killing at ordinary times was strictly forbidden, was on certain occasions solemnly killed by the clan to furnish a mystic meal by which the members of the clan strengthened their identification with the totem and with each other.[20] The author of this theory, however, could not adduce a single positive instance of such a sacrament in support of it.[21] Yet Freud maintains that in the *intichiuma* ceremonies of some Central Australian tribes a trait has been observed which fits in excellently with the assumptions of Robertson Smith.[22] But, as a matter of fact, their object differs radically from that of the sacramental meal postulated by the latter. Those natives eat a little of their totem as a magical ceremony intended to multiply the species in order to increase the food supply for other totemic groups;[23] hence their feast gives no support whatever to Freud's supposition that it is 'the repetition and commemoration' of the sons' killing and devouring of their father – that 'memorable, criminal act with which so many things began, social organisation, moral restrictions, and religion'.[24] Like Robertson Smith, Freud regards totemism as the earliest form of religions and the killing and eating by the clan of its totem animal as he prototype of the sacrifice of the alter, which was an essential part of every ancient cult.[25]

A custom or rite must not, of course, be interpreted as a survival of something of which it cannot be a survival. Yet this simple rule if often transgressed. Circumcision as an initiation rite, for example, has been represented by psycho-analysis as a survival of and substitute for an earlier act of castration;[26] which is absurd, considering that castration could have at most have taken place only in rare cases, while initiation rites, where they occur, are general. Or it has been said to serve the purpose of punishing and preventing incest. [27] But its generality as an initiation rite also makes it impossible to look upon it as a punishment, unless the offence too was general; and as a means of preventing incest it would of course be useless. It cannot prevent it by inspiring fear, when it is performed anyhow; nor does it produce physical incapacity to perform the forbidden act. Again, Dr. Briffault regards the custom of offering a wife to a guest – which is in fact only an incident of general rule of hospitality[28] – as a survival of group-marriage between two clans; he says 'we may be as certain as we can be of any inference in social anthropology that wherever it is observed clan-brotherhood is, or was formerly, considered to imply sexual communism, for it is by assimilation to a clan-brother that the guest is treated as he is.'[29] If this were true all inferences in social anthropology would be worthless. The guest is not assimilated to a clan-brother, hospitality does not imply that he is 'necessarily to be regarded and treated as a tribal brother'. It is probably always limited by time – often to three days, sometimes even to a day and a night. And while the custom of offering one's wife to a guest is widespread, it is open to considerable doubt whether there is any tribe in which all one's clan-brothers enjoy a similar privilege. Dr. Briffault has not told us how it is that sexual communism has survived in the case of a guest, although it has died out in the case of clan-brothers.

Another fundamental rule is that a custom or rite must not be interpreted as a survival of something which is not known to have existed or the earlier existence of which may not be assumed, or at least seems probable, for some other reason. This rule has been transgressed by those who have think they have discovered survivals of an ancient state of promiscuity of group-marriage between clans or of a general incest-desire. Psycho-analysts consider that such a desire is proved by the extraordinarily fierce laws which have been devised in the most varied parts of the world with the object of preventing incest.[30] They argue that the law only forbids men to do what their instincts incline them to do, and that we may accordingly safely assume that when crimes are forbidden by law there is a natural instinct in favour of their commission. This argument, however, implies a curious misconception of the origin and nature of legal prohibitions. Of course, nobody would ever have dreamt of making a prohibitory law if the idea of its transgression had not presented itself to his mind. When Solon, the Athenian legislator, was asked why he had specified no punishment for one who had murdered a father, he replied that he supposed it could not occur to anybody to commit such a crime; that wise man was not acquainted with the Oedipus complex. But though the prohibition of a certain act presupposes that it is considered possible, that it has occurred and is thought more or less likely to occur again, it does not imply that there is a widespread natural propensity to do it. Nor does the rigour of the law indicate the strength of the temptation to transgress it. Do the severe laws against bestiality prove that a large number of men have a strong natural inclination to copulate with animals? How then, could the severe laws against incest prove that there is or has been a general and strong tendency to incest? Customs and laws express the general feelings of the community and punish acts that shock them; but they do not tell us whether the inclination to commit the forbidden act is felt by many or by few.

I have so far spoken of cases in which I consider the interpretation of customs or rites as survivals to be illegitimate. But there are other cases for which no general rules can be laid down. Although a custom or rite which is not explicable by the present wants or beliefs of the people may be claimed as a survival, there may, of course, be a doubt as to the particular fact of which it is a survival. Moreover, although the present wants or beliefs of the people seem to afford a satisfactory explanation of a rite, it may nevertheless be a survival. I shall illustrate this by one of the most common marriage rites, that of throwing some kind of cereals or fruit on the bride or on the bridal pair or on the bridegroom separately or even on the wedding company, which has been found to prevail from India, Indo-China and the Indian Archipelago in the East, to the Atlantic Ocean in the West. In some cases the people who practice rites of this kind say that they are intended to promote fecundity, while in other cases they regard them as means of ensuring prosperity as well as offspring, or prosperity or abundance only. In Morocco I found yet other beliefs connected with them, though never the idea of ensuring fertility. The raisins, figs, or dates which are thrown over the bride are said to make everything sweet, or to make the bride sweet to the bridegroom's family, or to avert the evil eye from her; and the wheat, flower or other things which she throws over her head are represented as a means by which she rids herself of evil influences. In other countries, also, customs of this sort are not infrequently regarded as prophylactics or means of purification. Considering how many different explanations of them are given by the people practising them, even in the same country, there can be no doubt that, in certain cases at least, their real origin has been forgotten and a new interpretation substituted for the idea from which they arose. But on the other hand we should be on our guard against supposition, only too common in Anthropology, that similar ceremonies necessarily have their roots in similar ideas, even though practised by different peoples. Objects like corn and dried fruit may certainly be used for a variety of purposes, and there is no justification for the assumption made by several anthropologists, that the customs of throwing them at weddings, where ever it is found, originated in a rite the exclusive object of which was to promote fecundity; to ensure prosperity and abundance and to avert evil may have been equally primitive motives for it. I think it may be said in general that the more widespread a pretended motive is, the greater are the chances that it is a primitive motive. Yet certainty can hardly be expected.

While there is no doubt that in the marriage ritual new motives have often been substituted for old ones, it seems to me quite certain that the large bulk of marriage rites have sprung from magical ideas intimately connected with welfare of individuals, families or whole communities, and that their importance as means of studying earlier forms or marriage or relations between the sexes has been greatly exaggerated. We can only smile at the suggestions that the use of rings at weddings, the throwing of a slipper after the departing of the bride and bridegroom, or our honeymoon, are survivals of marriage by capture; or that the bride's dance with all the male guests at the wedding, and the kiss she bestows on them, hint at the former prevalence of group-marriage among ancestors of the European nations. If the right of kissing, or dancing with, the bride is to be interpreted as the survival of an earlier right of having sexual intercourse with her, what conclusions are to be drawn from the Swedish and Danish custom which prescribes that the officiating clergyman shall have the first dance with the bride, and from the Scottish parson's right to the first kiss?

Notes

1   W.H.R. Rivers 'Survival in Sociology', in *Sociological Review* vi (London 1913), p. 295

2   R. Briffault, *The Mothers*, i. (London 1927), p. 608 seq.

3   *Three Essays on Sex and Marriage* (London, 1934), p. 277 seq.

4   Ibid., p. 177 seqq.

5   S. Zuckerman, *The Social Life of Monkeys and Apes* (London, 1932), pp. 147, 212, 213, 314, seq.; F. Doflein, *Das Tier als Glied das Naturganzen* (Leipzig & Berlin, 1914), pp. 692, 694.

6   S. Freud, *Drei Abhandlungen zur Sexualtheorie* (Leipzig & Wein, 1926), p. 101 seq. n.2.

7   O. Rank, *Das Inzest-Motiv in Dichtung und Sage* (Leipzig & Wein, 1926), p. 391; J.C. Flügel, *The Psycho-Analytic Study of the Family* (London, 1929), pp. 91, 195.

8   Flügel, op. cit. pp. 93, 195.

9   Ibid. pp. 99, 195. Rank, op. cit. pp. 342, 408 seqq.

10 A.J. Storfer, Zur Sonderstellung des Vatermordes (Schriften zur angewandten Seelenkunde, xii [Leipzig & Wein, 1911]), p. 17; Freud, *Das Tabu der Virginität* (in *Gesammelte Schriften*, v. [Leipzig, Wein Zürich, 1924]), p. 225 seq.; Rank, op. cit. p. 341 seqq.; Flügel, op. cit. pp. 143, 195.

11 Rank, op. cit. pp. 391, 416 seqq.

12 *Three Essays on Sex and Marriage*, p. 43 seqq.

13 A. Adler, *The Practice and Theory of Individual Psychology* (London, 1924), p. vi.

14 C.G. Jung, *Psychology of the Unconscious* (London, 1916), p. 63; idem, *Collected Papers on Analytical Psychology* (London, 1917), p. 231.

15 Freud, *Totem und Tabu* (in *Gasammelte Schriften*, x. [1924]), p. 152 seq.

16 Ibid. p. 171 seqq.

17 See *Three Essays on Sex and Marriage*, pp. 90, 91, 185 seqq.

18 See my book *The Origin and Development of the Moral Ideas*, i. (London, 1912), p. 386 seqq.

19 Freud, *Totem und Tabu*, p. 130.

20 Ibid. p. 161 seqq.

21 Cf. J.G. Frazer, *Totemism and Exogamy*, iv. (London, 1910) p. 230 seq.

22 Freud, *Totem und Tabu*, p. 169.

23 B. Spencer and F.J. Gillen, *The Native Tribes of Central Australia* (London, 1889), ch. vi; *idem*, *The Northern Tribes of Central Australia* (London, 1904), ch. ix. seq.

24   Freud, *Totem und Tabu*, p. 172.

25   Ibid. p. 175.

26   Rank, op. cit. p. 308

27   Th. Reik, *Ritual* (London, 1931), pp. 105, 106, 116, 124; M. Zeller, *Die Knabenweihen* (Bern, 1923), p. 135; Flügel, op. cit. p. 85.

28   See my book, *The Origin and Development of the Moral Ideas*, i, 581 seqq.

29   Briffault, op. cit. i. 635 seqq.

30   Freud, *Totem und Tabu*, p. 150; *idem, Vorlesungen zur Einführung in die Psychoanalse (Gesammelte Schriften,* vii, [1924]), p. 347. Flügel, op. cit. pp. 35, 195, 200, 206 seq; Rank, op. cit. p. 405; E. Jones, 'Psycho-Analysis and Anthropology', in *Journal of the Royal Anthropological Institute,* liv (1924), p. 54 seq.

13

Methods in social anthropology

Huxley Memorial Lecture (1936)

The kind invitation to deliver this lecture in memory of Thomas Henry Huxley, with which the Royal Anthropological Institute has honoured me, is in a peculiar way calculated to call to my mind the first steps I ventured to take in Social Anthropology nearly fifty years ago. They were concerned with the origin of marriage. It was then very generally believed by scholars that primitive man lived in a state of promiscuity, where individual marriage did not exist, where all the men in a horde or tribe had indiscriminately access to all the women, and where the children born of these unions belonged to the community at large. I commenced my work as a faithful adherent of that hypothesis, and tried to discover fresh evidence of it in customs that I thought might be interpreted as survivals from a time when individual marriage did not exist. But I had not proceeded far when I found that I was on the wrong track. I became acquainted with the doctrine of organic evolution, and drew the conclusion that the social habits of the anthropoids might throw some light on those of primitive man.

The material in hand was scanty. As regards the gorilla and chimpanzee, however, the authorities attested unanimously the prevalence of the family consisting of parents and offspring among them. According to one informant it also existed with the orangutan, whereas others had come across only solitary old males or females with young or, like Wallace, sometimes females and at other times males accompanied by half-grown young. Nowadays the social life of the anthropoids is much better known. It has been amply proved that with the gorilla and chimpanzee the social unit is the family, although several families may associate and constitute a band or herd.[1] In the forests of Sumatra, Volz and Munnecke have found orangutans living in families consisting of one grown-up male, one adult female, and one, two, or three young ones;[2] and the monogamous family has also been found to be the rule among the gibbons.[3] Considering that the family is universal in mankind, among the lowest savages as well as among the most civilised races, an evolutionist who maintains, on the basis of morphological resemblances, that man and ape have evolved from a common type, is therefore naturally inclined to believe that it existed among primitive man as well.

But there were other circumstances besides the common descent that seemed to me to give support to this belief. If the question is raised why the family has come into existence, why male and female remain together not only during the pairing season but till after the birth of the offspring, the doctrine of organic evolution, as formulated by Darwin and expounded by Huxley, may again prove helpful, in this case through the theory of natural selection, which forms part of it. The family may be necessary for the existence of certain species because it has a tendency to preserve the next generation and thereby the species. The male not only stays with the female and young, but also takes care of them; and this I explained as the result of instincts acquired through the process of natural selection. In the case of the apes there are some obvious facts that may account for the need of marital and paternal protection. One is the small number of young, the female bringing forth but one at a time; another is the long period of infancy;[4] and none of these apes is permanently gregarious. The orangutan apparently never, or scarcely ever, congregates in groups larger than the family and is often found solitary. With the chimpanzee and gorilla, as already said, several families often associate and form a band; but even in the Cameroons, where the gorilla is particularly sociable, the herd scatters over a fairly wide district in search of food.[5] I concluded that the factors which necessitated marital and paternal relations among the apes also, presumably, operated among our earliest human or half-human ancestors. There is no doubt that in mankind, too, the number of children has always been comparatively very small, and that the period of infancy has always been comparatively very long; and it seemed to me probable that with primitive man, as with the anthropoids, the large quantities of food he required on account of his size were a hindrance to a permanently gregarious mode of life and therefore made family relations the more useful for the preservation of the offspring. There are even now many low savages among whom the separate families often are compelled to give up the protection afforded them by living together, in order to find the food necessary for their subsistence; and this is the case not only in desolate regions where the supply of food is unusually scarce, but even in countries much more favoured by nature.[6]

The instincts to which I have traced the origin of the family have also helped to preserve it, even though its biological cause, the need of the species, has ceased to operate. Mankind would not succumb if women and children nowadays and in the future had no husband or father to look after them. Certain writers predict that the time will come when marriage and the family will disappear. But I think we may safely say that this will not happen so long as the sentiments of conjugal and parental affection continue to exist and have a hold on human behaviour.

I have dwelt at such length upon my theory of the origin of the family because of its connection with the life-work of the great master whose services to anthropology this lecture is commemorating, as also because of its bearing on the influence that biological factors have exercised upon social phenomena. Such influence is found in the case of other instincts as well, that may be attributed to natural selection; for social institutions are to a very large extent primarily based on instincts. But apart from its role in the production of instincts, the principle of natural selection does not render us much help in our search for social origins. Herbert Spencer's suggestion that 'under most conditions polygyny has prevailed against promiscuity and polyandry, because it has subserved social needs better', and that during later stages of social evolution monogamy for a similar reason has prevailed against polygyny,[7] was merely an empty construction. In his study of social phenomena the sociologist is much better situated than the biologist in his study of organic evolution. Natural selection presupposes organic variations, but scarcely anything is known about the origin of these variations. The causes of social phenomena, on the other hand, are to an almost unlimited extent accessible to the sociologist, and it is his business to try to find them. The methods of sociology are therefore ultimately the methods of studying the causes of social phenomena. This is also true of social anthropology, which is only a branch of sociology. It has been defined as the study of the cultures of non-European peoples and particularly of those who have no written history, but I find no theoretical justification for excluding from it the folklore, or oral tradition, of the unlettered peasantry of Europe, which offers so many similarities to the cultures of uncivilised peoples.

One method of social anthropology is the comparative one. When applied to the study of human civilisation this method starts from the fact that there are great similarities between the products of culture – such as implements, weapons, objects of art, customs, institutions, and beliefs –

among different peoples in different parts of the world. They may be divided under different headings; and under these there may be sub-headings; as in the case of religious beliefs and practices, animism, totemism, ancestor-worship, polytheism, monotheism, and in the case of marriage, marriage by capture, marriage by consideration, monogamy, polygyny, polyandry, group-marriage. Such classifications are by themselves hardly less useful in sociology than are the naturalists' classifications of plants and animals into different species.

But the task of comparative sociology is not restricted to that of classifying the different phenomena of culture; its ultimate object is, of course, the same as that of every other science, namely to explain the facts with which it is concerned, to give an answer to the question, Why? Hence when similar customs, beliefs, legends, or arts are found among different peoples, the question arises how the similarity is to be accounted for. In answer to this question Tylor made the following general statement: 'Sometimes it may be ascribed to the like working of men's minds under like conditions, and sometimes it is a proof of blood relationship or of intercourse, direct or indirect, between the races among whom it is found.'[8] This statement appeared in his *Researches into the Early History of Mankind*, which was published in 1865; and in the same year Huxley declared in his essay on ' Methods and Results of Ethnology': 'The minds of men being everywhere similar, differing in quality and quantity but not in kind of faculty, like circumstances must tend to produce like contrivances; at any rate so long as the need to be met and conquered is of a very simple kind.' But he added: 'On the other hand, it may be doubted, whether the chances are not greatly against independent peoples arriving at the manufacture of a boomerang or of a bow; which last, if one comes to think of it, is a rather complicated apparatus ... The bows and arrows, the perched houses, the outrigged canoes, the habits of betel-chewing and of kava-drinking, which abound more or less among the northern Negritos, are probably to be regarded not as the products of indigenous civilisation, but merely as indication of the extent to which foreign influences have modified the primitive social state of these people.'[9] Sir James Frazer likewise speaks of 'the essential similarity in the working of the less developed human mind among all races, which corresponds to the essential similarity in their bodily frame revealed by comparative anatomy. But,' he adds, 'while the general mental similarity may, I believe, be taken as established, we must always be on our guard against tracing to it a multitude of particular resemblances which may be and often are due to simple diffusion, since nothing is more certain than that the various races of men have borrowed from each other many of their arts and crafts, their ideas, customs, and institutions.'[10]

I have quoted these statements in reply to the charge made by Rivers in a Presidential Address to the Anthropological Section of the British Association, that where similarities are found in different parts of the world it is assumed by the leading school of British anthropologists, 'almost as an axiom, that they are due to independent origin and development.'[11] So little is this charge in accordance with facts that Tylor, in his pioneer work, found it hard to account for the occurrence in so many distant times and places of customs like the cure by sucking and the couvade, and of superstitions like those connected with sneezing, 'on any other hypothesis than that of deep-lying connections by blood or intercourse, among races which history, and even philology, only know as isolated sections of the population of the world.'[12]

It is inconceivable to me how Sir G. Elliot Smith can call it simultaneous acceptance of 'two mutually contradictory views' when Tylor ascribes similarities in culture sometimes to the like working of men's minds under like conditions and sometimes to blood relationship or to direct or indirect intercourse.[13] Nor do I understand how he can speak of 'the dogma of the similarity of the working of the human mind' as an 'amazing psychological speculation' and a 'flimsy travesty of psychology'.[14] How would he explain the similarities found in the habits of animals belonging to the same species that live in different regions? Isn't there anything that may, broadly speaking, be called the human mind? Yet after all, when calling the views held by Tylor 'mutually contradictory', Elliot Smith makes his own views liable to the same accusation. He writes: 'The charge is repeatedly made that those who accept the validity of the principle of diffusion deny the possibility of a custom or belief being invented twice independently. What we do in fact maintain is not the impossibility of such a coincidence, but our inability to find any evidence to show that it has happened.'[15] So also Graebner admits that it is possible, although not proved, that similar culture elements grow up independently in different parts of the world; [16] and other diffusionists do the same.[17] Koppers summarises the present position of the *Kulturkreislehre* by saying: 'The culture historians do not wish to deny entirely the possibility of an independent invention of identical or similar culture phenomena at different places; they are, however, of the opinion, on the basis of observations and experiences at present available, that we do not so very often have to reckon with this possibility.'[18]

It is true that the question whether a certain custom or institution has sprung up independently among the people or tribe practising it, or whether it has been introduced from some other people or tribe, is seldom discussed in comparative treatises. But this by no means implies the assumption of independent origins; on the contrary, when the custom or institution occurs among related or neighbouring peoples there is, at least in many cases, a tendency almost to take for granted that it has been, derived from a common source – that its prevalence is due either to a common descent or to social intercourse. It need not be so, however. If it is possible that identical customs grow up independently among peoples in different parts of the world, it is obviously also possible that identical customs grow up independently among peoples who are of the same stock or have come into contact with one another. Indeed, the more similar two peoples are, the greater is the probability that also new details in their culture should resemble each other; from seeds of the same kind very similar plants spring up. If, for instance, the custom of providing a bride with a marriage portion is found among different so-called Indo-European peoples, we are not therefore entitled to assume that this custom is either an inheritance from a primitive Indo-European period or has been adopted in historical times by one people from another.

One reason why the question of transmission is not more often discussed is the lack of evidence in the case of peoples whose history is unknown to us. Tylor justly spoke of 'the constant difficulty in deciding whether any particular development is due to independent invention, or to transmission from some other people to those among whom it is found'[19] and this difficulty has been overcome only in a very limited degree by later investigations. Graebner lays down two main criteria which he thinks enable us to trace similar culture elements to a common source; first, the criterion of form, as he calls it, that is, correspondence of qualities not inherent in the nature of the object; and secondly, that of quantitative correspondence, that is, the coincidence of several phenomena between which there is no necessary and intrinsic connection.[20] Kroeber likewise maintains that 'if a trait is composed of several elements which stand in no necessary relation to each other, and these several elements recur among distinct or remote peoples in the same combination, whereas on the basis of mere accident it could be expected that the several elements would at times combine and at other times crop out separately, one can be reasonably sure of the real identity and common origin of the complex trait'.[21] If handled with sufficient discrimination, these criteria may without doubt be useful in various cases, such as the study of material objects of culture, of legends and folk-tales, and of proverbs.

Peoples have at all times taken adages from each other, and their wanderings are a fascinating study. But it must always be borne in mind that the resemblance between proverbs may have another cause than diffusion, namely people's tendency to express themselves in apophthegmatic sayings, which owing to their terseness are apt to become more or less similar in similar situations.[22] The real test of a common origin is therefore not the mere similarity of ideas and sentiments revealed in the proverbs, but the similarity of formal expression, with due allowance for modifications that are liable to occur when a saying is adopted from another language and transplanted into a new soil. Kroeber thinks that the absence of true proverbs among the American Indians tends strongly to establish the probability that the custom of using proverbs was borrowed, perhaps from a single source, in Europe, Africa, Asia, and Oceania.[23] This seems to me a very doubtful proposition.

Another branch of cultural phenomena in which diffusion has played a prominent part is decorative art. It may be taken for granted that it has done so within culture-areas where similar patterns and designs are found, although the diffusion need not in every ease refer directly to particulars in the design, but may also be independent effects of the idea underlying it. Several years ago I had the honour to read to this Institute a paper on the magic origin of Moorish designs, in which I endeavoured to show that the patterns used in Morocco were originally, at least to a very large extent, charms against the evil eye, as they still are besides serving ornamental purposes.[24] Nothing seems more natural than that people who have a strong belief in the evil eye should, to the best of their ability, try to protect themselves and their property from this dreaded enemy. Those Moorish charms are essentially based on two principles: either the hand or its five fingers and therefore the number five by itself as a means of throwing back the evil glance; or an image of an eye or of a pair of eyes, or something resembling an eye, as producing the same effect – if baneful energy can be transmitted by the eye it can obviously also be thrown back by a representation of the eye, in accordance with the general rule in magic that obliterates the difference between reality and image. Further investigations have convinced me that both types of charms and designs are spread all over the Mediterranean area and many of them also farther east, and they are proved to have existed since very early times. That they were meant to be charms against the evil eye in the past even in cases where no direct evidence can be produced is strongly suggested by the firm belief in, and great fear of, it which is known to have prevailed among those peoples from time immemorial. But this does not exclude the possibility of more or less similar representations of the protective objects having in certain instances originated independently.

I shall illustrate this by an example the hypothetical character of which does not prevent its representing a methodological principle of some importance. On leather bags made by mountaineers in northern Morocco and on a native gun from the south of the same country[25] I have found designs or charms that decidedly look like, or are actual images of, pairs of eyes, and at the same time have great similarity to the Ionic capital. My suspicion that the latter also was originally a charm against the evil eye was strengthened by various facts. Among the Punic inscriptions[26] there are representations of hands and eyes and various other charms against the evil eye side by side with drawings of an Ionic capital. This capital certainly bears a strong resemblance to a pair of eyes with their brows united. When I showed a picture of it to an old Moorish scribe, he at once exclaimed that it was the image of a pair of eyes. In the centre of either 'eye' there is often a well-marked 'pupil,'[27] which sometimes contains an eight-petalled rosette,[28] also by itself a common Mediterranean charm; and the frequent depression in the lower line connecting the volutes, which has been a puzzle to scholars and been simply ascribed to aesthetic motives, requires no further explanation at all if the line represents two eyebrows that are united over the bridge of the nose. It is significant that in ancient Greece such eyebrows were regarded as a sure indication of the evil eye – an idea which is also found in Morocco, where the designs or charms in question likewise present a depression in the connecting line – and the image of a pair of eyes with united brows would therefore, naturally, have been thought to be a particularly effective charm. I am not aware of any previous explanation of the Ionic capital that can satisfy me; neither a lotus[29] nor a lily nor, as Von Luschan suggests, the foliage of a date-palm,[30] has the faintest resemblance to it. It should be noticed that holiness is very susceptible to the evil eye, as well as to other evil influences. The ancient Greeks protected their holy lyres – musical instruments of harp kind – with a charm consisting of a very conspicuous representation of a pair of eyes with their brows, which was pictured upon them.[31] Hence it would be no wonder if they had protected their temples in a similar manner.

Now it is extremely improbable that the Moorish charms have been copied from the Ionic capital, whereas their resemblance is easily explained by a common belief that the representation of eyes serves as a protection against the evil eye. The same belief may possibly account for the eye design, which figures so prominently among the supposed instances of diffusion, also in other parts of the world. While the belief in the evil eye is particularly strong in the Mediterranean countries, it is found more or less prevalent among a large number of African and Asiatic peoples, in the Malay Archipelago and Polynesia, even among some

Australian natives, and among various aboriginal tribes and peoples in North, Central and South America.[32] But the eye ornament may also have a different meaning in different cases. It has been taken for evidence of diffusion without any inquiry into its meaning. This illustrates a general weakness in the method of diffusionists, who have a tendency to rely upon external resemblances only. They may of course be unable to do anything else when they study objects in museums which are silent upon motives. But this disregard of motives is also conspicuous in their treatment of customs, where there is no such excuse for it.

I doubt whether the diffusionists have really clearly realised the full implications of their theory that the occurrence of similar customs or beliefs of almost any kind, even among widely separated and unrelated peoples, is due to borrowing. It seems to me truly grotesque to assume that this is the case with such widespread or universal culture elements as, for instance, the right of property, punishment, the blood-feud, the various forms of marriage, the prohibition of marriage between parents and children and between brothers and sisters and other exogamous rules, slavery, a multitude of magical and religious practices and beliefs, and so forth *ad infinitum.* It should, moreover, be noticed that even when the historical connection between cultural elements has been well- established, their ultimate origin has not been explained thereby. It is not a sufficient explanation of them to say that they have been derived from ancestors or been borrowed from other peoples. This only raises the question how they originated in the first instance; for they must have had a beginning. It is with questions of this sort that the comparative school of sociologists have pre-eminently occupied themselves. And their comparative method has undoubtedly helped them in their task.

The simultaneous occurrence of certain social phenomena in many different groups of people may indicate that there is a casual connection between them, though no such connection is suggested by their simultaneous occurrence in a single group. It was this fact that led Tylor to his 'method of investigating the development of institutions' set forth in the Journal of this Institute in 1889; and a similar method was afterwards applied to the influence that industrial culture has exercised on social institutions by Nieboer, with reference to slavery,[33] and by Hobhouse, Wheeler, and Ginsberg in collaboration, with reference to other institutions as well.[34] Moreover, a comparison of the circumstances in which a custom is practised by different peoples may also without any correlation to other customs lead to the discovery of the motive underlying it. Thus a comparative study of the practice of human sacrifice shows that human victims are frequently offered in war, before a battle, or during a siege; for the purpose of stopping or preventing an epidemic; in order to put an end to a devastating famine; when the earth fails to supply the people with water; with a view to averting perils arising from the sea or from rivers; and in order to prevent the death of some particular person, especially a chief or a king. From these facts I thought it justifiable to draw the conclusion that human sacrifice is, largely at least, a method of life-insurance, based upon the idea of substitution;[35] and though the human sacrifice offered as a means of putting an end to or averting a ravaging famine and securing an abundant crop has been explained as serving as a magical manure,[36] it may be asked why this particular gruesome kind of manure was chosen if not because human life was in danger. Very frequently the knowledge of the cause of a certain custom found among one people is suggestive of the meaning of the same or similar customs among other peoples. Little details which by themselves would hardly attract our attention may, when viewed in the light of comparative material, become conclusive evidence or, in other cases, lead to valuable inferences which may be within the range of future confirmation. In this way the custom and ideas of savages have, in no small degree, helped us to understand culture traits in the early history of civilised nations. As Rose observes in his recent Frazer lecture, with special reference to custom and myth in classical antiquity, 'many points which were previously quite obscure assume a meaning, purely from the supposition that what is done by one group of human beings may have been done, for the same or similar reasons, by another group, without supposing any other bond between them than their common humanity.'[37]

The comparative study may further, if due caution is observed, enable us to discover that certain customs are vestigial forms or remaining traces of earlier customs – that they are so-called survivals. According to Rivers, a custom is to be regarded as a survival 'if its nature cannot be explained by its present utility but only becomes intelligible through its past history'.[38] I think it would be more appropriate to say: a custom which cannot be explained by present circumstances but persists, as Lowie puts it, in isolation from its original context.[39] There are customs that can scarcely be said to fulfil a useful, or even a presumably useful, function, but are simply expressions of emotional states, and are yet no survivals. On the other hand, a custom may be useful in some way or other and nevertheless be a survival, if that kind of usefulness was not the cause of its origin. The application of the principle of survival, however, may be beset with considerable difficulties: it may be difficult to decide whether a custom is a survival at all or of what it is a survival. That principle, however, has played a much more prominent role in social anthropology through attempts to prove the existence of certain customs in the past, than through assumptions that certain present customs are survivals of others, the earlier existence of which is known. Those attempts have often led to most unjustifiable results. In the study of the earlier relations between the sexes in mankind they were rampant towards the end of the last century, when leading anthropologists interpreted, in a most arbitrary manner, a variety of customs as survivals of an initial state of promiscuity. I do not know that any English writer nowadays believes in the theory of promiscuity. But that of group-marriage, according to which all the men of one clan or intermarrying group are married to all the women of another clan or intermarrying group, became its residuary legatee, and group-marriage was, and still is, regarded by many as the earliest form of marriage from which the others have gradually developed; and here again the chief evidence was derived from the interpretation of customs as survivals. R. Briffault, the latest exponent of this theory in his work *The Mothers* looks for proofs of an early stage of group-marriage in a variety of customs that were previously represented as survivals of promiscuity, such as the classificatory system of relationship terms, the practice of exchanging wives temporarily, the duty of offering one's wife to a guest, polyandry, the levirate, and the sexual liberty granted to unmarried women.[40] A detailed examination of all those customs, and of others that have been adduced as evidence of promiscuity or of group-marriage, has convinced me that none of them can be taken for survivals of either.

The interpretation of customs as survivals is also very prominent in the Freudian theory of the Oedipus complex as a universal human characteristic. As such it requires, of course, a great deal of confirmation from other sources besides psycho-analysis; and various customs are made out to be vestiges of the occurrence of incest in the past, such as brother and sister marriage in some reigning families, the levirate, the sororate, group-marriage, and the so-called *jus primae noctis*, the defloration of a woman being assumed to be originally performed by her father. And to the evidence drawn from customs psycho-analysts have added facts from mythology, arguing that when incest was repressed among men, the wish for it found an outlet in the fanciful creations of myths and legends. In a recent book I have scrutinised the evidential value of these supposed survivals of an original incest desire and found it to be none, since they are perfectly explicable without the assumption that there was any such desire. And the same may be said of the customs on which Freud has relied as survivals in his theory of the repression of the supposed original incestuous tendencies.[41]

In spite of the importance of the principle of survival, there has never, so far as I know, been any general theoretical discussion of the proper application of it where historical evidence is absent. I think that in this respect two definite rules may be laid down. An obvious one is that a custom must not be interpreted as a survival of something of which it cannot be a survival. From a logical point of view this rule is of course a sheer platitude, but it has nevertheless often been transgressed. For example, circumcision as an initiation rite has been represented by psycho-analysts as a survival of and substitute for an earlier act of castration.[42] This is absurd, considering that castration could at most have taken place only in rare cases, whilst initiation rites, where they occur, are general. Or circumcision has been said to serve the purpose of punishing and preventing incest.[43] But the generality as an initiation rite also makes it impossible to take it for a punishment, and as a means of preventing incest it would be useless. It cannot prevent it by inspiring fear where it is performed anyhow; nor does it produce physical incapacity for performing the forbidden act. Briffault, again, regards the custom of offering a wife to a guest – which is, in fact, only an incident of the general rule of hospitality – as a survival of group-marriage between two clans. He says: 'We may be as certain as we can be of any inference in social anthropology that wherever it is observed clan-brotherhood is, or was formerly, considered to imply sexual communism, for it is by assimilation to a clan-brother that the guest is treated as he is.'[44] If this were true all inferences in social anthropology would be worthless. The guest is not assimilated to a clan-brother, hospitality does not imply that he is 'necessarily to be regarded and treated as a tribal brother'. It is probably always limited by time – often to three days, sometimes even to a day and a night. And while the custom of offering one's wife to a guest is widespread, it is open to considerable doubt whether there is a single tribe in which all one's clan-brothers enjoy a similar privilege. Briffault has not told us how it is that sexual communism has survived in the case of a guest, although it has disappeared in the case of clan-brothers.

The other fundamental rule referring to the legitimacy of interpreting customs as survivals I take to be this: a custom must not be regarded as the survival of something which is not known to have existed or the earlier existence of which may not be assumed, or at least seems probable, for some other reason. This rule, too, has been transgressed by those who think they have discovered survivals of an ancient state of group-marriage to say nothing of primitive promiscuity or of a universally prevalent original incest- desire. Group-marriage has been found among peoples that practise polyandry, but then only as a combination of polygyny with polyandry and not as an original custom. There are many peoples that have a kind of sex communism, in which several men have the right of access to several women, although none of the women is properly married to more than one of the men; but the fact that some of our authorities apply the term 'group-marriage' to relations of this sort should not deceive us as regards their true nature. The belief in an original state of group-marriage was originally based on certain classificatory terms, but I have tried to show that the view which traces the origin of the classificatory system of relationship to communism in women, whether group-marriage or any other kind of sex communism, is not only unsubstantiated but inconsistent with plain facts.

Again, as to the prevalence of an original incest desire the Freudians consider it to be proved not only by customs that they interpret as direct vestiges of it, but also by the fierce laws which have been devised in the most varied parts of the world with a view to preventing incest.[45] If you thus have evidence of ancient incest both in the cases when it is allowed and in the cases when it is prohibited, you may be pretty sure that it was once universal. We are told that the law only forbids men to do what their instincts incline them to do, and that we may accordingly safely assume that when crimes are forbidden by law many men must have a natural propensity to commit them. This is a deceptive argument. Of course, nobody would ever have dreamt of making a prohibitory law if the idea of its transgression had not presented itself to his mind. When Solon, the Athenian legislator, was asked why he had specified no punishment for one who had murdered his father, he replied that he supposed it could not occur to anybody to commit such a crime[46] (that wise man was not acquainted with the Oedipus complex!). But though the prohibition of a certain act presupposes that it is considered possible, that it has occurred and is more or less likely to occur again, it does not imply that there is a widespread natural inclination to do it. Nor does the rigour of the law indicate the strength of the temptation to transgress it. Do the severe laws against bestiality prove that a large number of men have a strong natural propensity to copulate with animals? How, then, could the severe laws against incest prove that there is or has been a general and strong tendency to incest? Customs and laws express the general feelings of the community and punish acts that shock them. But they do not tell us whether the inclination to commit the forbidden act is felt by many or by few.

I have so far spoken of cases in which I consider the interpretation of customs as survivals to be illegitimate. There are other cases for which no general rules can be laid down. It may be that a custom *seems* to be explicable by present circumstances or its present utility, and yet is a survival; this might have been the case with the Sunday rest in modern civilisation if we had been ignorant of its history. On the other hand, a custom may seem inexplicable by present circumstances simply owing to our ignorance, and consequently be no survival at all. For this reason the popular marriage ritual has been a favourite playground for fantastic speculations about pre-existing methods of concluding a marriage or relations between the sexes. I have no doubt that the bulk of the wedding rites of simple peoples have a magical significance intimately connected with the welfare of individuals, families, or whole communities, or are more or less fossilised expressions of such emotional states as sexual bashfulness, anger, sorrow, or erotic feelings.

Connected with the extravagant and uncritical use made of the principle of survival there was another weakness that threw discredit upon the evolutionary school in social anthropology, namely the tendency of some of its leading writers to infer, without sufficient reason, from the prevalence of a custom or institution among some savage peoples, or from facts interpreted as survivals of it, that this custom or institution was a relic from a stage of development which the whole human race once went through. A classical instance of this is Lewis H. Morgan's suggestion that no fewer than fifteen normal stages in the evolution of marriage and the family 'must of necessity have preceded a knowledge of marriage between single pairs, and of the family itself in the modern sense of the term'.[47] Nearly fifty years ago I strongly opposed theories of this sort and, generally, the belief in a unilinear sequence of institutional stages; and in Morgan's own country they were subsequently contested by Boas[48] and other anthropologists. They nowadays belong to the past, even though traces of them may still be smouldering. I pointed out that we have no right to assume the universal prevalence of a social phenomenon in the past unless we may assume that the cause or causes to which it is due have been universally operating. If speculating on such problems, we have therefore first to find out the causes of the social phenomena; and only then we may, from the prevalence of the causes, infer the prevalence of the phenomena themselves, if the former may be assumed to have operated without being checked by other causes. It was on this method that I based my hypothesis that the family consisting of father, mother, and children existed already in primitive times. On the other hand, the causes, or hypothetical causes to which marriage by capture, group-marriage, and the so-called mother-right may be traced are not such as to justify the belief in the universal prevalence of any of these customs at any stage of human civilisation.

Nowadays the reaction against the methodological vagaries of evolutional anthropologists has become so strong that any attempt to conjecture the origin of a social institution or of an element of culture has been pronounced to be out of place in social anthropology. In his Presidential Address to the Anthropological Section of the British Association in 1931, Radcliffe-Brown said that the 'new' social anthropology rejects as being no part of its task the hypothetical reconstruction of the unknown past, and therefore avoids all discussion of hypotheses as to historical origins. By the origin of an institution he then understood 'the historical process by which it came into existence. Thus,' he said, 'we can speak of and actually study the origin of parliamentary government in England.' But this is not the sense in which the social anthropologists have used the term 'origin' with regard to social institutions: they tried to find out their causes, whatever the nature of those causes might have been. The advocate of the 'new' anthropology, however, makes the objection that the old school 'frequently sought the origins of social institutions in purely psychological factors, *i.e.* it sought to conjecture the motives in individual minds that would lead them to invent or accept particular customs and beliefs' and that 'any explanation of a particular sociological phenomenon in terms of psychology, *i.e.* of processes of individual mental activity, is invalid'. But who could deny that even collective behaviour involves the actions of individuals? And when we speak of the customs, ideas, or religion of a people we mean by it, of course, something which the individual members of it have in common, that is, something collective. Why, then, should social anthropology refrain from studying the origins of customs and institutions?

I think it is within this field that it has performed some of its most important tasks. Its results are to a very large extent as well established as any reached in any sphere of research; and when they can merely be regarded as more or less hypothetical, we should remember the saying that 'hypothesis is the salt of science'. Even Rivers, who once wrote that 'the proper task of the sociologist is the study of the correlation of social phenomena with other social phenomena',[49] admitted that 'in the last resort every custom and institution of human society is the outcome of mental activity'.[50] Indeed, the customs of a people are an outcome of collective mental activity in a much deeper sense than being merely a habitual repetition of certain modes of behaviour. Customs are not only public habits, the habits of a certain group of men, a tribal or national community, a class or rank of society. While being a habit a custom is at the same time a rule of conduct. As Cicero said, the customs of a people 'are precepts in themselves'.[51] They are conceived of as moral rules, and in early society as the only moral rules ever thought of; the savage strictly complies with the Hegelian command that no man must have a private conscience. Disobedience to custom evokes public, or moral, indignation. An exhaustive study of customs thus implies an investigation into the nature and origin of the moral consciousness, which, so far as I have been able to find by a considerable amount of detailed research, is ultimately based on retributive emotions collectively felt and characterised by disinterestedness and impartiality, at least within certain limits.

We now come to the positive side of the programme for the 'new anthropology'. Radcliffe-Brown says that it looks at any culture as an integral system and studies the functions of social institutions, customs, and beliefs of all kinds as parts of such a system. This principle must be accepted by everybody, and has, as a matter of fact, been more or less followed by writers of anthropological monographs on restricted areas. It has been a common complaint against the comparative method that it detaches the cultural phenomenon from the organic whole of which it forms a part. There is a tendency to assume that similar customs and rites practised by different peoples have the same meanings, and though it often has resulted in accurate classifications it is also apt to lead to ill-founded or inaccurate conclusions. This is largely due to the incompleteness of the sources at the sociologists' disposal. Hence the defects of the comparative method may be reduced by careful monographs on particular cultures; and I think indeed that, next to sociological field-work, no other investigations are more urgently needed than such monographs – just because customs and beliefs are not isolated phenomena but largely influenced by local conditions, by the physical environment, by the particular circumstances in which the people in question live, and are in fact expressions of their whole corporate soul-life.[52] The method nowadays called 'the functional' – which, as Malinowski puts it, 'insists on the complexity of sociological facts, on the concatenation of various often apparently contradictory elements in one belief or conviction; on the dynamic working of such a conviction within the social system; and the expression of social attitudes or beliefs in traditionally standardised behaviour –is thus not only indispensable for the study of any special culture, but also of the greatest value for the study of customs and institutions in their generality ; while, on the other hand, the comparative study may also help the specialist to explain facts that he could hardly understand in full if his knowledge were restricted to a limited culture area.'[53]

Another aspect of the 'new anthropology' as described by Radcliffe-Brown is its endeavour to discover general sociological laws. While it rejects all attempts to provide psychological explanations of particular social or cultural phenomena, it does so 'in favour of an ultimate psychological explanation of general sociological laws when these have been demonstrated by purely sociological inquiries ... It applies to human life in society the generalising method of the natural sciences, seeking to formulate the general laws that underlie it, and to explain any given phenomenon in any culture as a special example of a general or universal principle.' I doubt that such general laws, if discovered, would be of much service in investigating social phenomena. The thesis that every society or culture tends to function integratively is presumably one of them; but, as Kroeber remarks, neither as a tool for further inquiry nor as a final synthesis would it satisfy anybody. 'Every physiologist would accept the fact, probably takes it for granted, that there are strong integrative tendencies in the functioning of all organisms. But would any physiologist consider such a principle to be either the end result of his science or a specific tool for prosecuting it further?'[54] Radcliffe-Brown seems to regard the proposition that a social system is a special exemplification of laws of social physiology or social functioning as characteristic of functionalism.[55] But Malinowski does not professedly look for laws.

In order to illustrate the endeavour of the 'new anthropology' to demonstrate that a particular phenomenon is an example of a general law, Radcliffe-Brown describes its attitude towards the problem of totemism. To elucidate the nature of totemism, he says, we must aim at showing that it is a special instance of a phenomenon, or at any rate of a tendency which is universal in human society. For this purpose we have to compare totemism with all other related institutions in all cultures. And just as the question of the nature of totemism is part of a very much wider sociological problem, so the study of the functions of totemism is part of the general sociological problem of the function of religion. Radcliffe-Brown says he has chosen the subject of totemism to show the difference of method that distinguishes the newer social anthropology from the old 'because some of the most important steps of the passage from the old to the new methods are to be seen in Durkheim's treatment of the subject in his *Elementary Forms of the Religious Life.*'

This book, which was written a quarter of a century ago, has been subjected to much criticism, and it certainly bristles with fallacies.[56] In the present connection the main question of interest is that of method; and I cannot for a moment imagine that the new anthropology would benefit by any revival of Durkheim's methodology as demonstrated in that book. By analysing Australian totemism he alleges that he has found within it all the great ideas and the principal ritual attitudes which are at the basis of even the most advanced religions. One would imagine that such an allegation could only be justified by a supplementary study of the other religions, but he argues that 'when a law has been proven by one well-made experiment, this proof is valid universally. If in one single case a scientist succeeded in finding out the secret of the life of even the most protoplasmic creature that can be imagined, the truths thus obtained would be applicable to all living beings, even the most advanced.' His argument amounts to this: by analysing Australian totemism he has discovered a law representing the secret of religion, and the result of his investigation is therefore applicable to every other religion. This, however, is not an induction but a vicious circle. Yet Durkheim calls it an induction, which having at its foundation a clearly defined experiment is less adventurous than many summary generalisations that, while attempting to reach the essence of religion at once, without resting upon the careful analysis of any religion in particular, greatly risk losing themselves in space.[57] But an analysis, however careful, of Australian totemism cannot be a substitute for generalisations referring to the other religions. It is only by comparing it with the results of careful analyses of the latter that we can discover what they all have in common. But I cannot see that the study of the problem of totemism requires such an elaborate undertaking, any more than the study of any particular social institution presupposes a study of all related institutions in all cultures.

It seems to me rather singular that Radcliffe-Brown should have been so fascinated by the theories of Durkheim and his school of sociologists, who have been reluctant to embark actively on field studies, although he maintains that 'no insight, however genial, can fully compensate for the absence of direct personal contact with the kind of material that the anthropologist has to study and explain'. This is an opinion that I fully endorse. I took exactly the same view some forty years ago when I was preparing my book *The Origin and Development of the Moral Ideas*, and thought it might be useful for me to acquire first-hand knowledge of some forms of culture differing from our own. I intended to go to the East to study both civilised and savage races, but sailed first for Morocco. And I never went farther. I soon realised what a laborious undertaking it is to acquaint oneself sufficiently well with the natives even of a single country. Morocco offered the advantages of being little explored as a field for anthropological studies, absolutely untouched by modern civilisation, and within easy reach of Europe. I went there time after time, preparing my trilogy on the customs and ideas of the Moors, which was based on my experience among them during nine years in the course of more than three decades. I think therefore that I may venture to say something about the method of the field-worker, who is nowadays justly recognised to be the most important person in the sphere of social anthropology. But I shall restrict myself to some observations to which I attach particular significance.

The field-worker should have a solid knowledge of general anthropology, both its facts and its theories. When I first set out to improve my defective knowledge through personal experience of native customs and beliefs in Morocco I carried with me, besides tents and rifles and other necessary things, a fair number of books, one of which proved to be of inestimable value for my special purpose, namely *The Golden Bough*, then – luckily enough for my pack-mule – consisting of two volumes only, not of twelve. It drew my attention to facts that otherwise in all probability would have escaped my notice, since many customs are not discovered without being looked for. It offered suggestions and explanations, which were none the less valuable because they were not always applicable to the particular data that came under my observation. And it brought home to me the great lesson, which no field-anthropologist should ever forget, not to rest content with recording mere external modes of native behaviour without endeavouring, to the best of his ability, to find the ideas or sentiments underlying them. Even when the meaning of a custom is obscure or lost, the field-worker's knowledge of the native mind and its modes of thinking and feeling may enable him to make valuable conjectures. I trust it is nowadays an obsolete principle which I once heard expressed by an eminent reader of a paper on some savage tribes visited by him, at a meeting of this Institute, that the field-anthropologist should only aim at collecting facts and leave it to the anthropologists at home to explain them. But he must, of course, take the utmost care to avoid mixing up his own interpretation of facts with the observed facts themselves, and point out clearly the difference in the record of his work.

It has been said by one of the pioneers of modern anthropological research, Dr. Rivers, that there is no more depressing and apparently hopeless task than that of trying to discover why people perform rites and ceremonies: 'directly one approaches the underlying meaning of rite or custom ... one meets only with uncertainty and vagueness unless, as is most frequently the case, the people are wholly satisfied with the position that they are acting as their fathers have done before them'. I cannot say that this pessimistic view is supported by my own observations in Morocco. The native explanations often differed, and a probable reason for this was that the original meaning of the rite had been more or less forgotten and a new interpretation substituted for it. This, however, should not make the ethnographer less eager to find out the natives' own opinions about the facts they record; for whether or no they represent the original or the only meaning attached to them, they give us in any case some insight into the people's minds. But the direct inquiry into motives and ideas is not the only way in which they may be detected. The most convincing information is often obtained not from what the natives say *about* their rites, but from what they say at the moment when they perform them. I shall illustrate the value of such information by some examples.

In Morocco, as in many parts of Europe, smouldering fires are made on Midsummer Day or some other definite day of the year, and the people leap over them and also take their animals over the ashes. When they perform these ceremonies they may say some words like these: 'We shook on you the fleas and lice and the illnesses of the heart, as also of the bones; we shall pass through you again next year and the following years with quietness and health.' On the following morning the animals are taken over the ashes by their owners, who say: 'We shook on you that which again wanted to hurt us and also our animals; may you again take away that which is harmful, we shall take from you that which is useful.' In other words, purificatory effects are attributed to the fires and their ashes. Many similar sayings have more recently been collected from the south of Morocco by Laoust, but although he admits that the Berbers now regard the fires as means of purification or expulsion of evil influences, he still believes in the theory that they originally were designed to reinforce the sun's light and heat by sympathetic magic.[58] This idea is not found anywhere in Morocco, and the facts by which he tries to support the old solar theory seem utterly inadequate to its rehabilitation. He chiefly refers to the explanations given by Mannhardt and Frazer with regard to the European fire-festivals. But it has escaped his notice that in the last edition of *The Golden Bough* its author has changed his earlier views. Frazer points out that Mannhardt's theory is very slightly, if at all, supported by the evidence and is probably erroneous, and he now considers that the true explanation of the fire-ceremonies is the idea which I found in Morocco, that they are purificatory in intention.[59]

The Moorish rites of covenanting, and the utterances connected with them, may also be of some interest from a more general point of view. They imply some kind of bodily contact – by the exchange of turbans or cloaks, by the joining of hands, or by the partaking of a meal in common; and the covenanting rite derives its force from the idea that both parties thereby expose themselves to each other's conditional curses, in other words, that he who is guilty of breach of faith is cursed. By the contact the potential curse is transferred from one party to the other, and if the given promise is broken the curse is actualised. The nature of the restraint which a common meal lays upon those who partake of it is very clearly expressed in the words addressed to a faithless participant, 'may God and the *food* repay you,' and in the curse, which is a very dangerous one, 'I left to you the food that we shared'; the food embodies a curse. That rites of covenanting similar in principle to those practised in Morocco occurred in North Africa in very ancient times is suggested by a statement of Herodotus; [60] and among Semites a common meal was an early method of sealing a compact. There are instances of this in the Old Testament. Laban and Jacob made a covenant by heaping up stones – which is a favourite depositary of curses – and eating together on the heap;[61] and the Israelites entered into alliance with the Gibeonites by taking of their victuals, without consulting Yahve, and the meal was expressly followed by an oath.[62] In other instances, again, a covenant was made with the deity by means of a sacrificial meal[63] or in some other way. The Hebrews, as Robertson Smith observes,[64] thought of the national religion as constituted by a formal covenant sacrifice at Mount Sinai, where half of the blood of the sacrificed oxen was sprinkled on the altar and the other half on the people,[65] or even by a still earlier covenant rite in which the parties were Yahve and Abraham;[66] and the idea of sacrifice establishing a covenant between God and man is also apparent in the Psalms.[67] The same idea, according to Wellhausen, prevailed among the ancient Arabs.[68] Robertson Smith and his followers have represented these practices as acts of communion. At first, we are told, the god – that is, the totem god – himself was eaten, whilst at a later stage the eating of the god was superseded by eating with the god; communion still remained the core of sacrifice, and only subsequently the practice of offering gifts to the deity developed out of the sacrificial union between the worshippers and their god.[69] But the Moorish customs of covenanting, and the utterances connected with them, led me to believe that the whole of this theory is based upon a misunderstanding of the Semitic evidence, and that the very similar methods used by the ancient Hebrews in their covenanting with the deity were intended, not to establish communion, but to transfer conditional curses both to the men and to their god. In Morocco the practice of l-'ār, which intrinsically implies the transference of a conditional curse by means of a sacrifice or in some other way, is very frequently resorted to for the purpose of compelling not only a living man, but also a dead saint, to grant a request.

In all parts of Morocco rags or clothing or hair are tied to some object connected with a dead saint. In many cases this is done by a petitioner who thereby expects to profit by the *baraka*, or holiness, of the object; and the idea of disease transference may also be conspicuously present in his mind, as is proved by the words uttered, for example, by someone who ties a string from his clothes to a saintly tree, 'I left my fever in you, O wild olive tree.' But in other cases the utterances accompanying an act of this kind disclose a very different idea. In the Great Atlas I visited a place where the famous Mohammedan int 'Abd 'I-Qadir al-Jilani, buried at Baghdad, who in Morocco is more highly venerated than any other saint, has a small sanctuary, close to which there is a cairn with a pole full of rags stuck in it. When a petitioner fastens a strip of his clothes to the pole, he mutters some words like these: 'O saint behold! I promise you an offering and will not untie you until you attend to my case.' If his wish is fulfilled he goes back to the place, offers the sacrifice he promised, and unties the knot he made. A Berber servant of mine from Aglu in Sūs told me that once when he was in prison he invoked Lalla Ra ma Yusf, a great female saint whose tomb is in that neighbourhood, and tied his turban, saying: 'I am tying you, O Lalla Rahma Yusf, and am not going to open the knot till you have helped me, nor shall I ever invoke you if you do not assist me.' He said that on the same night his chains were opened by the saint, who was evidently frightened by his threat, and he escaped from the prison. These and other sayings of the same class, which so clearly express the idea of tying up the saint in order to compel him to render the assistance asked for, suggested to me the possibility of some similar idea underlying the Latin word for religion, *religio*, if, as has been conjectured, this word is related to the verb *religare*, 'to tie'. It might then have implied, not that the man was tied by his god, but that the god was tied by the man.

Besides sayings uttered on the occasion when rites are performed, which throw light on the meaning of the rite, there are sayings of another type to which the field-anthropologist should pay attention, namely the proverbs of the people, wherever such are found. By collecting and studying about two thousand Moorish proverbs[70] I have become convinced of the sociological importance of such a study from several points of view the proverbs of a people are valuable documents concerning its character and temperament, opinions and feelings, manners and customs. It is true that many of them are in all probability not indigenous. But a foreign proverb is scarcely adopted by a people unless it is in some measure congenial to its mind and mode of life; it is apt to be modified so as to fit in with its new surroundings when sufficiently deeply rooted, it may in turn influence the native habits of thought and feeling; and if it does not succeed in being acclimatized in its adopted country, it will wither and die. These facts are important on account of the frequent difficulty, or impossibility, of distinguishing indigenous proverbs from others which have crept in from abroad. A very similar answer may be given to the objection that proverbs are not creations of a group of people but of individuals.

But proverbs are not only reflections of life: they also play an active part in it. This functional aspect – which has also been emphasized by R. Firth[71] – should engage our attention not only because the study of it helps us to understand their intrinsic meaning and bearing on national characteristics, but for its own sake as well. I cannot strongly enough insist on the necessity of carefully recording concrete situations in which proverbs are used, unless the collector has made sure that they have no other meaning but that which they directly express. These situations give us an insight into the use that people make of their proverbs – teach us when and how and why they use them. Most proverbs are expressions of feelings or opinions, or are intended to influence people's wills and actions. One of the feelings that figure very prominently in the proverbs of the Moors, as well as of other peoples, is dissatisfaction. The world is full of evils of many kinds. The innocent is punished for the fault of the guilty: 'One eats beans, and for another they swell in his stomach.' Dissatisfaction also leads to disapproval or reproach; and here again a proverb is a suitable vehicle for giving vent to one's feelings. On the one hand, it gives the censure a semblance of public opinion; on the other hand, it makes even sarcasm less offensive by making it less personal. Generally speaking, the Moors are a polite race. If anyone shows you a thing he has bought, you should say it is good, whatever you may think of it: 'If you see him riding on a bamboo cane say to him, Good health to your horse.' This, however, is not a manner of mere politeness; there is an idea that the spoken word easily brings about its own realization. And there is yet another superstition that has been conducive to politeness, and at the same time to the use of proverbs as polite answers, namely the idea that a person by refusing a request exposes himself to the danger of being hurt by the other person's evil eye or his curse. It is obvious that a request cannot always be granted, and people often prefer running some risk to doing what they are asked to; but they may lessen the danger by politely couching the refusal in a proverb. In a country where charity is a cardinal duty it does not sound well to say 'no' to a beggar; it is much better to convey one's denial by making an excuse: 'What will death take from an empty house?', 'Our sickness is the same, and the one who cures is God.' In spite of their natural politeness, however, the Moors are excitable people and, when enraged, hurl at each other the most terrible curses. But the use of an appropriate proverb may serve to cool the rage, stop the quarrel, and make those who were cursing one another a moment before rejoice and shake hands with each other. Once when two of my servants from Tangier quarrelled I had only to recite the proverb, 'The quarrel of a native of Tangier is like fumigation with benzoin.' (which only lasts for a moment) – and the angry look was changed for a friendly smile.

The study of proverbs is also of great use to an ethnographer as a means of improving his knowledge of the native language. Such knowledge, which, strangely enough, seems to occupy a rather modest place in the equipment that Radcliffe Brown requires of a trained field-anthropologist,[72] is in my opinion an indispensable qualification for which no sociological training can serve as compensation; and I know that Malinowski, whose training of field-workers has been crowned with such signal success, takes a similar view. To be able to converse freely with the natives without the aid of an interpreter should be the field-anthropologist's most serious aspiration. In the beginning of my researches I had as interpreter a very intelligent and most trustworthy native, with a remarkable command of English, who also afterwards accompanied me on all my journeys in Morocco. But I came to the conclusion that even the best interpreter is apt to omit details which, though apparently trivial, might be of great importance for the right understanding of the custom or belief in question, or to let his attention slacken for a moment, or to give an inaccurate meaning to expressions which baffle all direct translation. Moreover, I made it an invariable habit to repeat to my informants their statements in full, and occasionally tested their accuracy and attention by deliberately misrepresenting their statements; and all this could scarcely be done through the medium of an interpreter. But I am happy to say that when I thus tested their trustworthiness they never failed to correct me. I found the accuracy of the natives even in the smallest details to be remarkable, and the patience of many of my teachers to be beyond praise.

Although the proper training of field-anthropologists is nowadays insisted on as a matter of first-rate importance, I thoroughly disagree with Radcliffe-Brown's statement that we can no more rely on information given by untrained observers in social anthropology than we can rely on the observations of an untrained person in such sciences as geology, physics, or chemistry.[73] If this were the case we should scarcely have any comparative anthropology at all, for the number of properly trained ethnographers has hitherto been exceedingly small. The untrained observers have often had the advantage of living for a long time among the people whose customs and beliefs they record and of possessing knowledge of their language which trained ethnographers have often lacked; and there is sufficient evidence that even ordinary travellers have been able to provide us with accurate information. Their chief fault is often the omission of valuable details which would not have escaped the notice of better-qualified observers. It is a common complaint against the comparative method that it does not allow a sufficiently careful scrutiny of authorities and sources, and there is certainly a great deal of truth in it. But on the other hand it cannot be denied that the comparative method itself offers a test which, if properly applied, may give the investigator some confidence in his fact, namely the test of recurrence. As Tylor puts it, 'if two independent visitors to different countries, say a mediaeval Mohammedan in Tartary and a modern Englishman in Dahome, or a Jesuit missionary in Brazil and a Wesleyan in the Fiji Islands, agree in describing some analogous art or rite or myth among the people they have visited, it becomes difficult or impossible to set down such correspondence to accident or wilful fraud'.[74]

Though I fully agree with the demand that the field-worker should be equipped with a thorough knowledge of sociological theories, he should accept none of them as an interpretation of his own facts until he has found the theory confirmed by his own experience. This has not always been the case. Morgan's interpretation of certain classificatory relationship terms as the outcome of group marriage has unduly influenced some field-workers in Australia[75] and among the Gilyaks.[76] The Freudian Oedipus complex has been applied as a matter of course to grotesque psycho-analytical experiments made on Australian savages.[77] French ethnographers have without a vestige of evidence explained certain North African rites by hypotheses based on Frazer's theory of the dying god;[78] and one of them writes point-blank that the North-West African carnival 'has well preserved its original character of an agricultural feast, with the murder of the spirit or divinity of vegetation and its resurrection for a new year',[79] although there is not a shadow of truth in any of these statements. Montaigne, who was a pioneer as a student of savage customs and one of the most sensible men who ever lived, makes the following remark in speaking of his informant concerning the cannibals of America: 'The man I had was a simple and ignorant fellow; hence the more fit to give true evidence. For your sophisticated men are more curious observers, and take in more things; but they glose them ... They warp them and mask them according to the point of view from which they see things ... Now we need either a very truthful man, or one so simple that he has not the art of building up and giving an air of probability to fictions, and is wedded to no theory. Such was my man.'[80] To be wedded to no theory is a warning that every ethnographer should have at heart.

Although it has been said that the 'new anthropology' avoids all discussion of hypotheses as to historical origins, I think on the contrary that, in many cases, it belongs to the task of the field-anthropologist to be concerned with the question of such origins, after he has studied the cultural phenomena and their relations as they exist at present. I fail to see how my researches in Morocco could have avoided this question, and how anybody but a field-worker could have tackled it with any prospect of success. The aboriginal culture of the Berbers was exposed to influences from various quarters. The latest, and from the point of view of religion greatest, wave of this kind came with the Arabic invasions, which brought to them Islam; but hand in hand with the rites and doctrines of their religion, the Arabs introduced other customs and beliefs, some of which were actually forbidden by it. The resemblances in these respects between the present natives of Morocco and the Arabs of the East are so manifold, even in little details, that we may assume a considerable Arab influence falling outside the pale of Islam. But it is also certain that many of these resemblances are not due to such influence; various forms of nature-worship were undoubtedly indigenous both among Berbers and Arabs. There has also been a Negro influence, which is very conspicuous in rites connected with the belief in *jinn*. In one or two cases I think I have identified traces of the religion of Carthage, due to the Punic colonisation; and ancient Roman influence is obvious in certain cases. In many traits of the North-West African carnivals we recognise the ceremonial of the Saturnalia, or rather of the feast of the Kalends of January, the New Year's festival, which attracted its ritual and in the fourth century was described as the great feast of the Romans which was celebrated all over the Empire. Finally, it should be noticed that a very large number of rites and beliefs in Morocco are identical with, or very similar to, such as are found on the other side of the Mediterranean, and there is reason to believe that at least some of them are due to the contact of peoples or a common descent. Whatever be the origin of the Berbers, it is difficult to doubt that a large portion or the bulk of them are members of a race which was once spread over the Mediterranean area and has been called the Mediterranean race.

Ladies and Gentlemen! I am afraid that I ought to make an apology for the rather egotistic character of my lecture. The greater part of it consists of an account of the methods, illustrated by examples, which I have applied in my own researches, both as an armchair anthropologist and as a field-worker. They are in essential points similar to those which have been characteristic of what may be called the classical school of English social anthropology; and I hope that this may serve me as an excuse for repeating much that has been said by others before. I have felt an eager wish to express my indebtedness to English anthropology for what I have learned from it. And at the same time I have desired to raise a protest against what has recently been said by the esteemed advocate of the 'new anthropology' about the 'unsoundness' of its methods, culminating in the allegation that 'in England we have very little of anything that is called sociology'.[81] I am convinced that there is no country in the world that can rival it in its achievements in social anthropology, whether pursued in the study or in the field, largely owing to its sterling qualities of lucidity and good sense.

Notes

1   See my *Three Essays on Sex and Marriage* (London, 1934), p. 181 seqq.

2   M. Volz, *Nord-Sumatra*, ii. (Berlin, 1912), p. 364; *idem, Im Dammer des Rimba* (Breslau, 1921), p. 57; W. Munnecke, *Mit Hagenbeek im Dschungel* (Berlin, 1931), pp. 77–9, 86 seq.

3   'See *Three Essays on Sex and Marriage*, p. 178 seq.

4   On this subject see R. M. and Ada W. Yerkes, *The Great Apes* (New Haven and London, 1929), p. 543.

5   E. Reichenow, 'Biologische Beobachtungen an Gorilla und Schimpanse', in *Sitzungsbericht der Gesellschaft Naturforschender Freunde zu Berlin*, No. 1, 1920, p. 15 seqq.

6   A different explanation of the origin of the family among primates has recently been given by S. Zuckerman in his book *The Social Life of Monkeys and. Apes* (London, 1932), who maintains that the factor underlying the permanent association of the sexes among monkeys and apes is their uninterrupted reproductive life: 'the male primate', he says, 'is always sexually potent, while the female is also to some extent receptive'. In the *History of Human Marriage* I considered the possibility of the family having such an origin as has been suggested by Zuckerman; but I found reasons to believe that the anthropoids have a definite sexual season, and that the pairing of our earliest human or half-human ancestors also was restricted to a certain season of the year. In support of the former opinion I quoted some statements then known to me – including one communicated to me by A. R. Wallace, which was based on his personal experience of the orangutan in Borneo – and in a more recent work I have added other statements of a similar character (*Three Essays on Sex and Marriage*, p. 199 seq.). Zuckerman's denial of a sexual season among the primates is founded almost exclusively on records concerning animals kept in confinement; he says (op. cit. p. 49: 'The Menstrual Cycle of the Primates', in *Proceedings of the Zoological Society of London*, 1931, p. 341) that definite knowledge about the breeding of wild Old World primates exists, so far as he is aware, only in the case of the Chacma baboon. Now it is a common opinion that animals in captivity do not

afford a reliable source of information about the breeding activity of wild ones, because the generative system may be affected by conditions attending captivity; and Zuckerman himself seems to have shared this opinion till quite recently ('The Menstrual Cycle of the Primates', in *Proceedings of the Zoological Society of London*, 1930, p. 693 seq.). Moreover, he has justly pointed out the danger of arguing from the behaviour of one animal to that of another, and has, curiously enough, illustrated this by the statement that the spotted deer of India breeds at all times of the year, whereas the red deer of Western Asia, which belongs to the same zoological family, has a short mating season, the only time when the sexes meet (*The Social Life of Monkeys and Apes*, p. 25). In no case could uninterrupted sexual stimulus explain the male's relation to the offspring and the paternal instinct underlying it, which have been noticed both in the anthropoids and several other subhuman primates. And that the lasting association of the sexes among primates by no means *presupposes* an uninterrupted sexual capacity is proved by the fact that similar associations are found in many species whose sexual life is restricted to a certain season. With reference to the anthropoids, R.M. and Ada W. Yerkes write in their exhaustive work on the *Great Apes* (p. 542): 'The facts available suggest that there is a definite breeding season, or possibly seasons, for each of the five types' (the gibbon, siamang, orangutan, chimpanzee, and gorilla). A more detailed criticism of Zuckerman's theory is found in my *Three Essays on Sex and Marriage*, p. 197 seqq.

7   H. Spencer, *The Principles of Sociology*, i. (London, 1876), pp. 696, 697, 701.

8   E.B. Tylor, *Researches into the Early History of Mankind* (London, 1878), p. 5.

9   T.H. Huxley, 'On the Methods and Results of Ethnology', in *Collected Essays*, vii. (London, 1894), pp. 213, 225.

10   J.G. Frazer, *Balder the Beautiful*, i. (London, 1913), p. vi. seq.

11   W.H.R. Rivers, *Presidential Address to the Anthropological Section of the British Association*, Portsmouth, 1911, p. 2.

12   Tylor, op. cit. p. 378 seq.

13   G. Elliot Smith, 'Edward Burnett Tylor' in *The Great Victorians*, edited by H.J. and Hugh Massingham (London, 1932), p. 556.

14   *Idem, The Diffusion of Culture* (London, 1933), p. 6.

15   Ibid. p. 218.

16   F. Graebner, *Methode der Ethnologic* (Heidelberg, 1911), p. 106 seqq.

17   See C. Kluckhohn, 'Some Reflections on the Method and Theory of the Kulturkreislehre' in *American Anthropologist*, New Series, vol. xxxviii (Menasha, Wisconsin, 1936), pp. 165 n. 12, 186 seq.

18   Koppers, 'Methodologisches zur Frage der Kulturbeziehungen zwischen der alten und der neuen Welt' in *Mitteilungen der Anthropologischen Gesellschaft in Wien*, lxii. (1932), p. 320.

19   Tylor, op. cit. p. 373.

20   Graebner, op. cit. p. 108 seqq.

21   A. L. Kroeber, *Anthropology* (New York, 1923), p. 199 seq.

22   *Cf.* F. von Luschan, 'Zusammenhange und Konvergenz', in *Mitteilungen der Anthropologischen Gesellschaft in Wien*, xlviii-xlix. (Wien, 1919), p. 89.

23 Kroeber, *op. cit.* p. 197.

24 The Magic Origin of Moorish Designs', in *Journal of the Anthropological Institute,* xxxiv. (1904). I have subsequently dealt with the same subject much more extensively in my book *Ritual and Belief in Morocco,* 1. (London, 1926), pp. 414-478.

25 See *Ritual and Belief in Morocco,* i. 461, and my book *Pagan Survivals in Mohammedan Civilisation* (London, 1933), p. 42.

26 See J. Euting's works *Punische Steine (Memoires de l'Academie imperiale des sciences de St-Petersbourg,* ser. vii. vol. xvii, No. 3, 1871) and *Sammlung der carthagischen Inschriften, i* (Strassburg, 1883).

27 O. Pucbstein, *Das ionische Capitell* (Berlin, 1887), *passim.*

28 Ibid. p. 11.

29 See W.H. Goodyear, *The Grammar of the Lotus* (London, 1891), 'Index', s.v. Ionic Capital.

30 F. von Luschan, *Entstehung und Herkunft der Jonischen Mule* (Leipzig, 1912), p. 7 seqq.

31 See my *Pagan Survivals in Mohammedan Civilisation,* p. 54.

32 See my *Ritual and Belief in Morocco,* i, p. 477 seq.

33 H.J. Nieboer, *Slavery as an Industrial Institution* (The Hague, 1900).

34 L.T. Hobhouse, G.C. Wheeler, and M. Ginsberg, *The Material Culture and Social Institutions of the Simpler Peoples. An Essay in Correlation* (London, 1915).

35 *The Origin and Development of the Moral Ideas,* i (London, 1912), p. 440 seqq.

36 R. Karsten, *The Civilization of the South American Indians* (London, 1926), p. 408.

37 H.J. Rose, *Concerning Parallels* (Oxford, 1934), p. 10.

38 W.H.R. Rivers, 'Survival in Sociology' in *Sociological Review,* vi (London, 1913), p. 295.

39 R.H. Lowie, *Culture and Ethnology* (New York, 1929), p. 83.

40 R. Briffault, *The Mothers,* i (London, 1927), *passim.*

41 'The Oedipus Complex' in *Three Essays on Sex and Marriage.*

42 O. Rank, *Das Inzest-Motiv in Dichtung und Sage* (Leipzig and Wien, 1926), p. 308.

43 Th. Reik, *Ritual* (London, 1931), pp. 105, 106, 116, 124; M. Zeller, *Die Knabenweihen* (Bern, 1923), p. 135; J.C. Flügel, *The Psycho-Analytic Study of the Family* (London, 1929), p. 85.

44 Briffault, op. cit. i. 635 seqq.

45 S. Freud, *Totem und Tabu* (in *Gesammelte Schriften,* x [Leipzig, Wien, Zurich, 1924]), p. 150; *idem, Vorlesungen* zur *Einführung in die Psychoanalyse (Gesammelte Schriften,* vii [1924]), p. 347; Rank, op. cit. p. 405; Flugel, op. cit. pp. 35, 91, 195, 200, 202, 206 seq.; E. Jones, 'Psycho-Analysis and Anthropology' in *Journal of the Royal Anthropological Institute,* liv (1924), p. 54 seq.

46 Diogenes Laertius, *Solon,* 10; Cicero, *Pro Roscio Amerino,* 25.

47 L.H. Morgan, *Systems of Consanguinity and Affinity of the Human Family* (Washington, 1871), p. 479.

48 F. Boas, 'The Methods of Ethnology' in *American Anthropologist,* New Series, vol. xxii (1920), p. 316 seq.

49 Rivers, in *Sociological Review,* vi, p. 304.

50 *Idem,* 'Presidential' Address' in *Folk-Lore,* xxxiii (London, 1922), p. 15.

51 Cicero, *De Officiis, i,* 41.

52 Cf. my *History of Human Marriage,* i (London, 1921), p. 15.

53 B. Malinowski, 'Foreword' to the third edition of *The Sexual Life of Savages in Northwestern Melanesia* (London, 1932), p. xxviii seq.

54 A.L. Kroeber, 'History and Science in Anthropology' in *American Anthropologist*, New Series, vol. xxxvii (1935), p. 561.

55 Radcliffe-Brown, 'On the Concept of Function in Social Science', ibid. vol. xxxvii (1935), p. 401 seq.

56 See e.g. A. van Gennep, *L'etat actuel du problems totemique* (Paris, 1920), p. 41; A. Goldenweiser, *History, Psychology, and Culture* (London, 1933), p. 361 seqq.

57 E. Durkheim, *Les formes elementaires de la vie religieuse* (Paris, 1912), p. 593 seq. (English translation [London and New York, s.d.], p. 115 seq.).

58 E. Laoust, 'Noms et Ceremonies des feux de joie chez les Berberes du Haut et de l'Anti-Atlas' in *Hesperis*, i (Paris, 1921), p. 419 seq.

59 Frazer, *Balder the Beautiful*, i, p. vii. Cf. ibid. i, p. 330 seq.

60 Herodotus, iv. 172.

61 *Genesis*, xxxi. 44 seqq.

62 *Joshua*, ix. 14 seq.

63 W. Robertson Smith, *Lectures on the Religion of the Semites* (London, 1894), p. 27; J. Wellhausen, *Reste des arabischen Heidentums* (Berlin, 1897), p. 124.

64 Robertson Smith, op. cit. p. 318 seq.

65 *Exodus*, xxiv. 4 seqq.

66 *Genesis*, xv. 8 seqq.

67 *Psalms*, 1. 5.

68 Wellhausen, op. cit. p. 124.

69 Robertson Smith, op. cit. lec. ix. seqq.; E. S. Hartland, *The Legend of Perseus*, ii (London, 1895), p. 236; F.B. Jevons, *An Introduction to the History of Religion* (London, 1896), p. 225.

70 *Wit and Wisdom in Morocco, a Study of Native Proverbs* (London, 1930).

71 R. Firth, 'Proverbs in Native Life, with special reference to those of the Maori' in *Folklore*, xxxvii (London, 1926).

72 See his Presidential Address in the *Report* of British Association's Meeting, 1931, p. 159.

73 Radcliffe-Brown, ibid. p. 154; *idem*, 'The Methods of Ethnology and Social Anthropology' in *South African Journal of Science*, xx (1923), p. 144.

74 E.B. Tylor, *Primitive Culture*, i (London, 1903), p. 9.

75 See my *History of Human Marriage, iii*, 258 seqq.

76 See my *Three Essays on Sex and Marriage*, p. 278 seq.

77 See ibid. p. 19 seq.

78 See my *Ritual and Belief in Morocco*, ii, 149 seqq.

79 A. Bel, 'Coup d'ceil sur l'Islam en Berberie', in *Revue de l'histoire des religions*, lxxv (Paris, 1917), p. 113.

80 Montaigne, *Essais*, book i, ch. 31.

81 Radcliffe-Brown, in British Association's *Report*, pp. 154, 166.

INDEX

Page numbers in *italic* refer to illustration captions.

CPSIA information can be obtained at www.ICGtesting.com
Printed in the USA
BVOW09*1129131114

374683BV00006B/119/P